With best wish

Terry Reeves

THE THREE
RINGS

BY

TERENCE REEVES

Grosvenor House
Publishing Limited

This book is published by
Grosvenor House Publishing Ltd
28-30 High Street, Guildford, Surrey, GU1 3EL.
www.grosvenorhousepublishing.co.uk

A CIP record for this book
is available from the British Library

ISBN 978-1-78623-024-9

Also by Terence Reeves

African Harvest

I dedicate this book to Andrea, Paul and Lynda
The three miracles of my life

CCC

ACKNOWLEDGEMENTS

I have been repeatedly asked by readers, 'So what happened next?' demanding a sequel to AFRICAN HARVEST.

So, again, I set off on a soul searching experience, necessary when you need to recall and set down the full details for an autobiography. To write anything but the truth and the full circumstance of events is to water down, hide and distort the essence of the story. It is a tough emotional experience but one you have to go through. Some people's names have been changed in order to protect them, but their personalities have remained. All the events are true with only minor dramatic liberties taken to illustrate the story.

African Harvest was an autobiographical story of what I personally harvested from my few years in Africa, with all its joys and emotions. The Three Rings takes up the story following those earth shattering experiences. Showing that with encouragement and determination a new life can be carved out despite all the adversities thrown at you.

My greatest thanks has to go to my wife, Andrea, who had largely lost sight of me for long periods of time as I pounded away on the key board. Her constant help at every stage with encouragement, copy editing, constructive criticism and patience and not least in keeping me adequately nourished, without her support I would never have completed either of these books.

My thanks go especially to Dena for her meticulous scrutiny of the manuscript making my thoughts readable and not least correctly punctuated. This transformed my ramblings.

I'd also like to thank fellow author Jennifer Elkin for reading through the manuscript, making her valued suggestions and giving her expert opinion, always with encouragement and enthusiasm.

In the publishing world, those who made the book physically possible, my thanks go to Kim Cross and his team at Grosvenor House Publishing Limited for their help, guidance and superb efficiency making the whole experience as painless as it can be.

CHAPTER ONE

October 1981

'I don't think I can continue living in this house,' Cecil remarked to his wife Margaret over lunch. It was the day after the funeral, in Yorkshire, of their daughter, Ann. She was just 41 years old.

'You don't expect your children to die before you do and this house has too many memories of time spent with her.'

Ann had suffered a long and exasperating illness with cancer over six years and he personally had grieved as much, if not more, than most and was finding her death very difficult to cope with. It contradicted so much all that he believed, and his faith in a God of love.

'How on earth are Terry and our two grandchildren going to cope with life now? It's so unfair that a beautiful, vigorous and gentle lady like our daughter should be taken from us all so early. How can they, and we, ever come to terms with it? They'd enjoyed only thirteen years of marriage and now this. Poor Terry, left to bring up those two children alone. How on earth will Paul and Lynda cope with it all I wonder? What a mess.'

Cecil was deeply concerned about the whole situation and feeling helpless. Ann's death had affected him deeply, as it had the whole family.

Margaret was shocked by his comments. She loved their beautiful house set on the hillside east of Bristol, just outside the village of Pucklechurch. Distraught as she was by recent events and the loss of their daughter, she felt she couldn't consider moving away from this house. They had both worked extremely hard over the past seventeen years at making it into a beautiful home. It was in a perfect location - one they had looked long and hard for and had had to really stretch themselves financially to buy it in the first place.

'I do understand,' Margaret replied, 'but surely it would be best to think about it for a while before deciding to move. It must be better to come to terms with the dreadful happenings of the past few years, slowly before we undertake such a huge change in our lives.'

'No.' Cecil barked. 'We have to find somewhere else. It hurts too much to remain here, and I can't do it.' He stormed off to wash his car.

He was something of a perfectionist and he washed it every day putting it into the garage at the side of the house; winter and summer alike. He had decided there really was no way that he could continue to live at Meadowland Cottage. It was so full of memories of Ann and was just too painful to contemplate, whatever Margaret said. Of that, he was quite certain.

There is a power and grace in experiencing sorrow and pain, but they found it hard to appreciate that fact amongst the heartbreak and misery they had all endured over the past six years.

Terry, Paul and Lynda hid their tears from each other, even now, in the aftermath of all the stress and sorrow they had experienced, when they could have let them flow. They had to continue about their daily lives, as fragile and frail as they continued to be, crushed and perplexed, abandoned and alone, numbed by grief. Could anybody be lonelier than a widow or widower or children without their mother? Terry began to think not. There was no darker place.

What he and Ann had shared was always there in his memory. Those carefree days and their hopes and dreams, but deep within him he remembered particularly her hate of any separation they might have to bear. How many times had she pleaded with him, whatever the circumstances, that they should never, ever, live apart for work or any other reason? But how many times had they needed to succumb to their destiny and accept it? How many times had they been forced to do the very thing they loathed and hated?

In order to prevent future separations, Ann, when forced to leave Africa in 1978 due to the recurrence of her malignant melanoma cancer, had to make the most difficult and heart wrenching of all decisions. She told Terry that they must give up their quest to live and work in Africa which was something they had hoped to dedicate their lives to and had become their life ambition.

Terry felt lost - totally inadequate and in a sort of panic since Ann had died on 7th October 1981. Grief had stripped him bare, left him heartbroken, vulnerable and alone. Part of him had been ripped away and he felt as if he were slowly dying.

Hanging over their house was a hollow emptiness. There was an eerie silence after the busyness and urgency that had plagued it for months, when doctors, nurses, friends and neighbours rushed in and out from sunrise to sunset, each day for months. They no longer felt it necessary to knock on the door to ask if they could come in. They had taken over their home as they rushed in and out importantly to undertake their respective mission of mercy. Now it had all stopped. The nightmare was over, the silence was deafening, the emptiness spine-chilling.

There were endless requests for him to go and have dinner with well-meaning friends and acquaintances as if that might return some normality back into his life. He laboured through as many as he could bear, but it served only to magnify his grief and loneliness. He and the children visited the grand-parents in an attempt to comfort each other. However, it only seemed to heighten all their feelings of helplessness and loss, achieving little, and making it more difficult to return to an empty desolate home there on the banks of the river Ure in Boroughbridge.

Letters and cards had flooded in and although Terry tried to answer and respond to them he was sinking fast under the weight of it all as the pile mounted on the dining room table. It grew daily as he quickly glanced at the contents of each new one that arrived in the post, assigning them to the growing hopeless pile of compassion that he tried to ignore. One such letter drew his attention. It was from George and Joan Hart at the Hombolo Leprosy Centre in Tanzania where Terry and Ann had met and fallen in love in 1966. They offered their condolences and advised him that their daughter Anne, who was now working in London as a nurse, would like to come to see Terry and would shortly be in touch with him. A kind thought he felt and one he welcomed as it reconnected him to those happy days in Tanzania.

A date was later agreed for her visit and on Friday 4th December Terry met Anne Hart at York railway station. The train arrived at 19.43 from Kings Cross. He wondered if he would recognise her, having last seen her a few years previously when she visited them in Boroughbridge with her parents for an overnight stay.

As the passengers alighted from the train and made their way off the platform Terry spotted her, dressed in three quarter length tweed trousers with matching jacket. She must have felt this was the Yorkshire code of dress! Anne was only about five-foot-tall with long fair hair down to the middle of her back. She pranced along towards him.

'Hello Anne, welcome to Yorkshire. Thank you for coming to see us.' She smiled shyly and let him take her case as they walked to the car park.

'How are you and the children managing? I was so sorry to hear of Ann's death. It has been a terrible ordeal for you all, tragic. Fate has not been kind.'

4

'Indeed,' Terry replied as he started the car and drove off to Boroughbridge.

'How are your Mum and Dad doing in Tanzania? I understand they are to move twenty miles away to work at a school for the blind near Buigiri? How do they feel about that, with so much of themselves having gone into establishing Hombolo over the years? It will have become so much a part of them.'

'Dad says he's happy to hand Hombolo farm over to Michael, the African Manager he's been training up, and with Buigiri not being too far away he'll be able to keep an eye on things for the Diocese and advise on any problems. As he says, one day soon he will retire so they need to have someone ready to take over and Michael is very good and capable.'

'Will your Dad retire to New Zealand? I guess he will,' Terry enquired.

'Where else?' Anne replied with a smile.

'He is a New Zealander and he hopes we will all be able to live there together one day. For so many years we spent long periods apart while he and Mum served in Africa. They felt that separation so much. My sister Margie and I were away from home at school either in Arusha or in the UK so he'd love to have us all around him in his retirement as he feels he's missed out.'

Those words would go on to haunt Terry sooner than he could ever have imagined.

After enjoying an evening meal and time with Paul and Lynda, Anne and Terry sat up into the early hours discussing their mutual interest in Hombolo, Tanzania and of course, George and Joan her parents. Anne had been only eight years old when Terry first met her. He was a volunteer who went to work at Hombolo aged twenty. He had only met her once since. He had grown to have a great admiration for her parents and all they had done and the sacrifices they had made in following their particular love for Africa and its people. Anne and Terry had an almost spiritual affinity in that respect. Terry was also interested to hear how Anne and Margie

5

looked upon their parent's dedication and if they felt they had suffered in anyway with the effects it had on them in their young lives.

It was a fascinating couple of days. Terry and the children were uplifted by Anne's visit and having a feminine presence in the house again, which took their minds off recent happenings. Terry put Anne back on the train to London the following evening and she invited them to come to London anytime they felt like it. They promised to meet up again one day, before too long if they could.

Christmas was fast approaching and there was only one thing Terry wanted to do and that was for him and the children to spend Christmas alone together, and yet it was so difficult to achieve. He felt he needed the time to rest, reflect and absorb all that had taken place since Ann's death, for it was only in the silence and solitude that he was ever going to find the way out of his suffering.

He was receiving so many requests inviting them to go and spend Christmas with other families. Many asked and would not take no for an answer, so he had to lie and say they were going to be away with the grandparents. That was partly true as they had planned to go and spend the end of the year with Ann's parents in Pucklechurch.

Terry used the Christmas mail he was sending out to thank those who had written to him and in so doing reduced the ever growing heap of letters on the dining room table.

They struggled through Christmas together. Terry tried to make it as enjoyable as possible for the children, ever conscious of their individual grief, while at the same time trying to manage his own and to avoid that paralysing depression hovering just below the surface. He had a craving for a complete night's sleep, free of the recurring nightmares he had been experiencing.

After Christmas, on 30th December, they left Riverside House Boroughbridge to go and spend a few days with Ann's parents. What relief Terry felt to be there, to feel he had someone else to share the responsibility of the children with, for he did not carry that task easily and felt inadequate in every way.

It was good to go walking in the beautiful countryside surrounding Meadowland Cottage and to feel free to remember all the occasions he and Ann had enjoyed there; the happy times together planning their marriage and their future in Africa which was the country that had brought them together. Here they fell in love with each other, the country and its people, never for one moment expecting life and its effects to dissolve those dreams.

He relaxed into those few days which gave him time to chat to Cecil and Margaret with long discussions around the table after each meal, providing Terry with much courage and support. Cecil had always been a great mentor for Terry. He had a deep affection for him. They were, in many ways, very alike and got on well together. Cecil would open up to Terry and discuss matters that he would never usually speak about with others. He was a very private man. His years in the army during the war had made him a much disciplined person, but he seemed able to talk frankly with Terry and the two had become quite close in the short time they had known each other. They had both, of course, lost Ann which bonded them still further.

Slowly with that short period of rest and freedom from responsibilities, Terry felt himself coming back to life, but in the center of every hurricane there is always absolute peace and quiet. He did not know it, but this was what he was enjoying, it was only the middle of his personal hurricane. He had been feeling much more relaxed, until he received a phone call from his neighbour in Yorkshire. She told him that after heavy rain and snow the river Ure had burst its banks and river water was entering under his front door fast. What should she do?

Terry's heart sank. He asked her to go to the Crown Hotel, which was in his charge and close to where he lived, to ask the staff if they would go into his house and move everything possible upstairs.

The following day, Sunday 3rd January, Terry and the children returned in haste to a flooded Boroughbridge, leaving their dog Duke in the care of Margaret and Cecil. The whole town was under water with house contents thrown out onto the streets and overflowing skips everywhere. The whole place looked like a war zone with groups of people standing around helping out where ever they could. Terry drove down towards their house and the river. He did not get far before an army officer stopped him to tell him he could go no further as it was flooded.

'But I live there, my house is the other side of the river on Milby Island.'

'Where do you live?'

'At Riverside House, just over the bridge.'

'Not anymore mate,' he replied, 'it's now in the river.'

'If you can get someone to take care of your children I'll row you over in a boat, well at least as near as possible if that's any help.'

Terry took Paul and Lynda to their school friends, Oliver and Emma, who lived nearby and asked their parents Jed and Penny if they would look after them while he went to the house to see how things were. It would probably have to be for the night. They agreed to do all they could to help which allowed Terry to leave them in safety. He then went back to the river and was taken in the army's boat slowly down the road and across the flooded bridge. They were able to get within five yards of the front door which, by this time, was underwater up to the middle, so about four feet deep with the water swirling by as it rushed on its way towards York.

'I'm sorry but this is as far as I can take you,' the army engineer explained to Terry.

'You'll have to get out here if you really want to go into your house. I'm sorry but I daren't go any nearer or I could get caught in the tide flow. Tie this rope around your waist, then, when you are safely in your house, untie it and I'll pull it back leaving you inside. You do know there is no electricity or gas don't you?'

'I guess not' replied a gloomy Terry, as he lowered himself into the freezing cold water and made a cautious journey to the front door. Gradually pulling it open he went inside.

He waded along the passage from the front door to the sitting room. The water was up to his waist by this time, and it smelt damp and dank. He pushed open the sitting room door. As he did so he saw that the Christmas tree which had been standing in the corner when they left just a few days before, was now floating on its side. What a sad and sorrowful sight it was.

He pushed his way through to the dining room. This had been almost emptied of furniture by the hotel staff and was taken upstairs to the bedrooms out of the way of the flood water. He continued on to the kitchen where the water was over four-foot-deep covering the worktops. Upstairs was in chaos with the contents from downstairs thrown anywhere and everywhere, stacks of books, boxes, chairs, electrical items, pots and pans, china, boxes of food, clothes, dog's bed - just about everything that had been downstairs. What a frantic and disheartening mess it all was. He sat on the stairs and cried as he looked down into the black water below.

There was little that could be done, but he felt he should stay in the house. He found some dry clothes which he changed into and some biscuits in their packets in a box that had been taken there from the kitchen. After having a good look around and making sure the power switch was turned off, he made a space on the bed and covered himself with blankets. He stayed there for the night, getting up from time to time to check on the state of the river and the level of the water.

By morning the water level in the river had dropped considerably which was reflected in the house. Everything was covered in a brownish green slime and smelt terrible, inside and out. The water in the house was about two feet deep and Terry was able to make his way out to the bridge. Thick mud and slim greeted him all around. There was a dead rabbit in the driveway and one, somehow, in the house. All sorts of debris were hanging from trees and piled up on the roads. Workmen had started trying to clear it all, which was a thankless task that would take weeks.

He suddenly remembered the six chickens they kept in a run in the garden and went to see how they were. Only one had survived and looked extremely sad and frightened.

He went back to inspect the house to try and decide what to do first. Everything was cold and clammy. He stood there in bewildered agony.

'What a mess' he said to himself. 'Why do all these horrors keep happening to me? How the hell am I supposed to cope with this?'

There was a knock on the door.

'Hello anyone here,' a voice called.

It was Jeremy, his work colleague, and Forester for the company estate where they were both employed.

'Come in Jeremy, I'm in yet another mess as you can see.'

'You're telling me, you don't do things by half do you?' he quipped, 'But don't worry we'll soon get this water out for you. Give me a hand will you to unload the pump from the back of the Land Rover.'

Jeremy, in his wisdom, had come prepared. They set up the pump, attached the hose and started pumping the water away over the now visible river wall. The house had been a pub in the past so there was a large cellar under the sitting room and of course that, too, was full of water. In the cupboard under the stairs was a small hatch which gave access to the cellar, so it was necessary to go down the steps and pump out all the water, which was likely to take ages.

Jeremy got on with the minimum of fuss taking it all in his stride, as he always did with life's problems. He was a good friend; the very best.

Terry started to hose down the inside walls of the house and later more help came when Penny arrived reporting that Paul and Lynda were fine and had managed to get off on the school bus. She had come to assist in any way she could, bringing along hot drinks and food that were most welcome. It felt odd to be standing in the lounge with a hose pipe, in what had been a beautiful sitting room, spraying water around on the walls and floor!

'I can't believe we are doing this Penny, can you?'

'It's totally bizarre isn't it. I'm so sorry you have all this so soon after Ann's death, just when you were picking yourself up again. Don't worry we are all here to help you get straight and somehow we will, I promise.'

Pumping continued throughout the day. The river level was steady and falling slowly which was a relief. It was getting colder but at least no more rain was expected so there was a good chance they might get all the water out and be able to start cleaning the house and dry it out.

By seven that evening Terry suggested to Jeremy that he call it a day and go home to his wife.

'No, I'm staying here until every drop of water is out of your cellar, even if it takes me all night,' he replied with rigid determination.

At four a.m. he was still there having spent the whole night in the cellar pumping the water, while Penny kept them all fed and made hot drinks which she brought from her house in order to keep them going. At five thirty in the morning Jeremy emerged, filthy, dirty, tired and exhausted. The petrol had run out for the engine pump and the water was freezing at the discharge end as it came out of the hose into the yard.

'Please, Jeremy go home will you?' Terry insisted.

By that time the water was freezing around the outside of the house and had turned into a sheet of ice with the temperatures plummeting, causing yet more problems, so they gave in and went off to their beds to recover from their endeavours.

Over the next few days Terry, with the help of friends, cleaned the house and tried to dry it out as the services were slowly reinstated. It was a huge and soul destroying task and it was going to take a very long time to get the house back to anything like it had been.

'You should take a few days away,' Penny suggested to Terry, seeing his strained and tired face.

'How can I? That's impossible.' He replied.

Penny insisted. 'I'm very happy to look after Paul and Lynda for a few days. You need to take a rest. Terry, if you don't mind me saying so, you look desperate. We're so worried about you. We don't want you to crack up and have a breakdown. You can't go on. The children need you to be fit and able, despite the distress you must feel in your heart. Please, for their sake, have a break away for a few days. It will give the house time to dry out a little too while you are away. You look shattered. I don't suppose you will have slept for many nights and you've been working hard all day, every day.'

'True.' Terry replied wearily. 'What is sleep? I don't remember when I last slept properly with one thing and another. I wouldn't mind a break if you're sure you are ok having Paul and Lynda, but I feel bad leaving them. My duty is to be here.'

'Your duty, as you call it, is to be strong for your children. You can't continue in your state. Just look at yourself. Of course you should have a break, take yourself off, you deserve it, you need it. The children are fine with me. They love being with Emma and Oliver.'

He was feeling very low, tired and depressed so felt it wise to do as he was advised by Penny. He was far too tired to argue, but where would he go and would he be able to take more time off from work?

He did not want to go to either of the grandparents, but then he remembered the offer Anne Hart had made for him to go and see her in London some time. He liked Anne and their past experiences in Tanzania meant they had a common bond, but was it right for him to go and stay with her?

He wrestled with the idea and finally rang Anne to see what she thought and if it was possible. She was delighted for him to go and stay and arranged to meet him at Kings Cross Station. Anne worked at St Thomas hospital and shared a house on Crane Grove, London N7. There was a small box room for guests at the top of the house and she told him he could use that. Fortunately, due to his circumstances, it was agreed he could have a few more days leave.

Terry set off on Friday afternoon, 15th January, for a weekend in London to return the following Monday. It felt good to get away. London for him was always an exciting place to visit and he might enjoy it. Anne met him at Kings Cross as they had arranged, at the top of the elevator to the Underground. It felt rather strange on one hand to meet her in such circumstances, but quite natural in another having known her during those days at Hombolo when he worked with her father at the Leprosy Centre in Tanzania. It seemed to bring them together, with Africa again being the link.

They went for a cup of tea just off Kings Cross Station and chatted like old friends. Terry thought that she looked much older than he had remembered from her visit to him in Yorkshire. She had her father's deep piercing and hypnotic blue eyes, brightening her good-looking girlie young face. They took the underground to Islington Station and walked the short distance to her place where she introduced Terry to her three housemates - a trainee doctor, a civil servant and a teacher. They all had a meal together and sat around putting the world to rights. Anne had booked the theatre for the Saturday evening to see 'Children of the Lesser God' featuring Trevor Eve, so he looked forward to that. They were going with two of Anne's girlfriends from work.

On Sunday she suggested they attend the evening service at All Souls, Langham Place. Anne went there often and had quite a few friends at the church. So it looked like a full weekend with plenty to take Terry's mind off the horrors of the past couple of months.

The play the following evening was very deep and not perhaps the best thing for Terry's state of mind, but he enjoyed the change and the company of Anne and her friends. Afterwards they went to a cocktail bar and tried different cocktails as they all sat chatting and laughing. That was certainly a new experience for Terry, rarely having had a cocktail before or indeed much to laugh about.

Anne's friends left after the drinks, leaving Anne and Terry to find a place for a meal to soak up the cocktails. On the corner of Leicester Square they found 'Brahms and Liszt' restaurant and, being quite high after drinking so many different cocktails on empty stomachs, they tucked into a hearty meal.

'What do you think of life in the city then?' Anne enquired as they sipped their Irish coffee.

'It's fast, busy and furious compared to life in the Yorkshire countryside that's for sure, but it's fun with so much to do and see. Yes, I love it, thanks for inviting me. It's been just the tonic I needed.'

She held on affectionately to his arm as they spoke. He was somewhat taken aback by her warmth and familiarity given his personal new found and enforced circumstances. He was not quite sure how he felt about it and was very slightly uneasy.

'The evening's only just beginning. There is plenty for us to do,' Anne suggested. 'We can go for a walk down by the river to see Tower Bridge if you like, and then make our way back to the house. We could even go by underground if you'd prefer. What do you think?'

'Sounds great. I always feel Tower Bridge is very much representative of England. A place you think about when you are in the heart of Africa or some other far away country and think – that's England. That's the centre of things.'

'I know just what you mean, coming from New Zealand we all feel like that and identify with London as being our natural home, hence its often referred to by us New Zealanders, as the 'Old Country'- a term of friendship and belonging.'

Terry felt comfortable with Anne, as she clearly did with him, but he was a little anxious about her sudden affection and closeness, and where it was all going. It was a wonderfully relaxing and head clearing experience as they walked on through the clear crisp evening air through the busy London streets. The cocktails and the Irish coffee took over and he went with it as they set off arm in arm towards Trafalgar Square and on to the Embankment towards Tower Bridge, which was lit up in the night sky.

They discussed her work as a nurse at St Thomas's, and her previous job at St Bart's where she had started her nursing career. She loved London, even if it was very expensive to live there. To help her budget Anne did a lot of sewing and was planning to make a friend's wedding dress. The wedding was to be in Jersey, in July.

They shared strong links, deepened by the allure of Africa and the life they had both known and experienced in their different ways. For Terry, his experience in Tanzania had touched a deep cord within him; far beyond that moment in time when, as a young VSO volunteer, he had gone to work at a leprosy centre. For Anne, growing-up as a child with her parents in Tanzania where they lived and worked was hard. They were continually on the move, often involving long periods away from her parents when only very young.

So Africa was never far from their conversation as they sat on the bench looking out across the river Thames on that crisp and gloriously tranquil evening in the heart of London. With the cocktails and coffee keeping them warm from within, they hung on to each other in the silence and historical shadow of Tower Bridge. She held on tightly to his arm as they kissed.

CCC

CHAPTER TWO

On their return to the house Terry laid on his bed in the attic unable to believe the events that had taken place that evening. Anne Hart and him an item? How could it be? How did that happen? Perhaps it was a dream. He felt confused, frightened and afraid, still numbed by grief from his wife's death. Perhaps he should never have come to London he thought, but did he not deserve some pleasure, some relaxation and fun after the misery he had endured over the past six years, and now the flood? He was still grieving for his wife Ann and couldn't imagine ever feeling any different. He missed her dreadfully, after all it was only three months since her death, and surely it was not right to be even thinking of a new relationship. But of course he wasn't. It had happened completely out of the blue!

Sunday was a busy day. Terry was up early and went alone to the local Catholic Church to attend Mass. Lunch was prepared and enjoyed by all members of the house, after which Anne and Terry went for a walk in a near-by park, with Anne hanging on to Terry's arm. He tried to talk to her about the situation, to explain, but neither of them could find the right words and things were left as they were. They went to the service at All Souls, Langham Place in the centre of London before returning again to Anne's house in Islington when at last, with the others being out, they could be alone and have time to talk.

'Anne, you know my situation. I'm in no position to get into a new relationship, you must realise that. Only a few months have passed since Ann died and I have two children. You are a lovely person and I'm flattered of course and very fond of you. It's been great fun and I'm so grateful to you for having me stay, but really, I can't do a relationship, not at this moment in time, if at all. I hardly know where I am myself or what I'm doing. Everything is moving so fast, I've yet to catch up with myself and my feelings before I can entertain any such possibility. I'm sorry, it's not you, it's me, I just can't do it.'

'Of course Terry, I do understand. I'm not trying to take advantage of your situation, but I can't help expressing what I feel.'

The following morning Anne was on late duty so was able to prepare a simple breakfast for Terry before he took the train back to Yorkshire.

'Anne, please don't come to the station. I hate goodbyes and there is no need. Its only one stop to Kings Cross on the tube and you'd better get ready for work.'

'I'm so glad that you came, I wanted to get to know you, I wanted to............' Anne paused.

'Please Anne, say no more. I have to return to my life in Boroughbridge. Paul and Lynda are waiting for me. They are devastated, too, by all this. They're broken and suffering deeply at the loss of their Mother, then the flood on top of everything else. They need me desperately. I'm all they have and I need them too. I'm flattered of course I am, but........'

'Terry I do understand you. I want to help. I need you as well you know. I want you, but I'm prepared to wait.'

'Please Anne stop. I'm going to go now. I can't let this conversation continue, not now, please.

He gathered his things from his attic room and prepared to leave stopping at the front door where Anne was waiting. She threw her arms around him and held him tightly, as he did her, as they kissed goodbye.

'I'll come up to Yorkshire soon to see you, is that ok?'

1 7

'Yes of course, but please leave it for a few weeks.'

'I will, but I want to help you, spend time with you, and be with you. Is that so bad?'

They held on to each other firmly in a warm embrace, and then Terry slipped away to catch the underground to Kings Cross.

He returned to face Yorkshire once more as he stepped onto the train north. It's never more difficult to pick-up your load than when you have put it down for a while. However, he was looking forward to seeing Paul and Lynda and to seeing how the house had recovered from the flood.

His time in London had been a tonic and given his spirits a much needed lift after all the emotional times that had befallen him in the last few months. He had felt as if he was somehow, 'outside of his life,' looking in at the worse possible nightmare - all a little unreal.

On his return to Yorkshire Terry drove straight to his house in Boroughbridge and was truly amazed at the progress that had been made to their flooded home. Penny and her husband Jed, together with Jeremy, had worked miracles so that when he walked into the house, apart from the dank smell, you would hardly know the place had been flooded. There were de-humidifiers buzzing away in various parts of the house sucking out all the moisture from the floors and walls while, at the same time, the boiler was working again warming the house and breathing new life into it. Terry was so surprised and taken aback by all that had been done for him that he sat on the stairs and cried. He seemed to do a lot of that lately, not knowing if they were tears of joy, sadness or relief.

He went up the road to Penny's house to thank her for all she had done and found Paul and Lynda had been fine, looking forward to seeing their Dad when they returned from school that afternoon. He had brought them both a gift from London and on their return they busied themselves unwrapping and playing happily with the contents. It was good to be back with them again and to see them happy. He had missed them so much.

The three of them returned home to find Jeremy emptying the water from all the de-humidifiers set up in the house. When he saw Terry he just stood there with a warm grin on his face, his dark eyes sparkling.

'Welcome back! How was life in the city?'

'Jeremy, what can I say. You've done a wonderful job, thank you so much, I'm totally speechless.'

'It's been worth it then' he smiled mischievously.

Terry stood and watched him in admiration as he continued his task.

'Jeremy, what would I have done without you? I'm so profoundly grateful for everything. How on earth did you get the boiler back on so quickly? Where did you get these machines? The electricity too, how did you get it dried out and working so speedily? Who has paid for all this? I must square up with you.'

Jeremy smiled with a broad grin. 'Got to go now, will you be alright? I'll see you in the morning.'

Terry was left just staring at all they had achieved in his absence. Penny had even made the beds and had stocked the cupboard and fridge with food. What wonderful friends, what stars they were! How could he ever thank them enough?

Soon life returned to something like normal. Terry was overwhelmed by the amount of paper work surrounding the insurance claim on the house, plus his own private correspondence that had piled up. The Missionary Sisters, his friends from Africa who were now disbursed around the world, some to their home countries and some to Africa, had deluged him with their kind letters of condolence since Ann's death. In her letters, his great friend, Sister Claire from Canada was most insistent that he should reply immediately to her many letters, at least two every week!

'You saved my life in Africa, now it's my turn to help you. Reply to me immediately,' she wrote.

She was a formidable lady so what else could he do but obey her!

Terry's new way of life continued, still tormented by a turmoil of mixed emotions and continuing nightmares. He struggled being back in his house without the love and support of his wife Ann. He had to play the role of both mother and father, caring for Paul and Lynda and keeping down a, sometimes, frantically busy job that seemed to grow and grow as more responsibilities were pushed upon him.

He had been promoted to General Manager of the property company, covering not only the 15,000 acres of farm land across Yorkshire with all the complexities of managing tenant farmers, but also three garage businesses with their car franchises, a large four-star hotel in a market town, a Motel and over forty-five residential properties in the Leeds area. Life was very full and often overwhelming with little time to consider his own loneliness and emotions.

He loved his beautiful children. They embodied him, and they characterised Ann. He wanted, like every parent, only the best for them, which he tried desperately to provide but always felt totally inadequate and vulnerable. He had a constant urge to get away, he knew not where, but any place to relax into his own thoughts and memories. He needed to step out of the situation he found himself in, and find time to try and understand it all, to seek answers to some of the many questions circulating in his mind as he was unable to come to terms with the how and why of his circumstances. For six years, since the nursing sister in the Seychelles hospital told him the likely outcome of Ann's cancer, he had carried alone the knowledge that Ann was very unlikely to overcome it. He shared this with nobody, in the hope that it was wrong, that it would go away, but it made no difference to the searing pain and heartache he felt deep within him.

The thought now of Anne Hart who had suddenly come into his life, right at a time he wouldn't have chosen, was a complication that made him even more confused. He had no clarity of mind to make such major and far-reaching commitments or to get into any sort of serious relationship, although the temptation was as great as the reality.

Anne had written two letters to Terry since his trip to London and rung quite a few times, as he had too. She asked if she could come to stay for the weekend of 6th February. What could he say? What should he say? In the end he agreed and was delighted to meet her at York railway station.

Anne was due to arrive at 7.30pm from Kings Cross but, because of a rail strike, she was delayed, eventually arriving at 10.20pm. She leapt from the train into the dark night with a certain positive quality and a cheerful engaging disposition, melting any of Terry's adverse feelings. Without any shyness or reserve she threw her arms around him and it felt quite natural to him to do the same as they kissed on the platform.

Paul and Lynda welcomed Anne to their home and seemed to enjoy getting to know her. Together they enjoyed a visit to Thirsk market on the Saturday morning and then on to see the 'White Horse' carved into the hillside above Kilburn village, before going on to the swimming pool in Harrogate that Paul and Lynda loved so much. The following day, Sunday, they all attended Mass at the Catholic Church in Knaresborough. It was certainly a full but enjoyable weekend.

The children had gone to bed exhausted on Saturday night having enjoyed a full and adventurous day. Terry and Anne relished an evening meal together with time to chat and get to know each other more. At twenty-four, Anne was still very young for her age with a certain naivety, but she had inherited her Father's drive and enthusiasm for life. She suffered from dyslexia which she dealt with very well, given her sometimes difficult background. Terry found her very pretty and attractive. She had a bubbly charismatic personality which he found refreshing, but he felt guilty for doing so, as he still carried the feeling that he was a married man. Of course he had been for the last thirteen years, so he was not going to easily feel any different for a while.

The house continued to dry out and the various trades moved in to repair and redecorate. It was agreed to fill the old cellar beneath the house with a hundred tons of stone, which was poured in and capped with concrete, thus avoiding any recurrence of flooding in the future. Slowly the house returned to something like normal. If only, Terry thought, it was possible for him to put his life back to where it had been so easily.

His friends made sure he felt their comfort and warmth. They had shared his sorrow and heartache and now his re-birth. Slowly he realised he could not go on feeling sorry for himself as he had been doing. It achieved nothing. He could not continue re-living those moments and suffering them over and over in his head. The only way out of his troubles was through them, not to go on being the one who was looked upon with pity and compassion, carrying an uneasy malaise with all the unanswered questions circulating in his mind. It would destroy him, his future hopes and his dreams. He had to break out. Not to forget, for he could never do that, but to learn to live with it, send life in a new direction, tough as it was going to be. He was alive. Ann had gone. The children would not remain such for long. Life stretched out before him and he must use it, fill it, and not allow his days to lay waste. He must drag himself forward not allowing the past to pull him back into the darkness of that uninvited sorrow.

Luigi Borgnis, Terry's Italian friend who he'd met while they both lived and worked in Malawi wrote to say he would like to visit for two weeks. Terry was so pleased to be meeting again such a good friend from his happier past in his beloved Africa. They had enjoyed so much together during those days in Malawi, sharing many difficulties, fun and laughter. They had helped and encouraged each other while both were far from home, they were like brothers, and Terry looked forward to his visit after so long apart.

Anne came to stay again at the beginning of March for a few days. They were getting closer each time and Terry tried to concentrate on his new way of thinking and not to fear either what people would say, or the future. They had agreed not to advertise the relationship yet letting it grow and settle on them both first. Anne was twelve years younger than Terry and he was conscious of that.

Luigi arrived on the 9pm flight from London to Leeds airport on Saturday 14th March.

'Mr Fodya, Welcome to Leeds, nice to see you again' Terry called out as Luigi arrived in the arrivals hall supporting a full beard.

'Fodya Ltd' was the name of his company in Malawi and Terry often addressed him as such.

He laughed as they embraced each other. They had not met for two years. There was so much to catch up on and for the next seven days they enjoyed each other's company as they reminisced about their time spent together in Africa. Luigi loved seeing Paul and Lynda after so long. They had grown up so much since he last saw them in Malawi.

A week after his arrival another sword was to pierce Terry's recuperating heart. His Niece, Anna-Marie, rang him from Weymouth to tell him that his Father had collapsed in church at the Convent of Mercy on Wyke Road where he had always attended Mass on a Sunday. He had arrived early to take a look at the reading before the service started. He died where he fell.

Terry was paralysed by shock and bewildered, distraught feelings crushed him once again. It was unbelievable. His Father had not been ill and was just going about his usual routine. It was less than two weeks ago that they had all been to Weymouth for the half term break and he had seemed quite well then. Shocked and stunned he didn't know which way to turn. He had been learning to cope, learning to manage each day and now another devastating blow. There is no greater loss than your father, your joint creator. He had felt closer to his Father since they had all stayed with him on their return from Malawi in 1979. Ann too had grown to love him, despite all his funny little ways. But this was totally unpredicted and unexpected. Paul and Lynda too were hit hard by the untimely death of their grandfather and silently sought refuge in their father's arms when he broke the sad news to them. How much more of all this can we take he wondered as he held them in his arms? How many more setbacks could they endure he thought to himself as he faced this latest grief and distress?

Anne Hart offered to come to be with Paul and Lynda while Terry went to his Father's funeral service in Weymouth. She dropped everything to take the train to York where Terry and Luigi met her. Luigi decided he would go and visit some of his friends in London under the circumstances and he left the following day. Terry made his way to Weymouth to be with his family for the funeral and to help with clearing the family home.

No 1, Tennyson Road had been the family home since the war. Terry was born there. His Mother and Father had lived in a council house on Devon Road in Weymouth when they were married in 1939 and after a few years were able to move to Tennyson Road. They had been happy there. The house was of a medium size but with poor facilities and had an outside toilet. It had a small garden at the front and rear of the house. Being high up on a hill it had commanding views of the countryside around. It may well have been partly this that gave Terry the urge to be in the countryside and to embark on a career in agriculture and to enjoy the remoteness of Africa.

On his return to Yorkshire after his father's funeral and helping his sister, Esmee, to clear the family home, Terry stopped off for an overnight stay in Pucklechurch to visit Ann's parents. They were delighted to see him, but sorry about the circumstances that led to his visit. He found them, for the first time, restless in their own home as they struggled to accept that their only child had pre-deceased them. Terry recognized their deep and helpless grief. He wanted to comfort them, to say something that would relieve them and assist in carrying their horrendous burden. There were no words. Again he felt totally helpless.

Cecil was always deeply concerned for Terry and how well he was coping and, when they took a walk up the lane with Rory their mad Irish setter, he attempted to express those concerns. He was not one to wear his heart on his sleeve, but he knew what it was to carry a burden, having himself seen some terrible things in the desert during World War ll. There, he had been missing for six months living in a cave waiting for supplies and trying to find a way out of his situation.

'Don't take too much notice of me.' Cecil said sullenly. 'I'm finding it all a bit hard. I've surprised myself. I've seen some things in my time in the army you know, the war and all that, but this, it's really knocked me back,' he said, as they climbed the stile and made their way across the field.

'I know; I think I understand that. It's not what you expect to happen in life. We have all been hit very hard it's not something you bounce back from.' Terry said sympathetically.

'Yes, but I should be able to, but somehow I can't.' Cecil replied angrily.

'You are still a young man; you have your whole life ahead of you. It's not going to be easy for you. Margaret and I understand that and you know, one day, you may meet someone you want to marry. We want you to know that it's ok with us. We hope one day you'll find that special one and when you do we know you'll choose the right one and we'll always support you.'

Terry was surprised and touched by his frankness and that he had even been thinking along those lines.

'Thank you for saying that. I do appreciate it, but I can't imagine marrying again. For one thing Ann was very special, very special indeed and a difficult act to follow. The scars are deep; the road was too long, and the horror of the last six years remains with me. I'd also be fearful that if I were to marry, the same thing could happen all over again and I'm not brave enough to go through all that for a second time. I haven't got the courage or the strength. I am physically and mentally drained.'

They walked on in silence across the field, both contemplating their thoughts, but there was a healing power in the beauty of the countryside around them as spring showed its reluctant face.

Terry left Pucklechurch the following morning to return home. He had been given much to think about but now had to return to reality and take up the reigns again in order that Anne, who had been looking after the children, could get back to her work in London.

It had been agreed that Terry, Paul and Lynda would spend the Easter weekend in London with Anne. It was also Paul's twelfth birthday on the Easter Sunday. They took the train from York to Kings Cross, which the children enjoyed. They stayed at the house of one of Anne's friends and enjoyed their time looking at some of the attractions in London like the Houses of Parliament, Westminster Abbey, Tower Bridge, Kew Gardens and Regents Park. Anne had prepared a meal for them all at her place and took the weekend off from work at St Thomas's hospital, to spend time with them.

On return to Yorkshire, after Easter, work became busy for Terry. There were a lot of problems surrounding his new responsibility in overseeing the company's four-star hotel. More food and drink was going out the back door than the front, and expensive cutlery and plates seemed to just disappear down a black hole. All this needed his immediate attention as well as the rental income that came in at this time of year on the quarter day from the farms.

Paul and Lynda continued to enjoy various activities like, Judo, Brownies, and Table Tennis as they all settled back into their enforced new way of life. There were school trips for both Lynda and Paul and they both settled down to a full and busy school life with the usual range of exams and challenges. Terry's evenings were often filled with being taxi driver for the children, taking them here and there, but he was happy to see them taking up new interests, developing and enjoying life.

Anne would ring him often, sometimes in the middle of the night while she was sitting watching over a ward of sleeping patients at St Thomas Hospital, when they would have long chats. It was good to have a telephone by the bed for that reason! She would also come and stay for a few days when she was off duty, sometimes for five or six days and slowly their relationship grew and took on a life of its own. As May moved into June Terry could feel that the relationship with Anne was going in only one direction, but he was becoming happier with that. In July the wedding dress Anne had been making for her friend Jane, would be ready to walk her up the aisle. She was to marry in St Paul's Church, St. Helier on the Island of Jersey.

'Mathew and Jane have invited us both to their wedding,' Anne said excitedly. 'Will you be able to come? It would be lovely if you could. I'd love to have you there. I know you have the children to think about but maybe they would like to come too?'

'We're going down to Aylesford in Kent to stay with an Aunty on 17th July, then over to Shaftesbury to see Dawn's sister Rosemary. She's invited them to stay for a few days with her and Heighway, so I won't upset that arrangement. I could perhaps come to the wedding with you while they are staying in Shaftesbury. That would work and might be fun with you and your friends renting a house together; that is if there is room.'

So that was agreed. They rented a cottage for a few days with some of the other guests at L'Etacq in the north of the island, ready for the wedding day of Anne's friend who was so delighted with the dress she had made.

Early in July after much consideration and reflection Terry and Anne discussed the possibility of marriage, but it was never going to be a straightforward issue for so many reasons.

Anne was very low Anglican Church and Terry of course, was Catholic. In itself that was not a problem, but Anne's father and mother, would certainly not be happy. Terry was also twelve years older than Anne. George and Joan had said many times that they would like to have their two girls around them when they retired to their home in New Zealand. A marriage between Terry and Anne was not going to allow that to happen with Terry being firmly based in the U.K.

'Mum and Dad are due home from Africa on leave for five weeks on 2nd August, so I'll speak to them and we'll see how they take it. I don't want to upset them of course and I'm very conscious of their feelings, but at the same time I've a right to my own life. I know how they feel about having lost all those years when we were away at school in Tanzania and the U.K. and they so much want us to be around them now, to sort of compensate for the loss of those days, so I'll have to tread carefully. For them to be missionaries was their choice, and I don't see why Margie and I should have to restrict our lives to living in New Zealand to be near them, as lovely as it might be. It was surely the price they had to pay to follow their calling to live and work in Africa it was their sacrifice not ours.'

'I'll speak to them first about us if you don't mind and convince them that we know what we're doing and have thought it through in some depth.'

'Of course Anne, that's fine, you know best. I can speak to them later when they come here to stay as they've asked if they could come for a few days. Your Dad is keen to see some of the farms around and pick up a few tips and it will be nice to see them after so long.'

CHAPTER THREE

Cecil and Margaret were as restless as ever.

'We're definitely looking to sell the house and move from Pucklechurch,' Margaret explained to Terry.

'Cecil is finding Ann's death extremely difficult to accept and feels a move from here will do us both good, a sort of new beginning. I'm not so keen, but it's no good if he's unhappy and can't settle, so we are looking around the Shropshire area.'

Terry was sad for them for he knew how they loved the place. He also particularly liked the house and the surrounding countryside and had always enjoyed his visits to Meadowland Cottage, as well as all the happy memories there for him. However, if Margaret and Cecil were not happy living there then a move might just be the right thing for them.

He continued to visit them at Pucklechurch with the children whenever he could, and sometimes on his own. He decided not to tell them about his new relationship with Anne as, despite what Cecil had previously said to Terry, he was not sure they were in a position to take it all on board so soon. After all Terry was finding it difficult enough himself. There would come a time when it would be right to tell them and of course he wanted them to know before he told anyone else.

Anne came up to stay in Boroughbridge every couple of weeks depending on her work schedule and Terry looked forward to those visits. Often she would work nights to earn more days off and use them to come to Yorkshire. Terry was becoming a familiar figure waiting around on the platform at York station for the 125 train to arrive from Kings Cross. Meeting a train is always exciting but, for him to meet Anne again after days or weeks apart it was always special.

When Paul and Lynda were away on school trips Terry and Anne took time away for a weekend. They would spend a lot of time discussing the likely reaction of her parents. Anne was unsettled by the thought, wanting to please them, but wanting to marry Terry. They were very difficult days.

On 17th July Terry, Paul and Lynda went to Aylesford in Kent to visit Aunty Smith for a couple of days before going on to Shaftesbury to stay with Rosemary and Heighway Bates. Rosemary was the sister of Dawn Timmis from Hombolo days.

He found it hard leaving them for so long, but being with Anne and getting to know her was important for all their futures, if they were to become a family. He still constantly felt driven by the desire to be away from home where he felt restless, so moving around suited this sense embedded within him.

After the lovely warm sunny relaxing days in Jersey and the joy of the wedding, Anne returned to work in London and Terry returned to Shaftesbury to be with the children before going back to Boroughbridge. A week later Paul and Lynda went to stay with friends Pat and David in Shropshire. The friendship with them had started when Terry and Ann were living in the Seychelles, where Ann's illness had begun. It had always been a special friendship, bonded by happy memories and later tragic ones. Pat, in particular, had been a very close and dear friend to Ann in her last days and a loving support to the children. While the children were away it enabled Terry to catch up on his work and all the jobs that had piled up at home while he had been away.

He was invited to spend the day in Lapworth, near Birmingham, on 4th August at the home of Anne's aunty, where her parents were staying while on 'home leave' from Tanzania. It was the first time he had seen them for a long time and the first time as a widower. Anne had told them about her relationship with Terry so it was going to be an interesting day.

'Hello Mate,' was George's usual opening gambit!

'How ya doing?'

'We were so sorry to hear about Ann. It must have been a very difficult time for you and the children. How are they coping?'

'Thanks George. It's been traumatic for all the family and for the children especially. They have had to come to terms with the situation and it's not been easy to explain these things to them at such young ages, nine and eleven years.'

Joan gave Terry a kiss and welcomed him, and they sat and chatted before having lunch.

Nothing was said about Terry and Anne's relationship. He felt they knew but did not wish to discuss it and later Anne confirmed this to be the case. Terry wanted to talk to them about it so they might understand how serious they both were, how wonderful it was that he and Anne shared their hopes for the future all linked to their combined African pasts. However, because of their silence on the matter, he felt they didn't want to discuss it, so avoided bringing up the subject.

Terry noticed that Anne was very quiet, red eyed and tired looking. He wondered if she had been crying. He sensed an atmosphere so they kept to small talk with her parents and news about Tanzania.

Less than a week later George, Joan and Anne came to stay with Terry for a few days, so there was time to open the discussion with them, reluctant as they may have been.

'You know that Anne and I have become very good friends don't you George,' Terry said as they sat across the breakfast table on the first morning.

'Yes, she mentioned it while we were staying with Meg. Perhaps a little more than just friends we understand,' George said with a twinkle!

'It just somehow happened. After you asked her to come and see us following Ann's death we found we got on so well.

Nobody was more surprised than me, but we have a lot in common with our mutual African bond, our love for the country and its people, as well as the past that we shared at Hombolo. We realise there's much to consider as we go further down this road, but you know me George, better than most. You know I would never rush into anything and would always consider Anne and take good care of her, you must know that?'

'Well, its early days yet,' George replied looking to one side and rather sheepish.

'Its early days mate.'

'As you say, you have a lot of things to consider. You have different faiths, different ages and very different backgrounds, not to mention the children. We'll talk to Anne about it all and we'll see how it all turns out,' George said thoughtfully, trying, which was unlike him, to side step the issue.

It was as if he didn't really wish to discuss it and Joan seemed to keep away from all such topics, leaving it to George as she often did. Even when Terry knew her in Tanzania, she was never one to express her own personal feelings openly.

They filled the next few days with trips out to the many attractions in the area. Terry and Anne enjoyed showing them the charm and beauty that is Yorkshire, a fantastic county with country houses and abbeys laying deep in the hidden corners of the county, rich in history and majesty.

Anne did seem a bit quiet and preoccupied, and Terry got the feeling that their new relationship was perhaps not going down too well with her parents, but it was difficult to discuss it with her while they were there. Anne enjoyed being with Paul and Lynda and threw herself into exploring with them, like punting on the river at Newby Hall near Boroughbridge, riding on the train with them and helping them enjoy the days out together.

Terry could feel that George and Joan were far away in their thoughts and seemed to be hiding something of what they felt. He was not totally surprised by their concerns. They may have known Terry well, but similarly Terry knew them too. He knew that George was troubled at having had to leave his daughters so often when they went off to school back in the 60's in Tanzania and had often spoken to Terry about it when they were working together. He knew George wanted to have the girls around him in his retirement and Anne's relationship with Terry would mean that would not happen.

Terry was aware of their narrow background, their strong Low Church Anglican roots with a suspicion and intolerance of Catholics, shown to him when he was working at Hombolo. He felt that was their greatest concern for Anne with this new friendship, but believed it best to let them digest it and for it all to sink in.

After their stay with Terry and family, George and Joan went off to Wales with Anne and their younger daughter, Margie, for a two-week holiday as previously planned. A period for them to spend time together as a family.

'Terry, I'll be up to see you again as soon as Mum and Dad have returned to Tanzania in September. It will only be a short time after our holiday in Betwsy-y-Coed. I'll miss you so much, but I must give them time with me as it'll be a long while before I see them again and I really want them to understand our relationship.' Anne explained anxiously.

'Of course you must spend as much time as possible with them, I can see that. We'll speak on the phone when you have chance and we'll get together soon. I'll miss you all, especially you Anne, and the children will too. They have really loved having you around.'

Terry had plenty to do. Time was not going to hang heavily that was for sure, but he was concerned, and in a quandary with it all, fearful that the path was getting rocky for them just as he and Anne began to fall for each other in a big way. Perhaps, he thought, it would do some good to pull back a little and get on with life, which he did.

His new responsibilities at the hotel nearby were growing. Sometimes it was too close for comfort and he had to spend a lot of time there trying to sort out various situations. This mainly concerned staff issues, as and when they arose and he was often called out late in the evening. The disappearing knives, forks, spoons and crockery were finally tracked down. An inspection by Terry, together with the hotel manager of the staff flats, revealed that the chef was allowing the staff to take them back to their flats each evening with any leftover food, rather than to throw it out. That in principal was fine, but the staff never returned any of the plates or cutlery to the hotel so they piled up in the flats. They found an amazing amount in the rooms, filling several boxes, which they returned to the hotel insisting that in future only paper plates left the hotel or the member of staff concerned would immediately lose their jobs!

Wine in the cellar did not tally with the amounts purchased. They were adrift by a wide margin, which was a big worry and cost to the business. This had to be investigated urgently as the total amounts were considerable. By trolling through all the invoices and records Terry discovered that the manager was removing the wine himself for his own personal use, so a trap was laid resulting in the manager being sacked and a new one appointed.

The assistant manager Carlo, an Italian, was put forward to be the new manager. He had a wonderful personality and the respect of the work force. He played the piano brilliantly to the delight of all who dined in the restaurant. Terry proposed to his chairman that he was made up to manager. He reluctantly agreed and Carlo went on to become a star attraction. The place began to hum with weddings and other functions as he brought the staff together to the benefit and success of the whole business. Subsequently it went on to become a very successful enterprise.

As harvest was completed on the farms there was a lot of drainage work to be done once the grain had been gathered in leaving only the stubble. There had been little or no capital investment over the past thirty years and there was need for that to change. Some of the farmland was so wet that production fell well below the potential and the farmers were struggling to make a living with land values falling as a result.

There were many agricultural grants available from the EEC, which Terry could see would not last forever, with drainage and barn building attracting around sixty percent grants. Even some of the new buildings that had been built in the previous five years could receive up to a forty percent back dated grant, which represented a return of capital already spent, so that had to be looked at! Most of the farmers did not understand the mechanics of it all or how they might receive these grants. Indeed, they had little time to pursue them being too busy with the practical side of their business. So Terry stepped in and worked out a plan in conjunction with the farmer to gain what he could from the grant schemes available, to the benefit of the Landlord and the Tenant. This took a lot of long term planning and financial assessment, form filling and meetings with the Ministry of Agriculture. Once agreed in principle, Terry had to sell the idea both to the farmer and the Landlord so they could see the short and long-term benefits.

Paul and Lynda were busy with their schoolwork and with many activities when school was over, leaving Terry to act as taxi driver. He didn't mind and was only pleased to see them follow some of their interests and to make new friends. They were handling life well, at least on the outside and seemed to be coping with one parent, despite his limited abilities! As Paul said one day when his Dad asked if it was ever a problem to him-

'A lot of the pupils at school have only one parent, as their mothers and fathers are divorced.'

Terry had never thought of that and it gave him some comfort.

The house was now pretty well back to normal after the flood at the beginning of the year, due to all the work that had taken place to put it right. For Terry losing his father was a tremendous blow coming so soon after the flood and the traumatic death of his young wife. It was so much sadness and heartache for him in five short months but he was doing his best to face up to it and accept life's new challenges. He'd be fine, he felt, as long as there were no more catastrophes around the corner. The least little wobble was likely to send him off in the wrong direction. Slowly he was beginning to heal. It did not bring either Ann or his father back and things would never again be as they were, but life changes and it's something we all have to accept. Healing takes you forward, but does not restore what was or what had been. The wounds are healed but the scars remain. Healing is not about yesterday, it's about tomorrow. It's about living the life God wants us to live from that day on.

Anne Hart had come into his life uninvited in a way, but perhaps, Terry thought, it was for the good. Good for him and good for the children. Not that he would ever marry someone just so that his children would have a Mother. That would never work.

He was growing to love Anne in a way he never thought was possible. She brought new life and light into their lives. However, he was not sure that he had the courage to put himself in a position where, once again, he might have to watch someone he loved die of a serious illness. He was often very doubtful that he could. It was his worst nightmare in any future new relationship. He had already lived through six long years of it. The horrors and memories still kept him awake at night with vivid flash backs. It was something he had to try to sort out in his own mind before ever being able to seriously consider marriage again.

Anne came up from London on Saturday 18th September, just after Terry's 37th birthday, for an overnight stay. She seemed nervous and quieter than usual. She told him all about her holiday with her parents in Wales and then she dropped a bombshell.

'Mum and Dad have given me a ticket to go and visit New Zealand. They want me to see the country as I don't really know it.'

Terry was astounded. Surely this was the old Victorian method of getting your daughter out of the way for a while.

'I see. Is it all booked up then?'

'I have to confirm it by 25th September for the flight out on 6th January next year, but I wanted to talk to you about it first. It's not going to make any difference to us. I'll only be away for six weeks and I can phone you often and write. It's just such a wonderful opportunity and I'd like to see the country of my father's birth as I was so young the last time we were there.'

'Yes I can see that,' Terry replied thoughtfully.

She wrapped herself around him in a reassuring manner, trying to convince him that all would be well.

However, Terry was concerned, upset even, that his long-time friends George and Joan had not had the courage to discuss it with him face to face, and to tell him what they thought and what they really felt about him and Anne. This method he sensed was all a bit underhand. It seemed to him that Anne had led him along a road that was fast looking like a cul–de–sac. He was most concerned for Paul and Lynda who were growing close to Anne. He could not, and would not see them hurt again, whatever the personal cost to him turned out to be.

October came around again all too quickly, with the first anniversary of Ann's death. Terry found that day the most difficult to deal with as memories came flooding back and the nightmares returned, keeping him awake night after sleepless night. The pointlessness of all that had happened, when his wife Ann, that shining light, had been extinguished at such a young age for no good reason, breaking five hearts in the process.

Sacrifice and dedication are not painful for someone you love, but necessary and often part and parcel of what it means to love. He had to step out of his comfort zone, endure whatever he was sent, and cling on with courage and fortitude. That's what love is, but it sent him into a spiralling decline and into a very dark place for weeks after the anniversary had passed by.

Both Paul and Lynda were shortly off on school trips, Lynda to the Yorkshire Dales and Paul on an exciting trip to France. This was the first of many in his life and, unbeknown to them all at the time, the place where he would go on to live and bring up a family as an adult in the years to come.

Terry used that time to try and pull himself together. Anne came up from London at the beginning of November for a week. It was a slightly strained time after which she went to stay with her aunt in Lapworth before returning to work at St Thomas Hospital. The hospital had agreed to keep her job open for when she returned from New Zealand. She was pleased about this and all was now ready for her to fly out on 6th January 1983.

A welcome visitor to Riverside House on 13th November was Terry's lovely niece Anna Marie from Weymouth, who had come to stay for a week. He took her around to see some of the farms on the estates that he managed, and she took charge of the children while he drove down to London to pick up Anne and bring her back for a long weekend. Anna Marie had no knowledge of their relationship but her stay did overlap a night with Anne's who came for the weekend. Anne came a couple more times before Christmas. The rail track from Kings Cross to York was becoming white hot!

Terry and the children spent Christmas at Pucklechurch with Cecil and Margaret who were pleased to have their grandchildren with them. He found them as restless as ever but they were hoping to move to Ludlow in Shropshire if they could do a deal on a house they had spotted in the newspaper. Cecil always had a good nose for property and he was hoping to complete the purchase sometime in February 83, depending on the sale of their own house. This made Christmas at 'Meadowland Cottage' a bit special, with it likely to be the last one spent in the house, a place they had all loved and enjoyed but, in the end, held too many memories when it came to it, for all of them.

On 29th December Terry and the children made their way back to Yorkshire calling in at Lapworth where Anne was staying with her Aunt Meg. They took Anne back with them for a few days. It was to be her last stay before she left for her trip to New Zealand on 6th January. They spent their time doing ordinary things together, sometimes alone, and sometimes with the children.

Anne had been such an influence in exorcizing some of the demons that had haunted Terry. She lit up the shadows, opened the windows, and helped the healing process with a flickering of romance. It was going to be a tough six weeks ahead with the force of Anne's family clearly pushing them apart. It was going to be hard, but what could he do?

Monday 3rd January had a slow unexciting start. School had not yet re-opened after the Christmas break, so the morning was a relaxed one, unlike the typical school day.

Anne had arranged to take the 16.48 train from York to Kings Cross, so they were all able to have lunch together and take a walk by the river before it was time for Terry to drive her to the station.

Anne was strangely quiet on the journey, carrying an expression of hurt and sadness on her face.

The 125 train roared in on time from Scotland, rumbling in alongside the platform to collect more passengers and to whisk her off to the city.

This was their bitter moment of parting. They embraced wordlessly as they stood on the platform, her dazzling sapphire blue eyes looked up at his, full of tears and longing. Her eye make-up was running down her cheeks giving her a melancholy expression, a look of sorrow, love, and affection.

Feeling a knot in her stomach she said,

'I'm deeply sad for us both, but I'll be back, I really will.'

Each knew the uncertainty of that statement as their intertwined fingers separated and Anne clambered aboard the train to London. The tone of the train's engine broke the bond between them and in seconds Anne had gone and Terry stood on the platform until the train was out of sight, swallowed up in its own pollution.

An empty feeling took over the house as Paul, Lynda and Terry ate a tea of boiled eggs and toast, followed by slices of sponge cake that Anne had made during her stay. The old pain of loss and loneliness returned with its memories and sleepless nights. How quickly life reverted back to what it had been before the flood. How hard he had to fight to keep above it all and not sink below life's waves.

Work and school the next day was a good antidote and Terry thought it might be nice if they all had a holiday together.

When the children returned from school he put the idea to them.

'Where would you like to go for a holiday?' They both looked a bit blank!

'Would you like to go back and see our old friends in Malawi, visit Bunda and perhaps stay with the Sisters at Mlale Mission?'

'Could we? Yeah! - please!'

'I'll look into it and see what I can come up with.'

Within ten days Terry had booked their flights and arranged with the Sisters for the three of them to stay over the Easter period for three weeks at Mlale Mission, just south of Lilongwe. With Luigi being just a couple miles from there it was a chance to spend some time with him too and to revisit Bunda College that was near-by.

Terry never needed an excuse to return to his beloved Africa and the thought of it lifted his flagging spirits.

CHAPTER FOUR

Anne left for New Zealand as planned on 6th January and quickly wrote a letter to Terry that arrived in record time on 12th. She had a steady programme of events which George and Joan had arranged. Various friends had her to stay with them as she slowly toured the South Island, starting at Christchurch where her parents had a small house into which they hoped to retire before too long.

Mike Baxter from Christchurch, New Zealand had, the previous year gone to Tanzania for six months to help George with the building of some new water tanks for Hombolo Leprosy Centre. George had arranged for Mike, who was about Anne's age, to keep an eye on her while she was in the country and to show her around. How thoughtful of him! Mike ran a small horticultural business on South Island.

Life back in Yorkshire took on its daily tasks and busyness and they all looked forward to the excitement of their planned African adventure leaving on 14th March and flying into Blantyre via Lusaka. They had a six-hour delay at Lusaka airport as the President was due to arrive back in the country from an overseas trip. The whole place was taken over by hundreds of people as they waited for him to arrive. The airport buildings were over-run, the café was full and the whole place jammed with people singing and shouting in praise of Kenneth Kaunda their President. When his plane finally arrived it touched down on the tarmac and without stopping immediately took off again and circled the airport. It did this six times as a sort of salute before finally stopping for the President to get out and greet his people with very long speeches.

Terry, Paul and Lynda finally arrived at Blantyre airport at 12.30 when they boarded another Air Malawi plane at 14.30 to fly up to Lilongwe where Sisters Irene, Marcelle, Laura and Genevieve, as well as Luigi were waiting to greet them. What excitement there was, so much so that Lynda was sick all down the steps of the plane - lovely!

They spent the next three weeks visiting faces and places they had known when they had lived and worked in Malawi. They so enjoyed being back to see, feel, and explore Africa again. It was a total change of routine, scenery and people and almost permanent blue skies. The warm heart of Africa with its depth, history and magic once again embraced them. It took them out of themselves, never forgetting the love Ann had too for the country and the joy they had all found while living there. But the past was in the past and Terry knew he had to climb on through it for his own and the children's sake. This was a valuable break, which gave him time to see life more clearly and to step away from everyday problems and cares.

He missed Anne Hart and all she had brought into their lives since they met last year. Now she was in New Zealand and he longed to see her again to hear how the trip had been, realising how very much she had come to mean to him, opening up their future. He feared, somewhat, her strong family ties and the persuasion and pressure George was putting her under, that she might be persuaded not to remain in England, that ultimately she would feel she had to follow him and live in New Zealand. Terry hoped she would be strong enough to do what she really wanted to do and not bow to such pressure.

They arrived back at London's Heathrow Airport on Friday 8th April, three days before Paul's 13th birthday, having had a fantastic three weeks in Malawi and determined now to get on with their life and work, come what may. Anne was back from New Zealand that same week and within a few days she came to stay for ten days. An unusually long time he thought, but tried not to read anything into it. They had exchanged a few letters and phone calls while she was away, and he was excited to be seeing her again.

Anne had gone to stay with her aunty Meg at Lapworth in the midlands on return from New Zealand, so Terry went to pick her up from there and take her to Yorkshire for a few days.

On his arrival at her aunt's Anne was looking out of the front door of the house in anticipation just as he pulled in and parked his car in the drive.

'So how was the trip? Did it live up to your expectations?' Terry shouted out from the car window.

Anne rushed over to his car and almost dragged him out of the seat.

'I've missed you, I've missed you so much,' she said as she threw her arms around him.

'It was an incredible trip, such a beautiful, peaceful and unpopulated place, I just loved it. I so wished you could have been with me.'

She was without doubt very excited by the whole experience, but seemed happy to be back in the U.K. again.

'Come on in and have a coffee. I'm nearly packed. How are Paul and Lynda?'

'They're fine. They had a wonderful time in Malawi and are now settling back at home. They'll be delighted to see you again. They speak of little else.'

That afternoon they drove up to Boroughbridge and arrived in time to meet Paul and Lynda off the school bus. They were thrilled to see Anne and took her off to their rooms to show her the things they had brought back from Malawi and tell her about their own exciting holiday adventures.

That evening Anne and Terry went for a meal at the Crown Hotel nearby, giving them time alone to chat and catch up on events. They were so happy to be together again and it was past midnight before they left the restaurant.

Anne was able to tell him all the details of her trip, how she had visited so many different families that her parents knew. Some they had worked with over the years in Tanzania as well as other family friends. She had travelled extensively around the South Island and part of the north and seemed very impressed by the beauty of the place.

'So how did you get on with Mike Baxter?' Terry asked.

'He was very kind and helped me a lot, showing me different places of interest. We talked about his days in Tanzania when he was helping Dad. He loved it, but said he couldn't ever live there.'

As the evening moved on the wine began to flow; freeing up their tongues.

Terry began to ask more searching questions of Anne.

'You do know why your parents wanted you to go out to New Zealand don't you?'

'Yes they wanted me to see their country, where Dad was born.'

'Is that what you really believe Anne?' He asked.

She looked a little surprised and concerned.

'Yes, it is, why?'

'Come on now, you must know they want you to go and live there to be with them when they retire and were encouraging you to do that by sending you on this trip. I feel, partly for that reason, they don't want us to get together or to get married for they fear you'll be living here and they'll rarely, if ever, see you. That's not what they want. It was an attempt to separate us. They don't approve of us do they?'

Anne was bewildered and thoughtful.

'They have their reservations of course, as they told me before they left - the children, our age difference, not to mention the religious differences. You know how Low Church they are. But I must be allowed to have my own life. Many people have contributed to all they did. They couldn't have served in Africa without any one of them. The help they received enabled them to live and work in Tanzania for all those years. Margie and I contributed too, in our own way, by not complaining when we were shipped off here and there; but that's done now. Why should we be expected to go on supporting them in their way of life. We need to go our own way. They must accept and understand that. You know people gave donations and raised funds from Dad's home town of Christchurch to pay their salary and supported them in so many other ways. Then there was my Aunt Meg - Mum's sister, who looked after Margie and me when we were at school or on holiday here in England. But why should Margie and I have to pay the price for their decision to work in Tanzania? It was their choice and they have no right to try and make us go and live in New Zealand if we don't choose to.'

'And do you choose to?' Terry swiftly enquired.

Anne hesitated.

'Your hesitation says a lot I feel.'

'Terry I love you and I want us to be together, really I do, wherever that has to be. Here, or in New Zealand, anywhere, but together. You know it's what I want more than anything else.'

'Are you really sure of that, because I'm not. It wouldn't work if you started to feel unhappy here in England, cut off from your family. It already looks as if Margie might go out to live in New Zealand, and your Aunt is talking of doing the same in the future, so forgive me when I say I'm not so sure it's what you want.'

Anne looked dejected, trapped like a rabbit in the headlights.

'I'm being torn apart by all this and it hurts. I have to choose, it's so unfair. I'm confused, I shouldn't be expected to have to make these choices,' she said tearfully.

Terry gently explained.

'Anne, we really do have to work this out now, before too many people get hurt. It's killing me and nothing must give the children anymore grief - that is paramount. I cannot see them put through any more heartache and pain. They have already had too much of that in their young lives, far too much. As their father I must and will protect them, as far as I can.'

They left the conversation there for the time being. They both had much to think over and they didn't want to spoil their first evening together after so long apart.

So Terry went on to tell her all about his trip to Malawi with the children and how he had fallen off a motorbike belonging to one of the Sisters which meant his arm was in a sling for several days. The tussle he'd had with a black mamba snake at Bunda College, as well as the joys of flying through Zambia with all its delays. Malawi was a place Anne had never visited, but it was not so different from Tanzania.

For the remainder of the week they were busy. Terry spent some days at work while Anne enjoyed being at Riverside House and recovering from her travels. Other days they were out and about together, often continuing with their in-depth discussions about the future, sometimes late into the night and early morning.

Terry noticed that Anne had received a number of letters from people in New Zealand since her return, which had been forwarded by her aunty, particularly from Mike Baxter whose name was on the back of a number of the envelopes! What was all that about he wondered? Anne dismissed it saying he wanted to know she had arrived back safely in UK and all was well with her. There was certainly nothing going on between them she assured him.

After the ten days together Anne had to return to London where she had to find new accommodation, before taking up her old nursing job. In the meantime, she was to stay with friends while doing agency work.

Terry, Paul and Lynda went to see Cecil and Margaret's new bungalow which they had bought following the successful sale of 'Meadowland Cottage.' It was in Vernolds Common near Ludlow, Shropshire. They had moved there while Terry had been on holiday in Malawi, so he was looking forward to seeing it for the first time. It was fairly typical of their usual choice, far out in the countryside with glorious views and a large garden. They seemed very happy and more content in their new surroundings, which Terry was pleased to see. Margaret enjoyed the new garden and Cecil had been able to purchase, and use for the first time, a ride-on tractor mower, so he was happy as he cruised around the garden. He loved walking, and took their madder than ever Irish Setter off most mornings on a walk to a near-by racecourse about three miles away. This provided the sense of freedom that he relished, and much delight to their dog Rory.

A week later Anne returned to stay again for a few days. She had been working nights so had earned extra days off, enabling her to come and spend time with them in Yorkshire.

Because of her indecision about the future it was a very difficult time. Terry felt Anne really had to make up her mind where their relationship was going. It was in her hands, she had to decide. The more they talked about it the bigger the circles seemed to go.

Terry was not easy about the correspondence that still seemed to be flowing in from Mike Baxter and suspected that he was encouraging Anne to return there to live so he could build on their relationship, and who could blame him. Maybe this was driven and supported by George and Joan in the first place, Terry suspected. Who knows?

In the end he felt he must bring the whole matter to a head and on the last night before Anne was due to return to work in London they both agreed that she must seriously consider what she was going to do and come up with her answer: either go to live in New Zealand to be with her parents, or to marry Terry and live in England. They agreed that within two weeks she would give Terry her decision, one-way or the other.

'I really feel Anne that I have to let you go. It's too much, too many pressures for you, for us both.'

'No, please don't say that, we have to fix it somehow, we have too,' she pleaded passionately.

'I know you say we could all go to New Zealand to live, but it's not really an option for me. The children and the grandparents have already made too many sacrifices. I can't ask them for more. I couldn't inflict that on them, however much I feel for you. They've been through far too much already,' he replied. 'And I made a promise to my wife Ann, that I would always care, and be there, for her parents. I can't blow their world apart by leaving the country, not after all they've been through and I must honour my promise to Ann.'

'Terry, I've been too selfish I know, but I will give you my decision, as we agreed, within two weeks. I promise. There's no way we can go on like this.' Anne replied unhappily and Terry agreed.

They were both in solemn mood the next morning, when in heavy rain, Terry drove Anne to the railway station in York to take the train to Kings Cross. There he carried her bag to the platform as she hung on to his arm, hardly daring to look at him as they slowly and deliberately made their way to the train that was now waiting to depart. It was a sad, emotional farewell as they once more said their goodbyes in this now familiar place. She was drenched from the rain; soaked from their slow reluctant walk from the car park. Water was dripping from her hair and running down her cheeks. In a speechless embrace he took her in his arms. She was trembling and crying in their blending moment of pain and sadness. With Anne's help, gradually his previously open wounds had formed a scar, but now they gaped open with unbearable agony. Slowly, the train pulled out leaving Terry standing forlorn, alone and wondering.

A little under two weeks later, on 16th June, Terry received a letter from Anne with her decision. She told him that with enormous difficulty and a broken heart she had decided to go to live in New Zealand and would leave in November.

It made heart-breaking reading, stopping his day, causing him to slide into a deeply depressive state. He could not go to work and stayed at home the whole day and most of the following week. He was at rock bottom. His heart had been broken again, he was absolutely shattered, disappointed and hurt.

The morning after receiving her decision he rang Anne, who was staying at a friend's house in London, to tell her the letter had arrived and that he had, very reluctantly, accepted her decision. They were both very upset throughout the whole hour-long tortuous conversation. Anne wanted them to remain as friends, but Terry said he couldn't do that and could only cope if there was a total cut off of their relationship.

They never met, spoke or communicated ever again.

CHAPTER FIVE

Since his wife Ann had died Terry felt he was travelling up the wrong side of a fast moving escalator. One thing after another came towards him in the opposite direction. He had to keep picking himself up to continue life's climb carrying a load he felt unable and ill-equipped to bear, drained of energy, fast running out of steam as he moved three steps forward and then four back. This latest setback had hit him hard. Was it tougher than he imagined it might be or had he become personally weakened by the constant and unrelenting barrage of events that had hit him over the past few years?

Terry felt he and Anne would have complemented each other. They had so much going for them. He was learning to overcome his hang-ups about entering into another marriage and felt it would work out and that, at last, life would revert back to a more level playing field as normality returned; but it was not to be. He seemed stuck in a vacuum.

He did not wish to lapse back into being self-centred and pre-occupied with sorrows that only shrank and narrowed his horizons, causing his troubles to loom ever larger in his mind. It would take him over, with nothing else able to enter his head but his own anxieties and he didn't want that. He felt crushed and perplexed and it was hard not to give way to despair, feeling persecuted, abandoned and alone. He needed to trust God in his life, frail and fragile though that trust may have been.

So that was what he did over the next few years. He stepped back and watched life, as if from the side-lines. The situation seemed to take on a life of its own, one he seemed powerless to change or influence. Daily he fought his depressive state of mind, fighting against the negative and corrosive powers that tried to drag him down. He walked miles with his dog Duke as he sought his identity and place in life, continually uplifted by his children and their needs.

Life's everyday events, as always came to his rescue and took over. The first started with Lynda's confirmation into the Catholic Church a few days later at St Mary's in Knaresborough which they celebrated with others from the church and school.

Paul enjoyed being a full member of the Air Training Corp, and Terry took him and his friends to and from their meeting place in Harrogate as required and enjoyed seeing him grow in that interest. He was keen to fly and to have a career in the RAF, before joining one of the international airlines as a pilot. Terry continually told him that there was nothing he couldn't do if he really wanted and was prepared to put in the work and effort. It was looking as if nothing was going to stop him as he worked away with enthusiasm.

Terry's colleague, Jeremy and his wife brought joy to the end of the year when they produced Laura, a 7lb baby girl on 25th November.

Christmas, was once again spent with the Grandparents until the last day of 1983 when they returned to Boroughbridge to start a new year; one that he hoped would turn out to be a happier one.

1984 had brought many challenges, giving Terry little time to look back. The company moved office from Harrogate, and the Reading Room in the village of Arkendale, to a new combined office in Boroughbridge. It took him only minutes to get there which was a great help when looking after the children and coping with their daily needs. His 'Home Help,'

Maureen, came once a week to keep the place in order and assist in keeping body and soul together which was essential.

In August he took a break to visit his friend Luigi, now back at his home in Craveggia, Northern Italy and in October, American friends Ed and Mary Lawson, from Bunda College days in Malawi, came to stay, from their home in Florida, for a week.

He had come to terms with his situation but still felt empty and forlorn and was still having the same recurring nightmares surrounding Ann's illness as he revisited them a thousand times having to face the pain of that irreplaceable loss. His sense of duty and his love for the children was the only thing that drove him on.

As Christmas 84 approached it was time to catch up with family and friends. George and Joan Hart sent him greetings as they always had done. A very subdued letter was enclosed which told that Anne had married Mike Baxter on 27th October 1984, less than a year after going to live in New Zealand. They lived a few miles away from George and Joan in Christchurch on South Island. Terry was not surprised at the news confirming what he thought might happen. George and Joan had now got what they wanted and Terry just hoped that Anne was happy.

One of Terry's tenant farmers near York had a daughter, Kate, who enjoyed singing and was an excellent opera singer. She had been to Music College near Leeds and was keen to have experience before an audience. Terry arranged with Carlo at the Crown Hotel, which was within his responsibility, for Kate to sing in their restaurant each weekend. She was a real star and sang in the style of Maria Callas, the American born Greek soprano. Kate, with Carlo on the piano, provided wonderful entertainment for those dining at the hotel. They packed the restaurant every Saturday evening for weeks. Terry became quite involved helping Kate as her talent and confidence developed and, in so doing, they became good friends, as did her wonderful farming family at Kexby near

York. However, he fought off any potential involvement with Kate following his heart-breaking relationship with Anne Hart which was still an aching wound.

On Wednesday 6th March 1985 while Terry was at work in his office he received a phone call from Paul's school, St John Fisher in Harrogate. They asked him to get to the hospital as quickly as possible as his son Paul had been admitted with facial burns. Distraught and upset he shot off at great speed to find Paul lying in bed with an almighty brown burn on the right side of his face covering his forehead and surrounding his eye over his cheek and ear.

'What on earth has happened,' Terry asked Paul who was sitting up in bed looking very pale.

'I was playing with a fire in the field by the school and it went up in my face!'

Once it was established that the burns were not too deep and that his eyesight was not affected, Terry calmed down somewhat. However, the Headmaster called Terry in to discuss the situation and it transpired that Paul and his friends had been playing with a can of WD 40 over a fire and sprayed it to make it burn. It would seem as if the jet from the can had been facing the wrong way when he sprayed the fire and it hit Paul's face. The flammable contents of the WD40 burst into flames! He was lucky not to lose his eyesight or to have caused longer lasting damage the doctor told Terry. As it was, it took the rest of the year for his face to fully recover, but a valuable lesson was learned.

Paul had a school trip to France in April and was well enough after his fire accident to make the trip. He enjoyed the holiday and it may well have planted the seeds for him to be attracted to live there in the future, as indeed he went on to do.

In mid-May it was Terry's turn to have an accident. His car, a sleek Italian Lancer, was involved in an accident when another car crashed into the back of him on the road near Kilburn village. It was a total write off with the impact to the rear bending the car into a concertina shape. Fortunately, he walked away from the accident, shaken but not hurt!

Later that month Terry and the children enjoyed a week's holiday in Guernsey flying from Leeds and staying in a hotel on the island. They enjoyed the break, visiting the beautiful outer islands of Sark and Herm, playing tennis, bike riding and walking.

With his heart always in Africa, Terry asked a Crown Hotel receptionist, Nicola, who he knew well, if she would come and stay to care for Paul and Lynda while he went to Malawi for a visit in November. They got on well with her, as Paul knew Nicola from his Saturday job at the Crown. So, once again, Terry found himself back in Malawi where he stayed with Luigi at Zanzi Estate close to his old college at Bunda and he was able to visit old faces and places. Two days after his arrival they had the first rain since early April with a useful 1.5 inches. This was just what the newly planted tobacco crops needed. More heavy rain followed bringing new life to the countryside all around. Luigi was going through difficult times with many staff problems. Clearly he loved the people of the country, but they did not see life as he did with clashes and governmental problems surrounding him on all fronts. He was playing with political fire and Terry feared for his future in a very sensitive Malawi, unless his attitude changed.

A lot of the time was spent at the Mlale Mission near-by, where the Sisters of Africa were running the hospital. They were the same Sisters who were there when Terry worked at Bunda and who Ann had worked with. It was a joy to be with them again and receive their words of guidance, wisdom and support. However, his life was now firmly in the UK and after this three week break it was time to return home to his children and to leave the warm heart of Malawi before again it took control of him. He was not free for such an event to even enter his thoughts.

His trip to Malawi had given him time to think about life. He was beginning to feel it was time for him to consider his own future as well as that of the children. They were getting older and one day would leave home. He was getting strong and clearer thoughts about marrying again, should the opportunity arise. The more he thought about it the stronger the desire became. He really did not relish living out his life alone. At forty he was too young for that. Ann had never wanted that for him, she told him he was not good alone and must one day consider marriage again. He would not be betraying her memory. The children would not always be with him and he had no wish to be a burden and responsibility to them in the years ahead. They had to be allowed to go out into the world to make their own way, uninhibited by their father's life.

Despite the prospects of history repeating itself, by any new partner becoming seriously ill, he was convinced that such thoughts were ridiculous. He could not go through life thinking like that. Was he a man or a mouse? The best way to love is to love like you have never been hurt. He made up his mind while on the long flight back from Malawi that he would take the chance and would seek to remarry, if the right person should come along. There were so many couples in his life who were wonderful examples but he could surely never match any of them. Their wives wonderful, loving and caring and who would surely raise the bar too high for the person Terry would love to share his life with. Then, of course, how do you go about meeting that special person? It seemed a hopeless task so he left it there in the back of his mind. After all he had enough difficulties in his life without adding to them.

All was well on his arrival back in Yorkshire at the end of November. Nicola, young as she was, had done a brilliant job, she was a little on the wild side but a lovely person and he was grateful to her. There was of course plenty of work to catch up on following the weeks away, his thoughts were forced to turn to work and Christmas that was fast approaching.

One of the difficult farm tenants who rented a 200-acre farm from the company, was proving very problematic when it came to agreeing his new rent, payable for the next three years. His rent review was well overdue. The company had let it slide, mainly because the farmer, Daniel Oats, was a friend of the family and in particular of Andrew Bowman the Chairman. Terry had been instructed to make sure that his new rent was in line with all the other tenants, but this did not go down well with Mr Oats

Terry made an appointment to meet Mr Oats at his farm at the beginning of the following week. He was a short determined sort of man in his late seventies. He had a sharp pinched face and wore a cloth cap, and he had a hard exterior, but with a soft inside. When Terry arrived he was invited to the kitchen where the discussion was to take place. The kitchen had a very old yellowish Belfast sink that had once been white. Alongside the sink at waist height was a long piece of board about two feet wide that stretched the length of the kitchen, some twenty-five feet long, with a similar smaller version above it with a few jars and tins scattered on the top shelf. That was the extent of the kitchen apart from an old freestanding brown cupboard and three very old tired chairs around a small round table. The lighting consisted of a single twenty-five watt single light bulb hanging uncovered from the ceiling. Mr Oats invited Terry to sit down.

'Aa suppose you'd better sit down lad and see if we can sort this out.'

He went to the upper shelf and removed a rusty tin and put it on the table between them.

'You'd best have one of those afore we start,' he said as he removed the lid and pushed the tin towards Terry.

Terry looked in the tin. It was half full of mint imperials. He couldn't believe his eyes; even those were yellow with age!

Not wishing to offend him he removed one and put it in his mouth pushing the tin towards Mr Oats who then did the same. They both sat there sucking the mints as Terry opened the negotiations.

'As you know you've had a beneficial rent for many years now, paying about half the market value and I'm sorry, but we now have to bring it in line with our other rents. We can't afford to go on subsidising your farm any longer.'

'Ah well, I'll have to have a word with Mr Andrew about this. We've had this arrangement for years. It's alright thou coming along here and pushing up me rent like that, but where do you think the extra brass is gonna come from. Tell me that young man?'

'Well I'm sorry,' Terry replied, 'but the farm estates have to start paying for themselves and that means everyone, without exception, having to pay a fair rent. You have a good business here with much of the land used as gallops for the local horse racing course, so I do know that you can afford it.'

'Well young man I ain't gonna to pay it so that's that and I'm gonna to speak to Mr Andrew about it.'

'Do that by all means, but it'll not make any difference. He'll only refer you back to me. He's asked me to get all the rents up to date and to their proper market value.' Terry replied firmly.

'You reckon so eh lad!'

'OK Mr Oats, I'll be coming back to see you next Monday morning at, say, 10 o'clock. That will give you time to think about it and then perhaps we can settle this.'

Terry left him at the table looking very flustered, muttering that there was absolutely no way he was going to accept an increase in his rent. He couldn't afford it and would never agree to it. Never.

The following Monday, as promised, Terry went along to meet Mr Oats at the farm, parked his car and knocked on the door. There was no reply! He set off to look around the farm buildings for him. As he walked across the yard a man in a suit approached him.

'Can I help you?' he asked.

'I'm not sure' Terry replied. 'I'm looking for Mr Oats. Who are you?'

'So you haven't heard then?'

'Heard what?' Terry enquired curiously.

'Sorry to tell you but Mr Oats died yesterday morning!'

Months later, Terry discovered that Mr Oats had left three million pounds in his Will!

Terry's thoughts continued to revert back to the decision he had made during his long flight from Malawi; that he would seek to remarry should he happen to find the right person. He so wanted to share his life with someone else, the joys and the sorrows. Without this life was empty. It would also be good for Paul and Lynda too. Nobody could ever replace Ann and that was not the intention. No one could replace their mother either, but it would be nice for them to have a friend in their future lives: someone who would come to love them as he did and to care for them in all things.

How on earth was he going to achieve it? that was the biggest obstacle. He met many ladies in his work and in daily life, but it was laughable to think of any one of them in that context. Apart from anything else his checklist would be too long and difficult for anyone to fulfil, impossible perhaps. He knew that she would have to be Christian with the same beliefs he had. Not necessarily a Catholic, but someone who had, at least, Christian values. The more he considered it all the less likely it seemed that he would ever realise his aim. His demands were set too high and he was not able to compromise them. Did such a person exist or were the stakes set too high?

1986 was off to a busy start for work and in the lives of the children. There was always some event needing Terry's attention. The weeks flew by. They visited Grandparents in Shropshire and friends in Devon and Sussex which all helped to break up his busy schedule of caring for the children and gave the opportunity to spend enjoyable days with family and good friends.

Aunty Lesley, Cecil's Sister who had worked for thirty years in Africa, died in Kent on 16th March, another sad family moment. She had followed Ann and Terry around the world and they both had a great love and respect for her in all she had done for the people of Africa. She had been a female Livingstone and was respected and loved by so many.

On 17th June Paul had an interview with the RAF at their office in Leeds, which he was most excited about. He passed all their tests and exams but failed his eyesight test. This meant he could not progress with his application. His eagerness to fly drove all his ambitions to achieve entry into the RAF so it was a very big blow that took a long time for him to overcome. However, many years later, when the fighter planes were leaving the U.K. to bomb Bagdad, they both recalled where Paul might have been on that night and thanked God he was not amongst them.

On the 21st August Paul went to school to collect his 'O' level exam results. He obtained six 'O' levels at 'C' grade and one 'O' level at 'A' grade, but was devastated to get only 'D' for maths, which his face revealed when he arrived home that evening. Terry's heart went out to him as he had worked hard, and this was yet another blow for him to deal with. The next day he had a weekend trip with the school at Scarborough which helped soften this traumatic time with a bit of relaxation.

Life at work was showing worrying symptoms of change for Terry. Andrew, the company chairman, was displaying disturbing signs of inability regarding his position inherited from his father who earlier, had wisely decided to leave the whole estate in trust, as none of his six children showed any sign of promise in business or had leadership qualities. As the eldest, Andrew had taken over as chairman on his father's death, but was clearly incapable of the challenge due, partly, to the way his father had suppressed him during childhood. Andrew was now under pressure from the other family members and the Group Trustees to provide some profits, and an income for them all. So far he had been unsuccessful and failed to show any success in running the group of companies. He had spent millions on his pet theme of refurbishing a hotel and, although it had been going for a few years, profits, when there were any, were very low considering the amount of capital invested. The board were aware of the vast inheritance from their father, consisting of land and property but they received no income from it and were rightly none too pleased to the extent that they were seeking to break the Trust, summoning the Trustee's to a meeting which caused Andrew a lot of grief.

Terry was beginning to feel the effects of all this when land and assets were sold off to provide money to pay a dividend. Not the way to run a healthy business! In desperation the chairman had also brought his nephew into the business in order to try and appease one of his sisters. Not a good move! He was a total waste of space, very unbalanced and totally incompetent. Even worse, the nephew was of the understanding that he, himself, was some sort of whiz kid! Having received treatment for a mental problem he was still very unstable, moving from being a very charming person to being totally obsessed and objectionable: a lethal mix in any business. He thought he was the 'great' businessman' but had no idea what he was doing and slowly, over the course of five years, brought about the decline of the whole multi-million-pound empire. Eventually and inevitably the family finished up fighting amongst themselves, and years later Terry was called to act as a witness in the Royal Courts of Justice in London. Andrew received his just deserts to which Terry was able to contribute. He felt he had to do this for the sake of all those who had suffered through Andrew's actions.

It was extremely difficult dealing with the volatility of these mad men on a day-to-day basis, with an incompetent Chairman running the business and neither knowing their own inabilities. They began to fire off all sorts of mad schemes and to accuse everyone of ripping them off or some other injustice when, in fact, they were actually surrounded by some wonderfully loyal and capable staff in nearly every aspect of the business. The effect was to drive the good staff away, or if they did stay, put them under a terrific strain to the extent some became ill, with a few deaths attributed to the lethal combination of stress. It was to this cause, that Terry, many years later in the dock of the Royal Courts of Justice had the opportunity to set the record straight even if those lost did not benefit.

Terry began to realise that the time had come when he should consider other employment, before he lost his job to this deranged and crazy family. Part of his remuneration was the house he lived in with a promise of its purchase from the company. He felt he should attempt to bring this about before things became really desperate. Apart from which, he perceived they would be more inclined to do a deal now with the company needing to liquidate some of its assets. He hoped to buy the house at a discounted price considering all the money he had invested in it himself over the years to make it comfortable.

In September Terry was invited to attend a dinner party in York with Allied Dunbar who managed his life insurance, pension and other minor investments. While he was there he met Janet who was the company's secretary for the York office. They chatted and seemed to get on well together. Janet was a smart tall dark haired lady in her mid-30's. She was not married and never had been. Terry invited her out and over the next few months had something of a minor affair. However, sometimes for no real reason, you find there is no fire or spark in a relationship. Terry began to feel this. He wanted it to work, but somehow could feel there was going to be no future in it. Was it him, his old fears and concerns perhaps? Who knows, but he decided to end the relationship before getting in too deep and causing upset for either Janet or himself.

Christmas 1986 was enjoyed at home. The grandparents from Shropshire came to stay to the delight of Paul and Lynda.

Terry too was pleased to have them, giving the Christmas celebrations another dimension and providing a much-needed lift to all their spirits. He was able to take time to chat with Cecil, who had always been a fount of wisdom and a valued mentor guiding him through many of life's major decisions.

'Have you managed to get out and meet new friends?' Cecil asked cautiously.

'You are, of course meaning lady friends I assume? Yes, I have, but it's not easy.' Terry replied with a smile.

'No it never is of course, but you know what I said, we don't want you living the rest of your days alone. You have a lot to offer and soon the children will be off on their career paths. Then what are you going to do?' Cecil asked.

'We would welcome whoever you choose you know, as I've told you before and we would welcome her into the family as if our own. We know you would choose wisely, so don't think otherwise and not go ahead because of us.'

'Yes I know. You are very kind and generous. It will not be easy for you and Margaret, I do realise that, and Ann will always be in your mind. Anyway the few I've met so far were not for me. Maybe I've set the bar too high. I don't know. It just seems an impossible task somehow. I'm finding it extremely difficult to meet the right people. For a start, where do you look? Pubs, clubs, work, church? I don't think so. Does it all have to be left to chance? Really Cecil, I do think about it and I do try, but you can't make it happen can you? I can't just spirit up a person who would suit me can I?'

'Maybe not, but try casting your net wider, much wider. You may be looking in the wrong places and you owe it to yourself to find someone to share your life with, so put every effort into it for all your sakes.'

Terry racked his brains throughout the year for new ideas but drew a blank every time. So the idea festered on in the back of his mind as he went about his daily life, but with no real idea of how, if ever he was going to resolve it.

Paul, who was seventeen in April, was eager to learn to drive so the early part of the year was spent giving him driving lessons whenever there was time to spare. He also took lessons with a driving school and showed great promise, being something of a natural driver. In March, Terry and Paul went off to look at a nine-year-old Ford Fiesta that had been advertised in the local paper for £800. It would make a good starter car so they went ahead and purchased it. Paul was thrilled and spent all his free time in the garage cleaning and polishing it.

At the end of May, they went to Jersey for a week where they stayed in a self-contained flat at a country house in Five Oaks, St Saviour. It was a lovely spot and very rural. They hired a car and enjoyed the various beaches, played tennis and took a trip for the day to Sark as well as other places of interest on the island. It was to be one of the last holidays the three of them would take together.

At 14.00 hours on 10th July Paul, aged seventeen, took and passed his first driving test. He was delighted and was now a free spirit, able to drive himself wherever he wanted to go. It inspired Lynda to start thinking about driving too and Terry agreed to give her some lessons when the time came.

CHAPTER SIX

Often Terry would have lunch at his desk despite working close to home. It helped him catch up with the mountains of paper work that was a feature of his day. It was on such a day that he read aimlessly through the Yorkshire Post as he often did while eating his sandwich. There seemed little news and his eyes turned to the adverts, cars and houses for sale, people looking for jobs and of course the personal columns. He had never really taken much notice of them before, but that day, for some reason, he started to read them. Maybe it was the effect of Cecil's remarks about spreading your net wider that led him to be more open to reading such columns. Well, he thought, there was certainly nobody there in the personal columns who came anywhere near the sort of person he would want to meet. Anyway the whole idea was ludicrous and not for him.

Then he had a thought. What if he were to put in an advert? What would happen then? Did he dare do it? No, that would be sheer madness. But there must be some nice people who read the personal columns or whose eye might catch sight of a notice and read it, as he had done. The more he thought of it the more it seemed a way forward for him. Could he dare to do it, he wondered? After all Cecil did say, 'Cast your net wider!' How much wider could it be than putting an advert in the local newspaper? However, he dismissed it as crazy and not for him, not ever.

Repeatedly, his thoughts kept coming back to the idea and every time he opened the newspaper it seemed to open at the personal columns. But, he thought, were these columns not full of dropouts and weird people. Was it right to get himself into that arena? Did he have the courage to join them? He kept coming back to the idea and day after day as he read more of the adverts in the Yorkshire Post his excitement began to grow. What if it did work, why not have a go? He was beginning to feel excited at the idea; daring and frightening as it was. He felt as if he was being guided to do it and read more and more about how you would go about placing such an advertisement. You were at least able to remain anonymous and if you had a box number, the newspaper took the replies and then forwarded them on to you. Nobody would know who it was. He was beginning to convince himself and warming to the idea. After all what did he have to lose. It would be quite an adventure, that is, until the time came to meet someone. That would be very different, terrifying in fact!

After spending a few hours compiling a suitable advert for the newspaper he couldn't bring himself to post it for several days, but then finally, on a whim he slipped it into the post box. He was petrified and watched the newspaper for his advert to appear!

Within two days the advert appeared in the personal columns. He could hardly believe it. There it was in the Yorkshire Post. His advert stated that he did not want to hear from anyone who was a divorcee and that she had to be a Christian. He felt that he could not get involved with anyone who had been divorced. At least if they were single or widowed there would be no ex-husband behind them to cause any problems.

Within two days replies started to flow. The first were from divorced people asking what was wrong with them and why had he put a ban on them; that they were as good as anyone else and it was not fair to separate them off! Terry responded with a polite letter of thanks but no thanks in reply.

Others were either too young or too old and after receiving around twenty-five letters he chose five that he would explore in more detail and wrote to ask more about them, but still under the anonymity of the box number. He felt as if he was interviewing for a job and it really wasn't so different in one respect. Of course once he started to meet them the emphasis would change and it would be all about chemistry and personality. He found the whole thing a bit sad and extremely difficult, but felt at least he was making contact with like-minded people and was swept along in the excitement and fear surrounding the whole exercise.

One letter from an Andrea Bowers attracted his attention, written with humour, caring and a sense of fun, which he liked. He put that on the 'to answer positive heap' with the others. There was a telephone number to ring so one evening he took his courage in both hands and sat down to ring all the positive replies he had received, including Andrea, to have a chat and see what he made of them.

This Andrea sounded a very chirpy, happy, sincere person as she told him a little about herself and her life. She sounded very nice, he thought, but there had to be a snag. She explained how she had lived with her mother since her father died when she was twenty-three years old. They lived in the village of Scholes near Leeds. They chatted on for some time. Terry knew Scholes and had a tenant farmer who operated from the centre of the village, so knew the area quite well and often visited the farmer, who Andrea also knew. Having talked for some time he liked the sound of her so asked if she would like to meet up for a drink and a chat.

'Aah', she said, 'that's a little difficult at the moment as I'm studying for my 'O' level exam in maths!'

Terry wondered if this was a put off because she did not really want to meet him. After all, why was a thirty-eight-year-old lady studying for 'O' level exams? What a shame he thought, she sounded so nice. She suggested he ring her again in three weeks after she had taken the exams. He wasn't sure but he felt that she was genuine and that he might perhaps call her, and made the appropriate note in his diary.

Meanwhile he went on to meet two other ladies who had written to him. The first one he met was again a bright bubbly lady but had been married before and was separated! She spent the whole time telling him about her terrible husband, all the things he had done and not done. It seemed she had still not come to terms with their separation.

The next lady he met in Harrogate, where they had lunch in Betty's. She was a very motherly person and would have been better looking for a son, rather than a partner to share her life. Not an attractive feature!

A few late letters came in following his advert and amongst those were three other ladies who he thought he might contact after he had met-up with Andrea Bowers. He thought back to his chat with her and was very keen to meet her to see how they got on, should he have the opportunity to do so. He was still not so sure that the maths exam thing was really true, but it was mad enough to be, or, surely, she would have come up with a better excuse. But he took the chance and, as they had agreed, he rang her at home three weeks later. They again had a pleasant chat and Terry was really warming to her. She sounded lovely and they seemed to have a lot of things in common, but he was ever cautious of the situation, keen to avoid another painful relationship at all costs. It was all unknown territory for him, never having done anything remotely like it. They agreed to meet up on neutral ground. Wetherby suited them both, being half way, and they agreed to meet in the square of that small market town, just off the A1 in three days' time at 8pm on Friday 20th November.

The fear and excitement grew as the day approached. Neither had even seen a picture of the other, so it was into the darkness, literally, for them both! Terry arrived early in Wetherby, parked his car and sat facing the square so that he could see any cars entering from the Leeds direction. The square was well lit by street lights on this damp and rainy evening. Andrea had given him details of her car, a White Datsun coupé, a real sporty job! Just before 8pm he got out of his car and stood at the edge of the square, so that Andrea could easily spot him in his long cream trench coat. She should easily be able to pick him out.

To the minute, she arrived on time, sweeping in to the square in a flash of white. She turned the car around in the square and Terry stepped out into the road as she drove towards him, winding down her window.

'Hello, you must be Andrea' he said.

She smiled shyly and said, 'Yes I am, you must be Terry?'

'Pull in over there.' he suggested, pointing to a space on a side road off the square. There was not a lot of space but he thought she could squeeze in and park her car there safely.

Andrea reversed into the space very professionally. Terry was truly impressed with her skill.

He thought she looked every bit as nice as he had hoped from their conversations. Pretty and dashing with an attractive smile and large striking cow like eyes as she looked up at him from the car window.

He could see she was shortish, slim and well turned out in her long white trench coat similar to his own and very suitable for the damp evening. Andrea stepped out of her car, locked it and then they shook hands nervously, but warmly. Terry could not believe his good fortune. His heart skipped a beat. What a beautiful young lady she was. Suddenly he couldn't remember what his fears had been!

'I thought we would go and have a drink and a chat up the road in a country pub away from these often noisy and smoky town pubs. Would that suit you?' Terry asked her.

'Yes that sounds good,' Andrea replied with a smile.

Terry pointed out his car to Andrea and opened the door for her to get in. Then off they shot to the nearby village of Cattal where they found the 'Huntsman Pub.' They went inside to the warmth of the bar. The bar was a little unusual inside. Instead of tables to sit at there were old trestle tables from sewing machines. Andrea sat at one of the tables while Terry ordered some drinks at the bar and brought them over. They were both clearly a little uneasy and nervous, new to this way of meeting and sat chatting about how they had both come to be doing it and trying to explain it away. Andrea explained how she just happened to be aimlessly reading the personal columns when she came across Terry's advertisement. They chatted for over two hours. She wanted to know, of course, about Ann and how those events sat on him in his life, what had happened and how he was managing. They discussed family matters, work and many other subjects before returning to Wetherby for Andrea to collect her car.

Terry asked if she would care to have dinner with him the following evening at the 'Grange Restaurant,' just outside York. He knew it well and they agreed that he would collect her from her home in Scholes at 7 o'clock.

The next evening Terry explained to Paul and Lynda that he was going out for a meal with a friend and gave them the telephone number of the restaurant, should they need it and left them to do their homework. The excitement grew as Terry made his way down the A1 from Boroughbridge to pick up Andrea for their date. He felt as if he were floating on air, hardly able to believe what was happening. It was a very much more relaxed meeting as they sat and enjoyed each other's company in the wonderful surroundings of the 'Grange,' which was a slightly eccentric restaurant with large and amazing dishes. It went on to become a favourite of theirs until, in later years, it closed and became a private residence.

Andrea, it seemed, had a very busy life and never stopped. She had so much energy, drive and enthusiasm with so many interests she had poured herself into. She had a very demanding job as Company Secretary of a privately owned investment management group in Harrogate, which she had helped set up in the early 1980's after leaving a larger company in Leeds. She appeared to be very hard working, caring, warm and compassionate, as well as extremely talented.

On top of all this she was a fully qualified glider pilot, which Terry knew would go down well with Paul! She was also very artistic using her talents in so many ways. One of her hobbies was the hand painting of plates and mugs which she had fired at one of the local Harrogate shops. Her Anglican roots and her Christian life were very important to her and she explained to Terry how she had a life long association with the Anglican Church in Scholes. For many years, too, she had been a member of Scholes amateur dramatic group. Terry thought how he was going to have to be careful with that!

Andrea explained she had lived and cared for her mother after the early death of her father when she was only twenty-three. She loved him dearly and it hit her hard with them having been very close. It was clear that she had needed great courage and strength in her life thus far, being the bread winner and keeping the home going and in good repair. She also cared for her mother and her great friend Toby, a little black terrier.

Andrea explained about her two brothers who lived in and around Leeds; about their work, wives and children. Her mother was obviously very dear to her and they shared a very close relationship as she was both a mother and a friend. She explained that, despite having twice been engaged, once against her father's wishes when she was very young and inexperienced, she had never married. The engagements had both been short lived after which she had poured herself into all these other interests which she clearly enjoyed.

Terry was quite exhausted listening to the list of activities but felt humbled and full of admiration for the way she filled her life and cared for her ageing Mother. After all, he knew how hard it was to be on your own, looking after a house and family with all the difficulties, worries and hardships and no one else to share them. He easily identified with that. He could see she was a person of tremendous strength and courage, shown over the years by being the head of the house. They both had this unexpected ingredient in common which was not something Terry had expected to find. They seemed to be made for each other. He already sensed a closeness to her as he hoped she felt for him. He was not expecting to find something as deeply meaningful as this, but there it was. He was in wonder and awe at how it had come about - a miracle indeed. He felt as if he had always known Andrea. There was a closeness through the hardships and sorrows they had shared in the early loss of loved ones in their respective rich and demanding lives.

Their conversation moved on at a rapid pace as they both dug deep into the other's life demanding to know everything. Nothing was off subject as they searched and prodded and poked while unwittingly moving closer together as their life stories unfolded.

Andrea wanted to know all about Ann and Terry's life and the background of their life together, fascinated by their days in, and love for, Africa. It was somewhere she had never visited.

He told her all about his two lovely children Paul and Lynda and how together they had to carry the loss of Ann, their mother, and his wife. Her six-year illness and the fight and pain they bore together then, and over the six years of emptiness since Ann's death.

He found himself telling her things he had never told anybody before, while trying to explain fully and honestly his situation with all the risks to their potential relationship in so doing. He did it without too much of the graphic detail of all that had gone on during Ann's illness which was not necessary. It was in a way a therapy in itself, if albeit a sad and tearful one.

His life history seemed to flow out fearlessly even though he wondered if revealing all in this way might kill the relationship before it had even started. He hoped the fact he had children would not put her off in anyway. The responsibility of such an undertaking, for her, could be quite daunting but, as he was to discover, for him to even think of such a thing was a failure on his part to understand her depth and the sort of person she actually was.

The hours had flown by. It was time to take Andrea back to Scholes where he returned her with a kiss just before midnight. Both were stunned by the way they had met and what they had found, hardly daring to draw breath in case it upset all that was growing between them. They both had much to think about and turn over in their minds.

Back in May Terry had purchased two tickets to see the singer Elaine Page who was to appear at the Harrogate Conference Centre on 26th of November. He had, at the time, no idea who he would take with him but he always enjoyed solo singers so had bought the tickets.

Terry phoned Andrea and invited her to the concert the following Thursday. She was delighted and said she would love to come. They agreed to meet outside the Harrogate Centre at 7-30pm, her office being immediately opposite the theatre. Terry was thrilled that the in-depth discussions they had enjoyed over their earlier dinner date had not put her off him.

So it was that their third date got underway and when Terry met Andrea outside the theatre. She was wearing a red jacket and black skirt and looked a million dollars. Terry was bowled over. From that evening onwards he knew that their relationship was heading only in one certain direction as far as he was concerned. The mixture of singing, music and style enriched their evening and they held hands throughout Elaine's talented and spectacular performance, never wanting it to end and sealing their relationship and the start of a growing love for each other.

Terry floated on air, he hardly knew what he was doing. The past was firmly in the past, and he felt he had definitely stepped out into the future with all the courage and strength it demanded of him, something he knew he had to do. He was at last feeling positive again.

Having opened his life to Andrea he thought she should come and see where he lived and most importantly to meet Paul, now seventeen, and Lynda aged fifteen; difficult ages for Dad to bring his girlfriend home and expect her to be accepted! He arranged to pick her up and bring her to Boroughbridge where he would make dinner for her the following Saturday evening.

'We have a guest coming this evening for dinner,' he explained to Paul and Lynda.

'She's a friend I've met and she'd like to meet you.'

They both seemed unsurprised and said, 'Fine, what's her name?'

'It's Andrea and she works in Harrogate but lives near Leeds. We've got to know each other and of course I'd like her to meet you both. I'm going to pick her up at six o'clock. She does drive but I thought it would be nicer for me to bring her. It won't take me long to go to Scholes where she lives. Is that alright with you both?'

'Yes' they responded, in a slightly disinterested way.

Paul and Lynda welcomed Andrea with a smile when Terry arrived home with her and it was not long before they were chatting away together. Terry could only wonder what was going on in their heads, but they were not children anymore and must have worked it out.

He never underestimated how they must have felt though. It was hard for them both he knew that. Lynda was still young and inexperienced and very hurt emotionally at the loss of her dear Mother. Paul too, but he was not one to carry his heart on his sleeve and Terry understood well the depth and the agony of his hurt, the loss he felt and the scar he carried that would never heal. He had to tread carefully and with compassion. They were all still very tender, very fragile and still hurting, even after nearly seven years. This was a huge step, made worse by the effect of Anne Hart, blowing in and then out of their lives which left a great deal of mistrust and hurt.

Terry somehow knew from the start that Andrea was very special and different from anyone he had previously met.

There was no fear, no concern that she was anything other than genuine. It is strange how you know and the certainty you feel. It is always so very obvious when it's right. If there is doubt in your mind, then it will almost certainly be the wrong thing to do.

A week was to pass before they met again. Work and life had taken over, so they were both excited to be meeting again the following Friday evening, when they were to have dinner at the Crown Hotel, just over the other side of the river from Terry's house. The company that employed Terry owned the Crown Hotel. It had become one of his responsibilities as General Manager of the group. His role was to oversee it and make sure that it fulfilled the aims of the business, together with assistance of the financial director Geoff Weaving who was a consultant employed by the company.

They had a delightful evening continuing to get to know each other and Terry enjoyed showing her around the very luxurious hotel including the haunted room. It resulted in a very late evening - or was it early morning - before Andrea drove off from Terry's house into the night and home to Scholes. He always asked her to ring him to let him know she had arrived home safely. Two days later on the Sunday she returned once more and they enjoyed a long walk along the river Ure to Milby Lock followed by tea with Terry and the children.

The following weekend they went out for a drink on Friday evening and on Saturday enjoyed a day in York returning to Terry's for a meal.

The relationship was growing fast and furious and the next weekend, after he and Andrea had spent the afternoon at Fountains Abbey near Ripon, he collected Paul from a school trip that he'd enjoyed in Kent. Terry agreed to pick up Andrea from her home later in the evening, take her for a meal at the well-known pub the 'Faulkenberg Arms' at Coxwold and to meet her Mother Helena, a tiny lady with a big personality. Andrea was all dressed up for the occasion and waved her

Mum farewell. Her Mother had been so pleased to meet Terry and to know who Andrea was going out with. So off they went on what turned out to be a momentous evening.

The Faulkenberg Inn was packed that evening. Fortunately, Terry had booked a table. They enjoyed much more relaxed chat and a wonderful meal finished off with an Irish coffee. They sat at the table sipping their coffee and Andrea was sounding forth, deep in conversation in Italian style moving her arms around when she accidently hit the tall glass of coffee sending it flying across the table all over Terry and over her dress. They both sat there with a look of amazement on their faces covered in coffee and, after the shock, burst out laughing as they attempted to mop up the coffee from their clothes and the table.

To compound their amusement Terry, when opening the door for Andrea to leave the pub, opened a completely different door that opened on to the wall, so that when he thought he was opening it to go out there was only a solid wall confronting them! They laughed all the way to the car as they looked at the coffee stains they were both covered in. Terry rang Andrea the next day to tell her that he found he had coffee stains in places he never thought possible! Poor Andrea's mother had gone to her kitchen the following morning to be confronted with all of Andrea's clothes soaking in the kitchen sink and was quite alarmed wondering what had gone on.

Christmas was fast approaching which was going to upset the flow of their regular meetings. They agreed that it was right for them to both enjoy their usual family celebrations - Terry with Paul and Lynda at home and Andrea with her mother in Scholes. However, they decided to meet up to enjoy the afternoon together in York on Boxing Day, which is what they did, leaving Christmas day to be spent with their respective families.

CHAPTER SEVEN

It was apparent to both Terry and Andrea that they had struck gold with their relationship. It didn't really matter how they had met, but they had and were both so happy with each other. Over Christmas Terry began to think about it all and was never more certain that Andrea was the person for him, and, although he had not known her for very long, he did know that he was fast falling for her and wanted to tell her. He considered where he might do this and thought as they were both Christians a lovely place to tell her would be in York Minster for it, too, was a place of great beauty and truth. So on Boxing Day afternoon they went into the Minster, and took a seat half way up the aisle on the right side; sitting admiring the amazing columns, structure and beauty of the place. It was there that Terry sprung it on her.

'There's something I need to tell you - well more ask you,' Terry nervously said to Andrea as they sat looking at the majestic beauty surrounding them.

Andrea looked a little alarmed, as if he was about to give her bad news. Terry was quaking, not quite sure what to say next.

'I've brought you especially to this magnificent place because what I want to ask you is very special, matching our surroundings. We have, I know, only known each other for a short time, but we're not teenagers and we know what we're doing. Andrea I've grown to love you and I know it's a lot to ask of you, with me having two children, but will you marry me? Think about it, you don't have to answer now I quite understand that you need time to consider such a huge commitment.'

Andrea looked happy, surprised, shy and thoughtful. She kissed him and said,

'Yes I'll think about it - Yes I will marry you!'

They both laughed and sat there in shock smiling and shaking as they kissed!

'I wondered how long you were going to have to think about it,' Terry smiled.

'Was it fifteen seconds? Far too long,' he laughed.

They sat there stunned but happy not quite knowing what to do next.

'When? Where? How?' they both enquired.

'First I must speak with Paul and Lynda and you with your Mum. I think, otherwise, we should keep it quiet to let it sink in, apart of course from Ann's parents and I'd like to get you approved by some close friends! Wow I'm so happy!'

Terry was quite concerned about telling Paul and Lynda. He felt they would not be surprised, but at the same time they might find it hard, even with it being nearly seven years since their mother had died. But life had moved on. Paul would soon be off to further education and Lynda not far behind; whatever their choice of careers turned out to be.

He need not have worried as they both seemed genuinely happy for him. He hoped they would learn that Andrea could become their friend too and would never try to replace their mother.

The next day Andrea brought her Mum to Terry's house to meet Paul and Lynda and after he took her to see the Crown Hotel and the restaurant that bore the same name as her mother, 'Helena.'

It turned out to be a stunning end to the year as life moved forward with plans and arrangements and so many changes to be made in both their lives.

They decided to tell only close friends and family then to go public with their engagement on 14th February, 'St Valentine's Day.'

On 31st December, Terry, Paul and Lynda went to Shropshire to see the grandparents when Terry broke the news to them about Andrea. They were delighted and looked forward to meeting her.

'So,' Cecil said, 'you've found what you were looking for, well done. Tell her she mustn't fear meeting us. If she's right for you, then she will be fine for us. We wish only that you'll have a full and happy life together. We'll treat Andrea as our daughter and welcome her, so don't worry.'

Terry was touched by Cecil's sentiment. He had always had the highest regard for him and the part he had played in his life as his mentor. They had also both shared a great loss in the death of Ann. Terry hoped that for Cecil and Margaret to have Andrea in their lives that it would help them, as well as Paul and Lynda.

On Friday 15th January Terry took Andrea to Devon to introduce her to his long time and dear friends Margaret and Philip. He'd known them since they first met in Tanzania in 1965 and they had shared so much over the years. Terry was so hoping they would approve of his bride to be and was anxious for them to meet. He need not have worried as they loved her and welcomed her into the family of friends.

Life took on a new and busy phase with all the planning and arrangements that had to be made. They agreed to get married in Andrea's church, 'St Philips' in Scholes where she had always worshipped. To do this it was necessary for them to get the permission of the Catholic Church. It was arranged that Fr. Gallon, the priest from Ripon in the Diocese of Leeds, would attend the wedding on 23rd July and celebrate the service together with Andrea's Vicar Rev Terry Monroe. It was a unique service and opportunity for the two churches to come together as one.

Paul and Lynda had accepted the new situation well and seem to be growing fond of Andrea too, which pleased Terry. Paul was now a young man and would soon be off to further education, wherever that would take him.

At the moment he had his eye on acquiring a car to replace the old one that had not proved to be so good, having been made up of two different cars! So, together, Terry and Paul went off to the car auctions near Manchester to buy a suitable one. They managed to find a good sound looking model. It was always something of a nerve-racking experience at the auction but they came away with a Ford Escort. Paul was able to spend the next few weeks polishing and caring for it, as he always loved to do, just like his father and grandfather had always done.

They were so busy with their work, the children and their plans for the wedding. Every day was another step along the road. However, there was still one very important task that had to be done.

'I'd like to take you over to meet Grannie and Grandad in Shropshire. They are looking forward to meeting you, having heard so much about you,' Terry explained to Andrea. 'How about we go on 30th January, stay overnight and then on to see my other long-time friends, Pat and David who live in Shropshire too? I know you're a little concerned at meeting the grandparents, but really you need have no fears. Pat and David you will love too and I'd like to ask David if he will be my best man at our wedding.'

'I'm sure it'll be fine,' Andrea said bravely, 'but I'll be glad when it's over as I know how difficult it must be for them, suddenly having me in the family.'

'Don't worry you'll charm yourself into their lives. They'll love you,' Terry said encouragingly.

After a meeting with the Vicar of St Philips Church in Scholes, the wedding date was set for Saturday 23rd July, providing everything else fell into place.

On 30th January Andrea and Terry had an overnight stay with Cecil and Margaret when they met and welcomed Andrea to their home. It was a momentous couple of days but with their kindness and warmth they made Andrea most welcome. There were no awkward moments or problems at all and Margaret, normally quite a tense person, was so overwhelmed by Andrea's warmth of personality. The fact that she had lived and cared for her own Mother since her Father died when she was twenty-three, made her realise what a caring person Andrea was.

Cecil whispered to Terry as he was preparing to leave at the end of their stay. 'Good choice. She is lovely, Margaret and I both like her very much, congratulations on your excellent choice. You will be good for each other. We're absolutely delighted.'

That meant so much to Terry. It was so important to him that they liked Andrea.

'Thank you for all your encouragement and support. I'm so pleased you like her. I do appreciate that it's not been an easy thing for you to do, but thank you for making her so welcome and for all your kindness and inspiration.'

Andrea had blown them away with her beauty and charm and they felt elated as they made their way after lunch to Shrewsbury to meet Terry's other good friends, Pat and David Cocks.

The snowdrops heralded the arrival of February with a hint of spring in the air. They had booked their wedding reception at the Crown Hotel, in the name of Mr and Mrs Smith planning to reveal their true names on 14th February when they were going to make the public announcement of their engagement.

On Sunday 14th February there was a big party held at Andrea's house in Scholes. Her two brothers and their families were all there and it was Terry's turn to be scrutinised for a change. They had a wonderful celebration of their engagement with a party hosted by Andrea's lovely four foot nine-inch

Mum, who had a ten-foot-high personality and who made the day a very special one to remember always.

While all this was going on dark clouds were pushing their way into this otherwise happy phase of life. Things at Terry's work were not good. The jungle drums were beating fast and furious with some very unhappy events going on around him. Staff in some of the companies that formed the group were being pressured and tricked into leaving their jobs by Andrew's unscrupulous behaviour. One case that hit the press involved a garage employee who took Andrew to court and a tribunal found Andrew guilty of constructive dismissal. He was ordered to pay £7000, plus legal costs to the employee.

Some employees from his other companies were also put under a great deal of strain and stress causing serious and long standing health conditions - good people who were being treated so badly that they become ill. Terry was most disturbed having to witness such behaviour and wondered where it would all end. Jeremy was also very concerned but kept his head down believing that if he did then things would improve.

'The man is mad,' said Jeremy when he heard all that was going on and the effect it was having on so many good people.

Andrew and his crazy nephew continued to rage around like a pair of mad bulls hitting out in every direction at anyone in their sights, making impossible demands and giving badly thought out orders and impossible requests. Terry realised they were slowly trying to push him, and Jeremy, out of the business. Andrew was trying to cut back in order to cover his own inabilities to raise the monies required to pay off his family members and to break the family trust that held the wealth. In so doing he left the business exposed with no management. It was clear to everyone but him that he was on a slippery slope to nowhere.

Pressure continued to mount around the time of their engagement and although Terry did not say too much he felt the wind of change was blowing, and, not in his favour. He wondered if he would lose his job and home which were a joint package, but tried not to let those fears spoil the joy and excitement that was going on around them.

Andrew had agreed that Terry could purchase the house he lived in from the company but, despite many memos from Terry on the subject, he could never get a price out of him or to how it would affect his salary package. If he no longer had a house as part of his remuneration, then he should expect to have an increase in his salary to compensate for the loss. But Andrew was being very difficult and un-cooperative about the whole matter.

'So, Andrea,' Terry said, 'how do you fancy a week in Holland - after all we've been engaged now for five whole days. It's time we did something exciting?'

'Sounds fantastic, why Holland? I've never visited the country before.'

'I'd like you to meet a long-time friend, Sister Anny Nijhuis, a missionary sister I've known from my time in Malawi where she became a close friend. She needs to give her approval before I can even think of marrying you,' he said with a glint in his eye.

'I'll pretend I didn't hear that, Terry, or this could become the shortest engagement on record.'

'I want to show you off of course and you'll love Anny. She is full of life and so funny in what she says in her Dutch style English!'

They flew out from Leeds and enjoyed four days staying with Anny's sister. Anny was so proud of her English friends that she wanted to show them to her whole family. She took them from one family member to the next to show them off. Somehow they all seemed to have the idea that because they were English they liked to have cream teas! Every house they visited brought out large quantities of cream cakes and scones. The first one was very nice but by the time they got to the fourth and fifth of the day they'd had enough!

'As its Saturday we'll go to Mass this evening in my local family church. Tomorrow we'll be busy visiting my brother.' Explained Anny.

Terry and Andrea laughed exclaiming, 'Oh Anny we are exhausted seeing all your lovely but kind family and we are absolutely full of cream cakes and scones.'

'We've already met so many of your family Anny, can there be many left in Holland?'

'I can't laugh at that. I've a very large family and I want them to meet you, all of them!'

As it was nearly five o'clock they set off for the church. During the Mass Andrea was kneeling for a long time, long after everyone had got up and moved on from that solemn part of the service. Terry wondered if she was alright and tapped her on the shoulder, but found her fast asleep on her knees!

'Come on wake up you can't sleep here you know,' he whispered to her!

At the end of Mass Anny said, 'Would you like to meet my Uncle?'

'Oh Anny we're exhausted, as you can see. Andrea fell asleep during the service. We've been around to see so many of your family today, I don't think we can see anymore. How far away is he as we would really benefit from some rest and if we eat another cream cake we'll explode?'

'Oh he's only over at the side of the church, not far.'

'O.K. then,' they agreed, 'but this really has to be the last visit today.'

They followed Anny to the side of the church and up to the front pew and stood waiting, looking around for her uncle.

'Where is he then?' Terry asked, as they stood there waiting and wondering.

Just as he'd asked that question the curtain covering the side altar in front of them opened and laying in his open coffin, surrounded by flowers, was Anny's 'dead' Uncle!

'Oh! He doesn't look at all well,' Terry commented looking up at him with surprise.

'I wish Anny you'd told us he was dead.'

'Well he wouldn't be in his coffin if he was alive would he.' She replied curiously.

They were both a little shocked by this event, but laughed all the way home. Dear Anny, her command of English and some of the customs proved a little challenging to say the least.

Their days in Holland had been a light relief from work with all its problems, but they had to return to it all and to the joy of planning their wedding day.

Lynda went to an interview on 7th March for a place at the secretarial college in Harrogate that would set her off learning shorthand and office procedures. They were delighted when she was accepted. Once enrolled she would be able to travel to Harrogate with Andrea each day who would continue, after they were married, in her job with the investment company, so it worked well.

Paul had his eighteenth birthday on 11th April so a special party was arranged for him at the Crown Hotel where one hundred and twenty of his friends and family had been invited for a Disco and Buffet Supper. Andrea's Mum had made a lovely cake for the occasion and everyone gathered to enjoy the celebration. The Disco started early with Paul's friends arriving from near and far assembling in the main restaurant bar which had been taken over for the evening. The older generation sat in the adjoining bar to begin to enjoy the evening as the young ones gathered.

At 8.45pm Carlo, the hotel manager came to find Terry and Andrea with an anxious look on his face.

'I think you'd better come to the car park. Paul is outside and is not feeling so well.'

They rushed out to find him with his head in his hands looking very pale and being sick.

'Whatever is wrong,' they asked? Paul could hardly speak.

'I think his friends put something in his drink,' Carlo explained.

They gave him lots of water to drink, but he continued to be sick holding his head and moaning.

'I think we had better take you home,' Terry suggested, 'for you the party looks as if it's over.'

With that Paul groaned and was again sick over Terry's shoe.

They got him to his feet and, with a friend, half carried him over the bridge and home to his bed. Andrea rang the doctor who told her to give him plenty of water to drink and to keep him lying on his side, which they did. The doctor said he should be O.K. He was probably suffering from alcoholic poisoning and if he did not improve, to take him to hospital where he would need to have his stomach pumped out. Terry & Andrea took it in turns to watch over him while the others went back to the party to see what was happening there. It became clear that Paul was not able to return to his party, so an announcement was made to bring the party to an end and everyone left by ten o'clock! It was an unfortunate end to what should have been a fun evening.

By 8.30 the next morning Paul was up and looking quite well. Perhaps he felt he should or he would be in trouble, but actually everyone was disappointed that he had not been able to enjoy the party because of the actions of one of his so called friends!

Terry and Andrea's wedding preparations continued. As there were two lots of clergy involved, the Catholic and Anglican, everything was doubled up. It was necessary to obtain permission from the Catholic Bishop for the marriage service to be held in St Philips Anglican Church in Scholes. It was not a problem, but a formality that involved much organisation. On 1st May, Andrea's 38th Birthday, they both attended the Sunday service at St Philips, giving Terry the opportunity to meet some of Andrea's friends from the many years she had attended that church. Contrasting this, they had, the following Tuesday to attend a funeral in Lincoln of one of Andrea's uncles who had died in tragic circumstances.

There was still plenty going on and things to arrange before the wedding.

Work pressures were mounting. Jeremy and Terry had always shared an office in the village of Arkendale that had been an old Reading Room years ago, where people from the village sat, read, and chatted. It was then converted into two offices, small in size, but adequate for them both to run their operations. They both enjoyed being there in the quiet country environment and got on with their work in relative peace and quiet. But of course instructions had been given by Andrew in 1982 that they should move from there to new offices in the centre of Boroughbridge where the whole team from Harrogate would also move.

Now, two months before Terry & Andrea were to marry, and under extreme pressure from Andrew, the group was again to split up with Terry and Jeremy sent to new offices in a converted barn back in Arkendale village. At first their immediate reaction was great relief. They were pleased to at least remain together and to be away from the main group, back in the freedom of a small village. Being together they retained a certain strength and were able to watch out for each other as the 'mad two' continued to rampage around the group of companies like two men possessed. But the move was to be only a temporary arrangement. Andrew told them that a single new and smaller office was to be set up in Harrogate, which Sean would organise. The pressure was enormous with the underlying threats designed to push as many employees as possible out and leave the business in the hands of the mad two.

Unemployment in the country at the time was at 2.5 million so it was not easy to find new jobs. This was very worrying for everyone and it became necessary to hang on to whatever job you had.

House prices were rocketing, but still Terry had no response from Andrew regarding the proposed purchase of his house from the company. This was strange as the company was seeking to sell whatever they could to raise money to buy out Andrew's brothers, once the trust had been legally broken. Terry kept the pressure on Andrew, as much as he could, but he was an impossible man to deal with.

Two secretaries had found new jobs and left the company, so the pressure on staff was working in some cases, much to the joy of Andrew and the mad Sean as they continued on their daily rampage. Jeremy's view was to keep his head down in the hope that it would all go away. He was convinced it would do and he spent as much time as possible out of the office working in the forested areas of the estates. Terry was not sure that it would all go away and really did not wish to remain in this dictatorship with two mad men driving the business into the wall. He wanted, above all, to get his house bought from the company before considering a move, so he soldiered on despite the enormous stress.

There was a long and tortuous meeting with Andrew on 20th May, which went nowhere. He made little sense nor had any idea of what he was doing, lost in his own mad world of frustration and wrong doing, misguided and muddled. The only thing Terry realised was that his days there were definitely numbered and for no apparent reason. Andrew had lost his marbles completely and was incapable of managing the group, running around like a headless chicken with his nephew clucking away behind him in a mad frenzy.

Mortgage rates were rising fast and were approaching 15%. Even if Terry did manage to buy the house from the company the repayments on the mortgage would be almost impossible.

Terry and Andrea kept their eye on the wedding day as the excitement grew and the plans were put in place. They were so happy and did not let the situation with work disturb them more than was necessary.

Saturday 23rd July was a cloudy but warm day and felt rather thundery. Cecil and Margaret had come over from Shropshire the night before the wedding, staying at the Crown

Hotel with many of the family and friends. They had all enjoyed an evening meal there to celebrate the great day and to meet each other.

Terry's friend David from his Seychelles days was his best man, and Lynda Andrea's bridesmaid together with her niece Louise. Cecil, and Terry's good friend Philip, did a reading. It was a wonderful day of witness and love as it should always be. Andrea, having made her own dress, looked stunning. They were both over the moon and enjoyed every minute of their special day. They never once revealed to anyone how they had met, despite the curiosity of many, then, and over the years since.

They had a wonderful honeymoon starting at Beatrix Potter's holiday home in Cumberland for two nights, followed by a week at the hotel Es Molí in the picturesque village of Deyà, on the island of Majorca, for a time of total relaxation and joy.

CCC

CHAPTER EIGHT

After the dream honeymoon they floated back on cloud nine ready to face life's challenges, and there were plenty. Returning to work Terry found a memo on his desk. It was from Andrew telling him that all future development projects were to be handed to Sean and that he, Terry, was not to get involved. Ah he thought, clearly more attempts by Andrew to undermine his job. Things had not improved in his absence.

Later in the day Andrew summoned Terry to a meeting in his office. There were no niceties or welcome awaiting him. The atmosphere was as ruthless as ever, creating a feeling of desperation and hostility for all who came in contact with Andrew. It was in stark contrast to the love and good feeling that had surrounded their wedding, and served to cast a worrying shadow over his and Andrea's new life together.

'You should know that I've sold the Kexby Estate consisting of 1,500 acres to the Oxford University Pension Fund for £1.1 million.' Andrew announced in his high handed manner. 'I want you to go and make available all the details of the estate from your files for their solicitors to commence the legal process. I want this done immediately. You have been away far too long.'

'Really,' Terry replied. 'I think you've undersold it. That's well under its capital value. I know where we could have sold it for far in excess of that; but if that's what you want me to do, fine.'

Andrew looked surprised and pale. 'What do you mean? How much more? And from whom?'

'Quite a lot more, but I'd need to look into it to give you an exact figure. If only you'd consulted me before agreeing to the sale, I am your property manager. I've worked with the farmers on that estate for years and know its worth from the capital that has been invested in its development. I'd need at least two weeks, but I'm sure I could produce a substantially increased offer. But if you've sold it without reference to me, your Property Manager, then it's too late. You'll have to go ahead.'

Andrew sneered, 'I doubt you could get anymore for the estate than I have. I doubt it very much. I do know what I'm doing you know.'

'OK that's fine, it's up to you, it's your money,' Terry replied as he turned to leave the office.

'Just a minute.' Andrew shouted.

'You know I need every penny I can lay my hands on for this buy-out so, of course, if you think you are so clever and can get more for it then do it. That's what we pay you for. I need to raise every penny to pay off my brothers so go ahead, but I've already secured a good offer and I doubt very much you'll improve on it. I've taken the very best advice.'

'Give me three weeks and I'll prove it to you.' He challenged Andrew.

'If you lose my deal with the Oxford University by your pratting around your job will go too,' Andrew shouted, 'I'm warning you.' However, Andrew was forced to agree to the challenge while at the same time beginning to regret doing the deal over Terry's head. He knew the legal work took time so all was not lost. He felt sure Terry would never find another buyer at such short notice, but he had to let him try as he needed all the money he could raise for his brothers.

As Terry left Andrew's office he paused and turned to look back at him.

'By the way Andrew, don't forget you promised to give me your figure for the purchase of my house from the company. That would give you much needed cash too. Shall we say you'll let me have that figure within the next three weeks?' Terry suggested with a half-smile.

Andrew's face reddened with fury and rage. 'I'll not be held to ransom by you or anyone, do you hear me?'

'I don't know what you mean. I'm only reminding you of your promise to me before I went on honeymoon. Being such a busy man, I wouldn't want you to forget!'

Terry left Andrew's office knowing there was a lot of tough negotiating ahead, both to obtain a price for his house and to realise an increased offer for the Kexby estate, if he could. There was no time to lose. It was a chance to link them together in an effort to finally get from Andrew a price at which Terry could buy his house from the company. Perhaps it was the lever that was needed to prevent it dragging on forever.

He always understood that the tenants of the estate would move heaven and earth to buy their tenanted farms from the company. It just remained for Terry to get them moving quickly enough and come up with an offer. That was likely to be the major problem. Time was short, but he felt sure if he were to get all four of the tenants together they would surely come up with a better offer than the one on the table from Oxford University's Pension Fund. He knew all the farmers well and held their respect for the drainage and improvements he had organised for them. It was time to call in the favour.

He went to each farm in turn explaining there was a chance for them to purchase their farms if they wanted, but for this chance, they had to act quickly. All were very keen but needed to arrange the finance and that was going to take time. One of the tenants proved very difficult over a block of woodland situated in the middle of the estate and there was a tremendous argument on how it should be divided up.

Terry called a meeting explaining they had about fourteen days in which to put together a collective offer for the estate or the opportunity would be lost forever. They agreed to try and find the collective finance then decide later how to divide up the woodland which was causing them such grief. There was much arguing and disagreement, with one of the farmers walking out of a late night meeting. Terry feared that an offer would not be forthcoming in time as they were unable to agree between themselves on how the woodland should be split, digging their heels in to the extent that they could lose the whole deal.

'Well it's up to you all to sort it out or lose this chance to own your farms. You need to know that if you don't take your chance now, plans have already been made to sell the estate; so over to you. There is no more I can do. You have fourteen days to make me your offer, after that it's off. You mustn't miss this opportunity if you really want to own your farms.'

They all looked very crest fallen but knew he was right. They could lose this once in a lifetime opportunity and none of them wanted that to happen if it could be avoided.

A final meeting was agreed for the morning of the fourteenth day. On that day they all assembled in the dining room at one of the farms.' There was a grim cloud hanging over the meeting. Terry feared the worst.

'Well, what have you all decided?' Terry asked the meeting.

'We can't agree the division of the farms I'm afraid, but if you give us one more day for clearance from the banks we can make a collective offer of £1.5m for the whole estate. Then we'll sort out the details of the boundaries later. Would that be possible?'

Terry was relieved that they had all seen sense and been able to work so quickly to get the monies together. He rang Andrew who was out and as usual nobody knew, or was saying, where he was!

He agreed to the farmers' request in principle, explaining the position to them but insisting they fax him confirming the offer, subject to completing the finance with their bank so that he could present Andrew with their offer for his approval.

The next day he managed to track down Andrew at his house.

'I can't come in to the office today' Andrew told him. My M.E. is playing up again and I don't feel good!'

Terry was continually given this excuse about him having M.E. and was never sure if Andrew did suffer from it or not. It always seemed to be an illness of convenience.

'I've news of an offer of £1.5m for the Kexby Estate.'

'Is it a firm offer in writing?' Andrew asked over the phone.

Terry avoided the question with one of his own.

'Do you have news for me on my house purchase?'

'I've spoken to David the accountant, but haven't made up my mind yet.'

'That's fine, well maybe if you decide and let me know then I will see if I can get a letter to confirm the offer of £1.5 million for the estate and, tomorrow, we can exchange information.'

'I will not be forced into this,' shouted Andrew down the phone.

'I'm not forcing you to do anything. You told me over a year ago the company would sell me the house and I need to get the purchase underway. Mortgage rates are rising almost daily, currently 15%. They were 5% when we first agreed I could buy the house. If you're not prepared to sell to me then say so.

I'm prepared to pay a reasonable open market price and the company is selling its assets. I don't understand your problem.'

'We'll speak in the office tomorrow morning,' said Andrew in annoyance.

'I do hope so. I might well have the confirmed offer for the estate, but it'll not be there forever, so it's up to you,' Terry replied equally annoyed. Andrew banged the phone down in fury.

The following day Andrew left a message that he was not feeling well enough to go into the office, so failed to come in, asking that any messages be sent to him via his secretary.

That afternoon Terry received a fax from the farmers at Kexby to confirm their offer of £1.5m. He did not contact Andrew but instead left his secretary a message asking for news on his house purchase. No reply was received.

The following morning Andrew blasted into Terry's office asking if he had received an offer for the Kexby Estate.
  'Yes I have an offer in writing.'
  'Who is it from?' demanded Andrew.

'Did you say you had come to a conclusion regarding my house purchase?' asked Terry casually.

'Look stop going on about your house. I've instructed our accountant to put your house on the open market through estate agents. Whatever is the best price from the viewers, that is the price you will pay the company if you want to buy it. You must deal with him in all future discussions, not me. I refuse to speak to you any further about this matter. Deal with the accountant. Here's a copy of my memo to that effect, deal with him.' Andrew shouted.

'Now are you going to tell me who the offer for the Kexby estate is from?'

Terry felt some relief that there was at last some movement and was pleased not to have to deal with Andrew in future as he was a total nightmare and unreliable. Not that the accountant was very trustworthy. He was always looking over his shoulder to protect his lucrative position in the group.

Reluctantly Terry revealed his hand to Andrew, not certain that he would finally agree the sale of his house. He didn't trust him one bit. However, what else could he do? Andrew was just being very difficult.

Terry passed the fax to Andrew confirming the offer from the farmers, much to Andrew's surprise and pleasure.

'You must instruct our solicitor immediately regarding the sale and get them to tell the Oxford people that their deal is off.'

Terry was delighted that the tenant farmers' offer had been accepted. He knew what it would mean to them and their families, they would be overjoyed. It was the right conclusion to the situation.

On the home front it was time for Paul to go off to take his place at college in Liverpool. He had, in one day, driven himself to Liverpool, signed up at the college, found accommodation on Rice lane, Walton and returned home. There was no stopping him once he made up his mind. They admired his tenacity.

Terry was always conscious that his children were his and Ann's and not Andrea's, but they discussed the possibility of having children, or not, as they set out on their new life together. Andrea said, had she been younger, then she would have liked to have children but, as it was, she considered Paul and Lynda to be the children that she never had and would always love them and treat them as her own.

On 27th September Paul left Riverside House to start his advanced computer studies course in Liverpool. They were sad to see him leave home so soon after their marriage. Andrea would have loved more time with him so they could get to know each other better, but they had to let him go to make his own way in the world. The time had come. They both felt very proud of his achievements and the way in which he had sorted out his accommodation and everything else with no help. Especially so as Terry was pre-occupied with work, busy fighting for the retention of his job and home while dealing with the bullying from Andrew and at the same time continuing to support the family. These were very very difficult times and so much depended on the outcome. If he lost his job then he would lose his home, which was not a very comfortable feeling with a new wife and two young adults about to launch themselves into the outside world.

Andrea and Terry always understood that they really needed to start their married life in another house; to move from Riverside House with all its memories and to start afresh. It was unfair to expect Andrea to live in the same house, but there was little they could afford so it was essential to buy the house from Bowman Estate as had always been promised. They could then sell it and move on. It now looked as if it could go ahead. Could Andrew be trusted? That was the big question.

Terry knew a local businessman, Mr Davies, who was very keen to buy Riverside House for his 'Lady friend!' Terry informed him he was looking to sell it and they agreed a figure that would represent a very good profit on the price he was likely to have to pay Bowman Estates, assuming the purchase went ahead as planned.

Terry and Andrea looked around at houses but found little available in their price range that appealed to them. Things were getting desperate. They had to have a place that was their own. Any day now Terry felt his job was likely to end and they would have nowhere to live and he remembered how that felt from past experiences. He was looking hard for other employment before that happened.

On a visit to the company's estate near Kilburn village, Terry visited a Colonel and Virginia Consett who owned Osgodby Hall on the edge of the North Yorkshire Moors. They were a likeable couple, eccentric, typical ex-army with the Colonel an epitome of an army officer. Virginia was from a very wealthy and privileged family with a back ground to match. She had fallen for this likeable rogue in his baggy cord trousers and decorative waistcoat. He had had a long and distinguished military career in the war years. They had recently purchased a piece of land from the company to expand their land holding and develop their farmhouse, so Terry did know them enough to approach them. With the land they had recently purchased came a house built with an agricultural clause barring its use from anyone who was not involved in agriculture. The Colonel was considering what to do with it and even pondered having it demolished.

'May have to pull the bloody thing down,' he announced to Terry.

'It's too bad, but the council wouldn't let us use it. They say we have to be working in agriculture. Unbelievable.'

When Terry heard this it sent his mind racing. Surely he was loosely working in agriculture and would qualify to live in the house? Maybe he should make them an offer. It was in a terrible condition as gipsies had been living in it for a while and had wrecked the place, but beggars couldn't be choosers he thought. Sure that he fulfilled the clause he offered to buy the house, relieving them of the problem and at the same time providing Terry and Andrea with a house in a wonderful position.

The old colonel blustered and blew with his roguish smile and a glorious twinkle in his eye as he stood there in his oversized cord trousers. 'Well its worth a lot of money you know.'

'It's a tip and unsaleable, as well you know,' Terry replied with a smile.

'Well how much bloody money will you give me for it - one hundred thousand should do it don't you think?' the Colonel bellowed in military style.

'Half that I think.'

More bluster and puffing came from the Colonel as his wife stood there mentally spending the money as they spoke.
'Too cheap, too cheap. You are a bloody fine officer, but I can't agree to that. What about seventy-five, yes seventy-five would do it.'

Terry walked away.

'Far too much, I'm only a poor employee you know. My best offer is seventy thousand pounds, but I'll have to bring my wife to see it before we'd be able to confirm the offer. There is a lot of work to do on the house and it's in a remote position for someone not used to country living, coming from near Leeds, as my wife would be doing.'

'Quite so, quite so, well I'll discuss it with madam and you speak to your wife Anthea and we can meet at the weekend.'

'No, it's Andrea, my wife's name is Andrea!'

'Quite so, quite he replied in his gruff manner.

The house was in a beautiful spot with magnificent views across to Sutton Bank and over to Wensleydale and Swaledale and not too far from Thirsk. It had only been built three years ago and was designed as two farmworkers cottages. However, a family of gipsies had lived in it and they had paid none of the bills for the services, so water and electricity had been cut off. The toilets were full and as a consequence the place was alive with flies. The radiators had, at some time, been frozen and needed replacing and many of the copper pipes supplying them had burst and leaked doing considerable damage. One of the reception rooms had been used to practise shooting a gun and the wall was pitted with shot gun pellets! In short the house was a disgusting tip. It was into this situation that Terry had to bring his new bride to decide if they had the courage to buy such a place and do all the necessary work to make it habitable.

'I don't want you to look at the inside of the house,' he said, as he brought Andrea to look at the property.

'Concentrate on looking out the windows. There are seventeen and seventeen different views. Don't look at the inside, that we can change.'

'What! seventeen windows?' she exclaimed.

'I've never lived in a house of that size.'

She was absolutely horrified at the state of the place. First of all, the house stood in a field and there was no garden, only an acre of rough grass around it. The door was boarded up having been kicked in at some time, probably by bailiffs. In every room there was another horror story that unfolded before their eyes. The smell was incredible, almost unbearable. Flies swarmed in every room, floorboards were up in some rooms, lights hanging off, lavatories full, baths broken and taps broken in the sink. Some of the ceilings had holes in them where someone had fallen through from the attic and, in the attic itself, huddled in the corners were large swarms of flies two feet or more across hanging there like swarms of bees. There was no water available in the house as the power, which was required to drive the motor for the private water supply had been switched off! Heating was provided by oil and a tank stood in the garden. Someone had been hitting the side of the tank and had made a small hole in it so any oil in the tank would drain away!

However, the views from the windows were magnificent and to die for. He kept repeating to Andrea, 'just look at the views.'

'What do you think, can we take this lot on, are we up to it? It'll be a lovely house once we've worked on it, as well as an excellent investment, but it's going to take time, a whole lot of work, and a heap of money!'

They walked around together in horror at what they saw in the house. There was not a good room in the whole place, not even a garden to console them, only about an acre of rough grass.

'Do we have any option? Not really, I think we have to go for it.'

Always up for a challenge, together they decided to bite the bullet and go ahead with an offer of £70,000. They agreed that it was a beautiful spot to live in and they could soon make basic improvements to make the place liveable. They planned to carry out most of the work themselves in the years ahead, as and when they could afford it. They would have to make it habitable before leaving Riverside House by spending every spare moment there to get it clean and to get the living areas in reasonable shape to move into. Their hope was that Andrew would not back out of the deal he had agreed for Riverside House. They needed the profit from that house to finance the purchase of Osgodby House. It really was going to be a balancing act, a big risk, but one they were forced to take as these were desperate times. It all depended on the unreliable Andrew signing the contract for the sale, once the price had been agreed by his bizarre method of calculation.

Terry made their offer to the Colonel and his wife Virginia, who insisted on meeting Andrea before accepting and signing any contracts.

While this was on going a number of people who showed an interest in buying it, came to look around Riverside House.

Unbeknown to them, their best offer was to be the price Terry and Andrea would pay for the house. When it came, they quickly agreed it with Bowman Estates before they changed their mind. The Estate was of course unaware that Terry and Andrea planned to sell it immediately and move on.

So, for a few months, they had two different contracts, one for Riverside House and the other for Osgodby House It was a very worrying time as negotiations were still going on with Mr Davies who wanted to buy Riverside House from them. It was a nerve-racking time, but they did finally pull it off. They felt a great relief when all the contracts were signed and they were out of the clutches of the mad Andrew Bowman; secure in the knowledge that, at last, they would have their own house. All they had to do was to keep up the 15% mortgage rates and of course, carry out the work to make the house habitable.

The sale of the Kexby Estate went ahead and, although Andrew had eventually kept his promise to allow Terry and Andrea to purchase the house in Boroughbridge, it was not without a sting in its tail.

With his terms of employment stating that a house would be provided as part of the remuneration, together with his salary, then it was only right for his salary to be increased to compensate for the absence of the provision of a house from the package. However, Andrew, ever sore from the pressure Terry had put him under and getting one over on him with the sale of the Kexby estate, would not increase his salary; he in fact reduced his salary by £4000, some 25%; Terry of course objected, but it fell on deaf ears.

This meant they had to support a mortgage with fifteen percent interest rates on a much reduced salary. Andrew was doing all he could to get Terry out by fair means or foul. It was a very clear case of constructive dismissal, but Terry decided to find another job as the preferred route, thus avoiding a legal battle which at that time he didn't have the stomach for, despite its certain outcome.

As Christmas approached the company moved offices yet again, bringing everyone into one first floor office on Forest Road in Harrogate. Andrew continued his quest to find enough cash to buy out his brothers and sisters from the group and stopped at nothing.

In the new offices everyone was jammed into a small open plan area, divided into units that resembled chicken coops. Except for the mighty Sean, who had divided up the space to provide him with a very large office overlooking everyone else, with a similar one for his uncle Andrew, and his secretary, who Jeremy had nicknamed, 'the poisoned witch!'

Andrew and Sean, a pair of mad bullying thugs, put everyone, at all levels, under extreme pressure. The results of this started to show. The financial consultant of the group, an ex-banker, resigned most weeks from his advisory part time-position, until Andrew persuaded him over a bottle of wine and a meal, to return, in order to retain the company's credibility in the eyes of his trustees.

On 23rd January Carlo, the manager of the hotel in Boroughbridge, resigned after severe pressure to fulfil impossible targets set by Andrew. One of Andrew's little side shoot building companies was also in trouble and due to pressure the manager went off sick from which he never recovered and later died.

Andrew had by this time taken over one of the main stays and the foundation stone of the group; the building company based in York. That was, under his management, failing fast with good staff and managers resigning daily from the various departments, increasing the speed of its decline.

Mad Sean, with his wide red braces and striped suit, pranced around the office giving orders and making outrageous demands to whoever he happened to bump into. Andrew appointed him as general manager of the group and, in so doing, kept at least one of his sisters onside. Terry was told by a memo on 3rd April to step down as general manager, handing over his duties and files to Sean.

Terry and Jeremy kept watch for each other as the pressures mounted. They felt nobody could be trusted as secretaries and staff looked to protect and save their own jobs and some didn't care how they did it. Jeremy and Terry kept their heads down trying to operate from their chicken coops in the new office. They spent as little time there as they could get away with, by going out on tasks around the properties. Sean continually told them that they must fill in a form at the secretary's desk, saying where they were going and when they would return. They had to be signed again on their return with an explanation if they should be late. Of course the two of them conveniently forgot to do this, or they would write a long funny story several sheets long as to why they were late back which infuriated Sean!

Andrew had instructed Terry, having taken his main job away that he was to work out a business plan for the development of one of the vacant farms into holiday lets. It was not a serious proposal, but something he asked hoping Terry would hate the task and resign under the pressure. However, Terry used it as an excuse to go out and meet all sorts of people on the site of the proposal, near Kilburn. He spent hours of his time measuring and drawing outline plans and anything to keep him out of the office, supposedly carrying out this fatuous task, much to the annoyance of the two mad men back in the office.

Terry was also applying for jobs as and when he saw anything suitable, but there were few available. Jeremy on the other hand hoped that if he kept his head down it would all go away!

In the meantime, every spare minute, weekends and evenings were being spent at Osgodby House trying to get it into some sort of shape. A firm of commercial cleaners had been employed to remove all the unsavoury contents of the two bathrooms ready for new suites to be installed. Terry removed some internal walls to make the five bedroomed house into four. Ceilings, pipes and floorboards were repaired and replaced so that painting of the interior could start in the main rooms. They would both spend Saturdays working on the house arriving around 10 am to start the day's work. They often brought a picnic to eat in the house or outside if the weather was good, taking in the magnificent views. On one such an occasion the Colonel arrived at the door shortly after they had started the day's work, standing there in his baggy light brown cords and green braces.

'Hello. How are you both?' he shouted.

Before receiving an answer, he would ask the next question, probably as a result of his poor hearing and his army background.

'Now then, we want you to come over and have a drink with us about 1 o'clock. As its race day, we often have a little sweep stake. I hope you have some bloody money with you. You'll need some money you know,' he exclaimed loudly.

'Well thank you Colonel but, as you can see, we are in our overalls and covered in paint. It's not really ideal to join you for a drink.'

'Doesn't matter, doesn't matter, come as you are dear boy, come as you are. Madam won't mind as long as you bring some money for the sweep stake. Come over at 12.30 and have a bloody drink with us first – see you later.' He shuffled off towards his house, a large converted barn, some hundred metres away. Clearly he was not taking no for an answer.

They both laughed and at 12.30 in a rather grubby state they set off still in their painting clothes that were spotted with paint, as were their faces after painting the ceiling of the sitting room all morning. They pressed the button on the post at the entrance to the drive to the Colonel and Virginia's house. Slowly the gate opened and they walked down the drive towards the house feeling like two tramps. They pulled the knob that rang an inner bell. The Colonel opened the door. 'Come on in, come on in, welcome. Come through and have a drink.'

He directed them down the hall and they were bundled into a large drawing room where, to their horror and amazement, were a few more people all chatting, looking very smart and with glasses in their hands. As soon as Terry and Andrea entered a silence fell over the room as the gathered elite looked down their noses at these two much underdressed people.

'Good afternoon,' they said meekly, 'sorry we didn't know this was a party. We are in the process of moving into the house next door.'

Out of the crowd came Virginia. 'Hello' she called in a shrill voice, 'nice to see you.'

They again apologised for their appearance and explained that the Colonel had asked them to come over, and said it didn't matter about their dress, but he failed to tell them there were other guests!

'Sit down. We are just going to start the sweepstake.' Virginia quickly placed a copy of the Telegraph on their chairs before they sat down, in case the paint on their clothing came off onto the furniture.

The other guests moved uneasily away as they clutched their drinks looking down on these poor urchins that had suddenly arrived in their midst.

'Now then, you all have to put £2 into that bowl and take two pieces of paper which have the names of horses on them. The first race starts in five minutes, so all please take a seat and I'll turn on the television. The idea is that whoever has the name of the horse that comes in first wins the kitty.'

Virginia went around the assembled guests. 'Now come along everyone before it starts, take your horse.'

By the end of the third race Terry and Andrea had taken all three prizes. They made their excuses and left the gathering with £16 in their hands returning to their picnic lunch at Osgodby House; much to the surprise of the flabbergasted gathering. They laughed to themselves for the rest of the day every time they thought about it, comparing themselves to Tom and Barbara on the 'Goodlife' television series.

CHAPTER NINE

There was hardly a minute to spare in the newly marrieds' life. Andrea, after finishing her own demanding job in Harrogate, faithfully did the hundred-mile roundtrip to visit her Mum in Scholes every Wednesday evening to help her with her health problems, her house and general well-being, not returning until 10 pm; by then quite exhausted. They were both run ragged and under a great deal of stress and strain but managed to keep it all going.

On 2nd May they completed the purchase of Osgodby House from the Colonel and Virginia. They had to wait another week before the purchase of Riverside House was complete because of a last minute legal hitch over the footpath that ran alongside the property to the riverbank. It was with great relief, on 9th May that the purchase was completed and on the same day resold to Mr Davies, releasing an immediate £30,000 profit to put towards the Osgodby House deal and provide funds for the serious improvements to start.

At work, further pressure was put on Terry when his name was removed from the company's bank mandate for no apparent reason, only to squeeze him further!

Monday 12th June was a blisteringly hot day. It was a sad day for Terry when the time came to say goodbye to his old home after nine years there as a family with all its memories, its sorrows and yes, joys too. But it was right to move on and to start this new life at Osgodby with Andrea. So after a tearful farewell to Boroughbridge they were ready to leave.... a true rebirth.

The fear of the past continued to hover in Terry's mind. How illness had suddenly come, from nowhere, attacked Ann and struck her down as it did. From the time he even considered marriage again, the thought of putting himself in a position where it could all happen again filled him with a renewed fear. He tried to muster the courage to put it behind him and hopefully this move would help. Andrea was a diamond amongst jewels and the very thought of seeing her go through the same hell that Ann had, filled him with fear and loathing. It was hard to kill the demon within, no matter how desperately he tried.

At 8.30 am the removal van arrived and they slowly loaded the contents of their home onto the lorry transferring it to their new home and life at Osgodby House. They had taken a week off work to settle into the new house and assist the builders who arrived the following day to start on the structural works. Removing walls, building new ones, fitting new bathroom suites together with all the works necessary to make it a fully operational house. They shovelled brick rubble as the building team set to work removing some of the interior walls, wheeling barrow load after barrow load outside making a huge heap that grew and grew.

'Who has been repairing this wall and plastering it?' Ian the builder enquired eyeing an adjoining wall that Terry and Andrea had spent several hours plastering.

'We did, why?'

'It'll be ok when it's finished,' he laughed.

'Oh we thought it was finished.'

It was apparent that their skills were not quite as good as they thought, at least not in the eyes of the professionals!

They worked hard with the builders to try and keep the cost down. Slowly with the aid of good weather the progress of their design for the house revealed itself. The whole of the ground floor was full of dust and brick rubble, but over the course of the next few days it began to take shape as the shell was created for them to work on with fixtures and fittings and new decoration.

'I don't know about you,' Terry said to Andrea, 'but I'll be glad to get back to work for a rest. I never thought I'd hear myself say that but my back is killing me!'

'Just think what we've saved by helping out,' she replied.

'True enough, but I've found muscles I never even knew I had.'

The week passed quickly and it was soon time for them to return to work life.

On return to work, waiting on his desk was a memo from Andrew telling him to hand over all his files to the agricultural agents Savills and Carter Jones at a meeting on Monday 18th September. Sean would be present and Terry was to make sure everything was in order for the transfer to take place that day. This was the final straw when Andrew was prepared to pay outside agents considerably more to do his job. He was so misguided and foolish to think they would provide a better and cheaper service.

Terry returned home to his 'work in progress' in something of a depressed state to tell Andrea the news - there was now no doubt that Andrew was looking to push him out.

'That's terrible. Surely he can't do that can he? Could we change our minds and take him to a tribunal? We certainly have an open and shut case.' Andrea asked.

'I rang a top employment lawyer in Leeds today for a chat and explained my situation to him. He assures me I have a cast iron case, but it'll take time and of course money.'

'I hate to see you treated like this after all you've done to make his business a success and pouring money into his pockets. It's the Lord Burnham situation all over again. What is it about employers?'

'Yes I know, but let's wait another few weeks to see how my job applications turn out. I know there's not much around at the moment, but if that fails we'll go for him in court with all guns blazing. What else is there?'

The following week, when Terry was in his office, Andrea phoned him.
    'Have you seen the job section in the Yorkshire Post today?' she asked.

'Yes, but there's nothing in it that I could apply for, sorry.'

'Well,' Andrea replied, 'what about that 'Property Manager' job based in Wakefield? It's on page twenty. Take a look.'

'But that's for a 'Commercial Property Manager,' not agricultural. I saw that. I don't know anything about commercial property.'

'It can't be so different, can it? It's all property.'

He laughed. 'Only almost everything about it, that's the difference - all the legal side and tenancies.'

'You should write off for it, you have nothing to lose.'

'Mmmm - OK, but I don't hold out much hope, it's a totally different sort of business.'

A few days after the application had been sent off he was invited to attend an interview by a firm of employment consultants on St Paul's Street, Leeds for the position of 'Commercial Property Manager.' Nobody was more surprised than Terry.

The consultants explained the detail of the job and what was involved. The company had recently purchased large amounts of property all over the north east, south and west Yorkshire, as part of a bus company, with land holdings valued in the region of £20 million. The group were looking to improve the income and develop their property portfolio and needed a manager for that purpose. It had a very dynamic and talented chairman who would, they informed him, want to interview the successful candidates before a choice was made.

Terry was somewhat taken aback by the immensity and magnitude of the job. Where would he even begin?

The consultants seemed keen to push him forward, but he was unsure of his ability to do the job. However, a few days later he was called to attend an interview with the Chairman of the company and found himself waiting in the secretary's office to be called through for an interview.

'You may go through now; the chairman is free to see you.' His secretary said as she guided him along to the main door of his office on the first floor.

Nervously, Terry entered the office, a large room, where a window occupied the full length of one wall overlooking a busy road. Mr Hodgson, the chairman, shook his hand firmly as he seemed to be quickly summing Terry up. He then sat at his desk, indicating for Terry to sit in the chair in front. He was a very tall alert man immaculately turned out in a smart grey suit. He leaned forward and played nervously with a decorative glass ball on his desk while giving a half smile.

'You seem to have had a lot of experience with your company in North Yorkshire. Tell me a little about it.'

Terry explained how he had found absolute chaos on taking the position with the Bowman Estate. Nobody knew who owned what, or where anything was. How he had to search out all the land ownership and tenancies through solicitors and then establish the boundaries of each of the properties. He had to deal with farmers, solicitors, land agents, councils and the ministry of agriculture, slowly pulling it all together and developing various properties or selling them for housing or commercial development. Over the nine years he worked for the company he built up the rent roll from £70,000 to £1.5m a year.

Mr Hodgson listened intently with a fairly unimpressed expression on his face, as he stared forward in deep thought listening to Terry.

Surprisingly after a long silence he said, 'I see you are a 'Holy Child.'

Terry looked at him inquisitively?

'Your school, I see it was the Holy Child School.'

'Oh yes, I see what you mean,' Terry replied smiling.

'So are you a Catholic?'

'Yes indeed, since aged five when my parents became Catholics.'

With that Mr H. walked over to the coat hanger standing in the corner of his office and put on his overcoat as if to leave.

'OK we'll be in touch, thanks for coming,' he said in a matter of fact way.

Terry stood up, shook his hand and went out the way he had come in. That was strange he thought what an abrupt end. He went to see the secretary to tell her the interview had ended and he was leaving.

He really didn't know what to expect. It was one of the strangest interviews ever! However, on 17th October, a letter arrived from the consultants offering him the job, and setting out the terms. Terry was ecstatic. It was an enormous step to take, going away from agriculture into commercial property management, one he was not confident he could easily make. However, it sounded like a fascinating, if demanding job, one that he was prepared to have a go at and learn on his feet as he got into it. The company, born from within a bus group, was looking to develop its land holdings to develop them and to vastly increase the rental income, and he was to be at the top. It was a clear case of sink or swim and he was determined to swim.

He was able, with great joy and relief, to give notice to Bowman Estates on 25th October 1989 that he was terminating his employment with them. Andrew looked surprised and aggrieved, saying he didn't want him to work out his notice. He probably feared he would cause too much havoc among the remaining staff, who mostly congratulated him for getting out under the wire! So instead he enjoyed two paid weeks off before starting his new job on 27th November. The start of yet another new beginning.

That month saw Margaret and Cecil's fiftieth wedding anniversary so they all went over to Shropshire to celebrate and organise a surprise party with a few neighbours and friends. It was a lovely celebratory evening, one of happy memories and joy, which brought the grandparents so much pleasure. They loved relating the stories surrounding their wedding day at Hatfield Hyde, near Welwyn Garden City in

1939, at the outbreak of WW11. Remembering they only had a few months together before Cecil was sent off to the Middle East with the army in the 3rd Battalion Royal Tank Regiment as a Tank Commander. During that time, he had many close escapes with death and was lost in the desert for nearly two years before returning to a very surprised, but overjoyed, Margaret carrying their pride and joy Ann, born just before Cecil left. Indeed, they had so much to proudly celebrate in their fifty years of marriage, as well as being a fine example to the rest of the family. It was blighted only by the loss of their daughter Ann at such a young age.

The rural life style at Osgodby House was relaxing and rejuvenating after a working day. They slowly worked away at the improvements and decorations bringing new life into the house. Lynda, who had found it hard leaving Boroughbridge, began to settle. She was busy with driving lessons, with an eye to having her own car one day bringing with it her freedom, as she saw it!

Paul, was enjoying life in Liverpool. He worked hard with his studies and in the evenings and weekends in a bar to raise money to cover some of his expenses, which helped Andrea and Terry. Paul was always pleased to come home and crash out in his own room while enjoying life in the country for a change after the hustle and bustle of Liverpool and they loved having him around.

Lynda took her driving test on 2nd November and passed first time. She was delighted. Shortly after her eighteenth birthday in March 1990 she purchased a car from Ruth a retired teacher from Knaresborough who had become a family friend. She enjoyed the freedom the car gave her to come and go as she wished. Terry and Andrea were pleased for her, always being aware that living in the country was not so easy for Lynda and the car allowed her to go out more and make friends.

It was fun having Colonel Christopher and Virginia as neighbours and they grew to enjoy each other's company. There was never a dull moment. They were from entirely different backgrounds that fascinated them both! Virginia was absolutely amazed that in Terry's childhood and upbringing he never had a 'Footman.' She found it hard to understand how on earth he was able to manage without such assistance! They enjoyed the friendship with Christopher, as they knew him. He was quite a character and often came to their joint boundary fence for a chat, usually after he had fallen out with Virginia, who he always referred to as 'Madam.'

He would often say to Terry in a very serious manner
   'Funny things women, funny things. Is your wife funny? – Mine is.'

'Now then. How are you both? You must come around for a bloody drink and tell us all about the business and about 'your God.' I'll speak to Madam.'

'That would be lovely Christopher, perhaps at the weekend.'

'You moved in very quickly - jolly good, jolly good. If you ever feel that you haven't paid us enough for the house, well you can always give us some more bloody money. It was too cheap! Too cheap!' Christopher said with his roguish smile.

'And if you feel you've over charged us, and you are having problems with your conscious then you can refund some to us too!'

'Ha! Ha! Bloody fine Officer! What regiment did you say you were in eh?
   What regiment was it?'

'I wasn't in the army.'

'What, not in the army? Are you a bloody conscie then?'

'No I wasn't in the war,' Terry replied.

'Not in the war? Christopher shouted surprisingly, 'Why ever not?' he demanded unbelievingly.

'I wasn't born until the end of the war.'

'What! Not born? Oh I forget you are so bloody young,' he exclaimed as he went off tutting away to himself and shaking his head.

It was a conversation that Terry was to have with him so many times over the years. Christopher really had the greatest difficulty accepting that he had not served in the war and was not even born at that time.

One of the drawbacks to living in the countryside was the lack of proper sewers with everything having to go into a septic tank. This is fine when they work, but a nightmare when they don't. Something they were about to learn when, one morning, they awoke to a blockage in the pipe to the septic tank with the resulting back up into the house! On investigation they found that the septic tank was outside their boundary fence and the feed pipe from the house had been cut by the neighbouring farmers plough! Terry had to locate the pipe, dig up the broken section and make a repair, not a good way to start the day!

Terry's new post as Commercial Property Manager started quietly. It was a bit of a shock having to drive for one and a half hours through busy suburbs to arrive at the company's office in Wakefield for 9am. Previously his journey had only been a short distance which had been very handy. Driving those long distances seemed such a waste of valuable time each end of the day, but it had to be done.

His large oak panelled office was on the first floor. It contained a vast desk with numerous phones, each with a panel of buttons and names. This was one of the mysteries that he had to resolve. Next to his office was his secretary Margaret who had two filing cabinets containing some of the few records the company had available. On the first day Terry sat there not quite sure what he should do. He admired the oak panelled walls and wondered about all the past occupants who had sat in this historic looking office where he now found himself. Then suddenly one of the phones rang. Which one he wondered? He picked up each in turn until he heard a voice.

'Good morning, when you have a minute would you come along to my office please?'

'Oh yes, of course Mr Hodgson.' Terry replied.

Terry nervously entered his office remembering the last time he had been there at his interview. Mr Hodgson outlined the group, the different companies in it and how it had all come about. He explained the likely areas for expansion, as well as some of the projects that were on going at the moment, giving a rough brief of where Terry was to become involved.

'First you should visit all the properties and familiarise yourself with them, where and what they are. Your secretary will give you a list of them all.'

He then tossed a large grey book at Terry.

'We've just completed the purchase of this company in the north east. This is a report from our solicitors who checked out all the properties and advised us on the purchase. There are over thirty different properties, mainly bus company premises, depots and bus stations. Read the report, look at the maps and plans and then go and have a look at each of the properties and report back to the next board meeting in two weeks. Can you do that?'

'Yes, I'll get on with that straight away.' A stunned Terry replied.

Mr Hodgson leaned forward playing as usual with his paperweight.

'Each month we'd like you to produce a report for the board on all property matters and circulate it before the meeting, especially where there is something going on. You will then attend the monthly board meetings to discuss the content of your report. It's held in the boardroom, which is in the basement. Your secretary will show you where that is. In that way you can keep us informed and we can give you our decisions and requests in connection with the matters arising, thus enabling speedy progress. However, it's my intention that you and I will work closely together on the day-to-day detail, where you will always be directly responsible to me. We will, at first, both attend meetings with all those necessary as they arise. I'll then slowly pass these over to you, depending on what we are dealing with at any one time; that's solicitors, agents, planners and the like.' He said in his very business-like manner.

'All matters involving the properties will be passed to you and will be your responsibility to progress and deal with. Nobody else in the group may make decisions about property without first referring to you, and that includes me. Is that clear, as its very important?'

'Crystal.' Terry replied.

'We've had too many people in this organisation thinking they can do as they wish in property matters, but they'll all be informed that, in future, they have to go through you. You are therefore, likely to get quite a few visits from the different managers within our bus group. I'm sure you'll deal with them effectively.' He smiled for the first time and his face lit up.

He was very different from the Chairman of Bowman Estates, efficient, progressive, and focused. Coming from a very good accountancy background he used it with skill and effect. Terry liked his manner and could already see they would get on well together. He was clear, fair and firm, knew what he wanted and what he was doing.

Terry set about his task, looking around all the properties and speaking to the managers and staff at the different sites. He knew that the very best knowledge is gained from those on the shop floor, not necessarily the managers, as they are the ones likely to know the most about the site and the business. Some of the employees had probably been there for years and would gladly impart their valuable knowledge if only asked.

Terry arrived at one of the newly purchased bus depots having looked in the record book of properties the solicitors had provided in their advice to the directors. In it there were valuable photographs and plans of each of the properties, aiding Terry as he toured around the northeast area fulfilling his mission. Somehow one particular property didn't look quite right, being very different in appearance from the photographs in the report which showed an old brick build property. However, Terry was looking at a large newish modern building of some 30,000 square feet. Unable to reconcile what he could see with the plan in the book he went to find the manager of the depot.

'I'm the new property manager for the group and it's my task to look around all the properties we own and familiarise myself. I'm having problems with this one. Am I in the right place? This photograph shows a series of old brick buildings, but you have one large modern building here.'

'Ah yes, that was how it used to be, but this new building was put up six years ago.'

'Are you sure?' Terry asked the manager.

'Oh yes, it's your photograph and description that's out of date.'

'Well it shouldn't be. This was drawn up by our solicitors who went around all our properties making this record.'
Terry was confused, as the report was only a few months old and the preface said that all the properties had been inspected and photographed by the solicitors before compiling and reporting on the holdings in the company.

As he drove out of the car park he stopped to chat to another man busy sweeping up leaves at the exit.
'Good Morning, I'm the new property manager for the company. You're doing a very valuable job there keeping us all clean and tidy. It's very exposed, so a lot of rubbish must blow in.'

'Oh aye it does, but I like to keep it tidy.'

'You worked here long?' Terry enquired.

'Been here for twenty years, but I'm only part time now. I'm supposed to be retired.'

'So you know all there is to know I guess,' said Terry with a smile.

'Oh yes nobody knows more than Jeff. I've learnt a few things since I started here.'

'You'll have seen a few changes too in that time, I bet.' Terry volunteered.

'Oh yes! - see that coal yard over there.' He pointed over the boundary fence to heaps of coal. 'Well its owned by Mr Price.

He's a friend of mine from the village. He owns all of this corner right up to that there building where he keeps his pigeons. He never uses it and we get a lot of his rubbish blowing across here. I keep telling him but it makes no difference, so I put up a fence to catch his rubbish and to try and keep it tidy.'

'Surely, that can't be right, he can't own that area as it's shown on this plan as being ours. We own it. See the red line on the plan.' Terry showed the plan to Jeff.

'I don't know about your plan, but I've known Mr Price the coalman for more years than I can remember and he said, as a favour to me, we could use it for our buses to come in and out this way and over his land. That was back seven or eight years ago, about the time the bus company put up this new building, but they don't own it, he does.'

'Jeff, are you sure of that?'

'Of course, I know everything about this place. If you need to know anything else, you come and see Jeff. I've got to get off now though taking the Mrs to the shops. You'll know how it is.'

'It's been very interesting to meet you Jeff and thanks for all your help. It looks as if we don't own the access to our own property, which is quite an omission,' Terry said as he thoughtfully drove off into the stormy morning sky towards his next site inspection.

The next morning Terry made an appointment to see Mr Hodgson and reported to him what he had found out about the bus depot and the whole boundary situation within it.

'Yesterday I was up in the northeast starting the inspection of the properties in the report. I went to Trimdon bus depot. It's a very wild and windy spot.'

'So anything exciting to report? Mr Hodgson casually asked.

'Not exciting, but very concerning. We appear to have no rights of access to the site. You see the report gives you, the directors, several pages of written details about the site, together with photographs. These, and the report bear no resemblance to what I found there. Even worse, it appears we don't even own the entrance or the exit. Without which the site is pretty valueless. It seems that our solicitors only did a desk top exercise and didn't visit the properties despite what they said.'

Mr Hodgson's face went whiter than it normally was. He never generally had a lot of colour.

'Are you sure?'

'Yes quite certain, but it's something we need to check out as it's a very serious omission. I have it on the best authority about the ownership of the access. I found a smart modern building on the site, not the one described in the report from the solicitors. It appears they have never checked the detail and certainly have never been on site as they said and charged us for.'

'But we made that purchase partly on the basis of what they told us. This is appalling!' Mr Hodgson said furiously.'

Picking up his phone he rang the solicitor concerned with the purchase, who also did all the company's property work.

'Could I speak to Mr Webb please,' he said sharply.

'Mr Webb this is Ken here. Something has come up and I need to see you urgently. Tomorrow morning at 9am in your office and I'll be bringing Terry Reeves our new property manager with me.'

'Is there a problem?' Mr Webb asked.'

'That's what we will find out tomorrow.' Ken replied.

Being the sixth biggest fee payer for this large law company they were not going to say no to his request for an urgent meeting!

'OK Terry, I'll meet you tomorrow at the Queens Hotel in Leeds. We can have coffee there first. Let's say 8.30 and don't be late.'

Mr Hodgson was calm but rightly furious.

The next morning Terry arrived in Leeds at 8.10 parking his car at the multi storey car park. As he locked his car he could smell bacon cooking which lit-up his taste buds. How he wished he were going to have a cooked breakfast and not going to a meeting in a solicitor's offices!

KH was late arriving at the Queens, but it didn't seem to worry him. They had coffee and went over the details to make sure he had the facts straight before going into the meeting. Together they made their way to the office block and checked in at reception. In minutes Mr Webb came out and greeted them both before taking them off to his office deep within the premises.

'So what can we do for you today Ken.' Mr Webb asked with some intrigue. 'It sounded important when we spoke yesterday.'

Ken as always went straight to the point, never a man to waste time on pleasantries.

'It's regarding the report you recently carried out for us on the northeast bus company purchase. That's the depot at Trimdon.

Did you visit it before you drew up the report for us?' KH enquired.

'Yes, we visited all of the properties as you asked and then followed it with a comprehensive report and photographs.'

'Oh did you?' Ken questioned.
   'So you personally visited all the properties did you?'

'Well not me personally, but one of my colleagues, a Mr Blake.'

'I see; then would it be possible for me to speak to Mr Blake?' KH enquired.

'Why, is there a problem?' Mr Webb asked with some concern.

'Can we just have a word with him please, if he is available?'

Mr Webb picked up the phone and asked for his colleague Mr Blake to attend the meeting. He was a tall dark haired man in his thirties who quickly breezed in to join them and they all shook hands.

'Can I help you?' asked a buoyant Mr Blake.

'Yes,' replied a cool KH. 'The report you recently made for us on the northeast companies, did you visit all the properties?'

'Yes, of course, all of them.'

'All of them?' KH questioned again.

'Yes, all of them.' A puzzled Mr Blake replied.

Terry was cringing as he realised the trap KH had laid.

'So how do you explain the fact that the buildings on the Trimdon site are completely different from your description and, more importantly, the fact that we don't own the access to the site?'

Mr Blake looked shocked and surprised, then very embarrassed.

'I'll speak with you later,' said Mr Webb uncompromisingly as Mr Blake left the room in shame.

KH was, as always, quick to take the initiative and maximise his position. He went for Mr Webb, guns blazing.

'We paid you over £10,000 for this report, on which the board based its decision for purchase. We now find the report is full of errors and lies that have far reaching consequences for us. You didn't carry out an inspection of the property or establish the legal boundaries from the deeds.'

'I want you to refund the fee we've paid you, investigate the boundary matters and rectify them at no cost to us. What's more, I don't want Mr Blake to ever have any further involvement with any of our properties. Is that clear? If you don't agree to this, we will expose this whole matter and your incompetence to the media and cut all ties with your firm.'

'Of course we do accept your terms and would offer you nothing less. I would like to express my regret that this ever happened in the first place and assure you that a full investigation will take place to make sure this never happens again,' replied an embarrassed Mr Webb.

Terry and KH left the office to find their own way out.

'Well done, good work,' KH expressed to Terry as they made their way back to the car park.

'All part of the service, but we do expect better from our professionals don't we?' Terry replied.

'Yes indeed we do.'

CCC

CHAPTER TEN

While at work things were slowly progressing with Terry gaining confidence, getting used to his new position as commercial property manager and quite enjoying the challenge. At home storm clouds where gathering on the horizon.

Andrea had been told that her directors were selling out their investment company to a London based investment company. They explained she need have no worries as the new company would take over her employment and had invited her to a day at their London offices in order that she could get to know more about the company. However, Andrea was not interested in the offer of a job in London, and was assured that, in such circumstances, her existing employers would pay any redundancy payment due.

Discussions took place, but they refused to accept their legal obligation for paying redundancy and tried, wrongly, to pass that obligation to the new employer.

War broke out between the two over a relatively small payment, but finally through the advice taken from the Citizen Advice Bureau a court case was avoided. The C.A.B. took up the case on Andrea's behalf against a firm of top London lawyers and won the day at the eleventh hour, settling the question of responsibility, and the amount due. It was a long, emotional and stressful battle, one that Andrea did not deserve and could have done without. She had given many years of loyal service to her employers and this was the thanks as they tried to flout the law. It left her without a job at a critical time when she needed most to be able to support Terry and the children in keeping up the mortgage payments, as well as funding Paul in college.

On 28th March Lynda celebrated her 18th birthday with a party for her friends and purchased a car with money left to her by a relative. She began to enjoy the freedom it gave her and was a very careful driver. She would often spend a weekend with Andrea's mum in Scholes, which they both seemed to enjoy.

Never one to be out of work for long, within a month Andrea was offered a new job as accounts manager with a fabrics company at Kirbymoorside on the North Yorkshire Moors. It was a small business with a large order book, sending fabrics that were produced in West Yorkshire all over the world. Very different from the finance industry and not far for her to travel. It was also a new challenge within a small team of employees.

Tuesday 1st May was Andrea's 40th Birthday for which Terry had arranged a surprise party at Osgodby House. The night before he crept out with posters he'd printed announcing, **'Andrea 40 Today'** and attached a copy to every tree and post he came across all the way along the road that she would take to work the following morning.

It was a fine evening and twenty-four friends, neighbours and family arrived from near and far to enjoy the party in the garden, which was now beginning to take shape. It was very different from the rough grass field it had been. Helena, Andrea's mother, made a beautiful cake and everyone enjoyed the warm sunny evening with family and friends, celebrating the occasion as it should have been with loved ones around.

Osgodby House had an agricultural clause on it limiting its use to those employed in agriculture only. This reduced its value by a third, but if they could persuade the council to remove the clause it would be a great financial benefit to them making it available to anyone when sold in the future on the open market. This was part of the reason for buying such a property and Terry always hoped they might be able to get the clause removed. It was never going to be easy and was a risk.

They put an application in to the council for its removal but unfortunately it was turned down. They then appealed against the decision, but that too was turned down.

The advantages of its removal were enormous, enough to make them doggedly continue with the process refusing to take no for an answer. It took hours of time to prepare all the documents and to collect the evidence against retaining the clause and, despite the costs involved, they continued to try. It was a battle they continued for fifteen years until finally it was removed, but only by their steely determination and the help of a very switched on lawyer.

As life's current problems were getting sorted Terry felt it would be interesting for Andrea to see some more of the places he had lived and worked in. Africa had played a big part in Terry's early life and had come to mean so much to him. He felt that if she was to really know him, then she had to know Africa.

'How would you like to go out and visit Malawi?' Terry asked Andrea.

'Is it safe and where would we stay?'

'I'm sure we could stay with the missionary sisters. They have always said they are keen to see us and would love to meet you. It would be so exciting and I'd love you to see where I used to live and work. We could spend some time with them and then go off on Safari and stay at a game reserve, as well as visiting one or two of my African friends out in the bush.'

'It sounds very exciting, when would we go do you think?' Andrea asked.

'How about September or October, depending on flights and when we can get time off work, and making sure first that the Sisters can have us stay?

'Sounds good to me.' Andrea said excitedly.

They made contact with the Sisters at Mlale mission in Malawi and established it was a good time to visit. They were ecstatic and looked forward to meeting Andrea and to seeing Terry again after so many years. They booked their flights and would fly out on 6th October from Manchester direct to Lilongwe in Malawi, returning on 26th October.

Amongst the excitement they heard that Jeremy, who Terry had left working at the Bowman Estate, had been given his notice on Friday 13th July, the very day that they had arranged to meet for a pub meal. At seven that evening Jeremy and his wife, Gabrielle, pulled into the car park of the Faulkenberg Pub, Jeremy still with a sparkle on his face.

'So you got out under the wire Jeremy? Sorry to hear it worked out that way.'

'Yes, Andrew finally got his way and, like so many others, he pushed me out with no real reason.'

They discussed it all, trying to give some encouragement and support. He took it philosophically, as Jeremy would. It was his way and perhaps it was also with some relief, for it had been a very stressful situation for several years. He was not so much surprised as sad, as he really did love his work in Yorkshire. He now had to look around and see what else was available. It wouldn't be easy as management positions in forestry for a man of his calibre were few and far between at the best of times.

'Well Jeremy, I managed to find employment so I'm sure you will too, you just have to get out there and see what's on offer. If there is anything we can do you only have to ask, but you know that.'

Terry felt that his days at Bowman Estates were now far behind him and looked back on the latter days with some horror and he didn't envy the position that Jeremy now found himself in. Terry's new position was very demanding and he did miss the contact with the agricultural community. They were, on the whole, lovely people, straightforward and hard working. But life changes and he had to change with it if he was to continue to support his family and have a full life.

Ken, the Chairman of the group was a complicated and unusual man who didn't trust people easily. He was direct and sometimes cutting in his approach, but he also had a soft side, keen and able to help whenever called upon to do so. Terry was to be availed of that very genuine warm man with his exceptional kindness and compassion when, in later years, crisis again visited Terry's door.

Ken was, at the same time, a very intelligent and able man. The only man Terry ever met who was capable of chairing a meeting, reading his notes, writing intricate new notes with his fountain pen in his day book, while, at the same time, recording events and conversations with inordinate detail. Attending a meeting with him was like watching an accomplished musician at work. Terry grew to admire and respect him and his abilities. Nobody could read a set of accounts more lucidly than Ken and sum up the value and direction of a company in a flash. Terry watched with awe when he was in action, commanding the meeting with vigour, but always in a gentlemanly manner, totally outwitting anyone around the table, whoever they were.

Terry was beginning to get to grips with all the different properties, the subtle difference between a bus station and a bus depot and to finding where they all were geographically. He was slowly overcoming the fear of his monthly presentation to the board as he became more involved and familiar with the situation. Property was his expertise. He soon learnt that he had a far greater knowledge of property matters than anyone else on the board. They themselves had their own individual expertise and talents which they brought to the board meetings and which contributed to the overall success of the group.

At the next monthly board meeting he was delighted and excited to be able to drop them all a bombshell. He would point out ways in which they could make money from the sites and property they owned, claim back considerable monies already paid out, and make large savings in costs.

He sat at the long boardroom table, surrounded by the ten directors of the group, who were either moneymen or managing the bus companies. There was silence with all eyes and ears on Terry as he begun to address the meeting in his usual manner. They sat with their papers strewn around them listening intently to the new boy, ready to fire questions and make enquiries, in order to test him. He had not told Ken Hodgson what he was about to say and it did not feature in his report sent to the board before the meeting. He wanted to surprise them with it!

'I'm able to inform you,' he voiced to the board, 'that I've arranged for over thirty advertising boards to be erected in strategic places across the portfolio - these will produce £1000 a year for every board, a direct income on an annual licence, so not tying up the site should we ever wish to develop it. A total sum of £30,000 a year. The advertiser will even apply for the planning approval and erect the boards, so no costs fall to us, only income!'

The Board members were never ones to show much excitement or joy, but on this occasion looked surprised and delighted at the information, as they sat there peering at this 'new boy' in their midst who was bearing such gifts.

'Furthermore, I'm even more delighted to be able to tell you that I've identified savings in business rates that will, across the whole range of properties, reduce your annual rates payable by £350,000.' They all looked shocked but alert.

'In addition to this I have already started to reclaim back rates already paid, to the tune of £150,000 in this first year, with more to follow in the second year. That's money already paid out that will come back into the group. You may well have to adjust your accounts for those years!'

Silence fell on the meeting with a look of shock and disbelief on their now white faces. The statement had gained the attention of them all, as they were people totally motivated by money. They had all invested every penny they had into buying the bus companies from the government in the first place, and had collectively taken a huge risk.

The chairman Ken Hodgson was excited and sat with a broad beam on his face.

'How on earth have you been able to do that in such a short time?' he enquired?

'That's why you employ me,' Terry replied grinning.

'Most of your properties have not been assessed for business rates for many years,' Terry explained. 'During that time many of the old buildings have either been removed or fallen down, but no notification ever given to the local authority. Many of the sites have changed beyond recognition since they were last assessed. On looking into the detail and structure of the rating system I found also that it's possible to backdate the rating assessment so I asked for a refund from the council for some five years. That's what I'm in the process of doing and the figure of £150,000 is my lowest estimate of the likely refund. It will most likely be quite a lot more.'

They were stunned. Chairman Ken looked on proudly at his prodigy.

Terry continued to go through other property matters with the board, but they seemed to have little appetite for any more information. He then left the stunned meeting feeling he'd proved himself and earned his keep! It had been the result of a great deal of investigation and hard work on his part poring over papers and figures, but it proved very rewarding.

At home it was time to have all the vaccinations necessary for their travels to Malawi, so a visit to the doctor resulted in them having a series of injections for Poliomyelitis, Tetanus, Typhoid, Yellow Fever and Hepatitis. Quite a cocktail over the next few weeks and not one they were looking forward to but, as the doctor said, no one ever died from the vaccinations but many died from the diseases!

The first vaccinations were arranged and happened to coincide with the evening when neighbours Christopher and Virginia had invited them for dinner. The nurses at the health centre told them that they were now injecting some of the vaccinations into the thighs and not, as traditionally, in the arm. Surprised by this, they agreed and went ahead receiving some of the injections in the leg and then set off to prepare for the meal with their neighbours. It was the usual warm friendly visit with drinks flowing as always and Christopher in his usual exuberant mood. They had a wonderful meal of Virginia's delicious homemade game pie followed by a selection of sweets. When the time came for them to adjourn to the sitting room for coffee, Andrea and Terry were alarmed to find they were unable to get to their feet. Their leg muscles seem to have locked and were hard and unable to function. They seemed powerless to move and had to work at forcing themselves onto their feet by pushing on the table with their hands, to lift themselves up. They then realised that this must have been caused by the injections earlier, especially the ones in their legs. After a while they managed to get sufficient feeling into their legs for them to function but they decided they should really go straight home and wondered if they would ever make it. They slowly dragged themselves back to their house like a couple of ninety year olds and, when they finally arrived home, they had to go up the stairs on their bottoms as they had little use in their legs!

By morning they were able to move slightly better and rang the health centre to inform them what they had been through. 'Oh yes,' they said, 'we don't inject in the leg anymore. That must have been done by mistake but don't worry you'll soon recover.'

They left for Malawi on 6th October and were greeted at Lilongwe Airport by four of the Missionary Sisters of Our Lady of Africa, Terry's ex-assistant farm manger, his wife, and their three children, together with his long-time Italian friend Luigi. It was quite a reception committee. What excitement there was. The sun was high, bright and burning on that hot dry afternoon as the ceaseless warm winds blew across the plains of central Africa. A long exchange of greetings took place as the Sisters met Andrea for the first time with non-stop chatter and so much to catch up on. Slowly they all became one, blending all their joys and sorrows. Terry felt it was so necessary that Andrea should go to see and understand something of Africa, a place where he had once lived and to which he felt he belonged, beyond explanation or reason. It was a place that had had such a profound effect on his life since he first went to Tanzania as a volunteer with Voluntary Service Overseas at the tender age of twenty in 1965. Somehow to know Africa was to know him.

They stayed at the 'Mua Mission' on the edge of Lake Malawi, an incredible lake that runs the length of this relatively small country, providing fish and water to its population. It was good to smell the dryness and to again experience the heat of Africa's warm heart; to feel the lively winds and see the cloud shadows galloping across the plains of Africa creating the most amazing patterns; to again see the unfamiliar tropical plants with their beautiful blooms and to be able to take for granted the Bougainvillea strung out along the fences, and the magnificence of the gigantic Baobabs scattered throughout the region as if planted upside-down.

The Mission at Mua had been a Leprosarium in its early life, back in the 1950's, but was now a hospital and a school, full of life and death. The long-term aim of the Sisters was always to train the local people, who would eventually take over the work, while the sisters and fathers slowly withdrew to start other projects. You could feel the history in the very dust of the place; the endless hours of work, sweat, blood and toil that had resulted in it being the refuge for so many poor and desperate people.

Terry and Andrea stayed there for a few days with the sisters and then moved on to visit another mission up in the mountains at Dedza, on the border with Mozambique. They slept in the schoolroom there where Sister Laura had made up a bed for them. It, too, was a small hospital and a base where the sisters worked to help with the organisation of orphan children as well as many refugees. These had amassed on the border and lived and died there whilst seeking protection, care and shelter. The refugee camps stretched out along the whole border with thousands of people seeking refuge, fleeing war in Mozambique. Thousands upon thousands of round thatched huts had been built from local materials - grass, sticks, cow manure and mud in the long held traditional manner and stretched across the plains in a rash of mankind. It was a sad reflection of man's inability to coexist with his neighbour; and scarred its beautiful setting in the backdrop of the mountain hills that themselves looked as though they had been tipped up by a giant lorry and left there on the vast plains. They made long shadows on the unending dry land along the grim border where thousands had gathered.

The missionary sisters were outnumbered thousands to one in their quest to help the refugees. Were they ever dispirited? No never. Sister Laura, a lone figure on a small two-stroke motorcycle carrying a large red box on the back, risked the sandy dangerous roads visiting the camps to help the people in any way she could. She taught the women how to sew and helped them with cooking in the poor surroundings in which they found themselves, occasionally bringing them little luxuries like a small bar of soap.

Sister Anny, a midwife, sought to bring comfort to those in child birth as one after the other, day and night, they arrived on her doorstep in urgent need as the birth of their child was upon them. She and her team of nurses - local people who she had trained - endeavoured to bring them comfort with the limited tools, equipment and drugs available. Aids was everywhere; from which so many died. Men who had contracted the disease from their promiscuous life style passed it on to their innocent wives and, in turn, they to their unborn children, creating a deep pit of sadness, grief and horror beyond belief and understanding. These wonderful sisters and their team fought against all odds to bring some hope, comfort and relief to those in need.

Sister Genevieve tried to educate as many as possible with classes for the people. She also trained trainers who would then go out and inform and educate others to create centres of influence in all health and birth control methods. She battled on. The challenge was immense but, never dispirited and always in faith, she gave everything to helping the people she met, no matter their nationality religion or creed. Every hour of every day, and often at night, she sacrificed her sleep to bring help and support to such desperate people.

All the sisters and nurses were an inspiration to Terry and Andrea who on their return home and for the next fifteen years, held a fundraising event in their beautiful garden in North Yorkshire, enabling them to send money to the Sisters to help in their service of the people, providing education, medicine and support.

While in Africa Terry was keen that Andrea would not merely carry a dark image of the under belly of Africa, but that she would also see the beauty of the country, and there was plenty of it to see.

Malawi – the word means, literally, fire flames and is associated with some of the most ancient sacred sites – is a small, landlocked country in the heart of East Central Africa. It is almost one-fifth water. Its vast lake, southernmost in the chain of the Great Rift Valley waters, is 580 km long, the third largest in Africa, and is linked through the Shire River to the Zambezi and the sea. It encloses a variety of terrain unparalleled for its unsurpassed beauty and magnificence. Steep, often precipitous, escarpments form the edge of the Rift Valley. To the north west of the lake the table land reaches its peak at 2,500 m on the beautiful, rolling grasslands of the Nyika Plateau and south to the forested Viphya mountains. Rich alluvial farmlands stretch along the lakeshore, between Viphya and Dedza, where the Missionary Sisters were based. There is an extensive plain some 900 m high, which gives way at the southern edge of the lake to the tropically hot, low-lying Shire Valley.

In the Shire Highlands to the east of the rift in southern Malawi at an elevation of 600 to 900 m, the climate is cool and stimulating, with very heavy rainfall in the summer. The beautiful plateaux of Zomba Mountain, 2087 m and Mulanje, at 3000 m the highest mountain in Central Africa, dominate this area clothed with cedar and pine forests, with fields of wild orchids when in season. This entire area once teemed with wildlife, whose descendants now roam the country's national parks. The Malawian people themselves, wherever they are encountered, are always courteous, friendly and helpful earning their reputation as 'the warm heart of Africa.' This is the Africa that Terry wanted to leave in Andrea's mind, not for it to be totally taken over by the horrors, corruption and terrors that it also portrays.

They visited the Kudya Discovery Lodge on the Shire River, a river unchanged since 1859 when David Livingstone steamed up the Shire River in his vessel the "Ma Robert." He sought to use it as a gateway into the heart of Africa but was halted by a series of cataracts extending some 64 km up stream.

Terry and Andrea found it very relaxing, a place where time seemed to have stood still. Hippo came out of the river at night and lay by the cars in the car park, chewing some of the vast quantities of grass that they consume daily and, in so doing, cause a problem, if you wished to gain access to your car!

Before they left England they had met the Bishop of Zomba area, Bishop Nat Aifa, at a local church while he was on a visit to the U.K. They told him they were going to stay at the Kudya Lodge, gave him the dates and he said he would try and visit them, but they didn't really expect him to.

While looking around the hotel and enjoying its wonderful riverside surroundings they saw a man in a colourful shirt rushing through the outer lounge calling out to them.

'Hello! Hello there, Pink People, how are you?'

Somewhat confused they went over to this flamboyant character to see if he really was addressing them.

'Hello,' they said, 'do we know you?'

'You must remember me, we met near Leeds.'

Suddenly it dawned on them who he was. He looked so different in lightweight ordinary clothes and not in his usual Bishops outfit!

'Hello, how good to see you. However did you remember we were here this week? So nice to see you again Bishop.'

'I never forget my friends. I've come to invite you to my house. I've a boring meeting on Saturday, followed by lunch with lots of my priests, deacons and the members of the Mother's Union. Please come and join us. Here is my telephone number. Call me, if you're not able to come or to find my house. The phone line is my private one. Its next to my bed.'

'We're going south on Saturday so we could call in on the way to Zomba. Thank you so much, we'd would love to come.'
    They sat and chatted with him while looking out of the open lounge with its round windows onto the Shire River with the mountains on the horizon. Hippos were basking in the water below and snorting as if they were chatting to each other.

Later in the day they took a trip in the hotel's flimsy boat that looked as if it was made of balsa wood. It had a framework that took you up to a higher deck, in order that you might view the amazing bird life, while dodging the hippo and the odd local fisherman in his dugout canoe that passed along the gently flowing river. Reeds towered twenty feet high on either side of the river. It felt as if nobody had passed along there for many years as it sort of hung there in the heat of the day. After about an hour they came to a herd of elephants on the bank, elephants of every age from the tiny one to the large grandad figure undisturbed by man. They were not happy with the invasion of their privacy so after watching their antics with delight, they left them in peace, feeling it safer to turn the boat around and go back the few miles to the hotel. They ploughed on across the still waters of the river dangerously close to large herds of hippo in their family groups, quietly dozing in the sun. They felt quite vulnerable, a quick swipe at them in the matchbox wood construction that was their boat would have sent them into the water providing fodder for the Hippo family. The river was wide merging into the swamp of the area, with no other people to be seen in the vast oasis of water. It most certainly was time to return.

On the Saturday they enjoyed lunch with the Bishop and his team of pastors. He was a very friendly jolly man and he and his wife made them very welcome being genuinely delighted to have them at his house for lunch on route to Zomba.

Zomba, a thriving business centre and the base for Parliament and the Government buildings, stands amongst the impressive grandeur of Mount Chiradzulu towering above the town. Zomba was also the home of the University of Malawi and the exceptionally beautiful Botanical Gardens with a scenic road leading past the State House up to the 2133 metre plateau, from which magnificent views can be enjoyed across the vast plains below overlooking Lake Chilwa.

It was there they stayed at the Kuchawe Inn for a couple of nights, absorbing all that was Africa. How beautiful was the sunset casting that special light across the plain, high-lighting the thorn-trees waving in the slight breeze of the evening. The clarity of the air filled their lungs with the aroma of local herbs giving out their spiced scent that mingled with the stars displaying their glory, one by dazzling one, revealing their radiance in the new night to the only sound to be heard; the song of the cicadas.

Then it was onward to Blantyre the capital city of Malawi where they had to visit the imposing church of Saint Michael and all Angels, the first permanent Christian church to be erected between the Zambezi and the Nile. Dedicated in 1891, the Church of Scotland missionary David Clement Scott, with no previous architectural or building experience, had designed it; they learnt their crafts as they went along! The dazzling roof looked as if it were covered in snow - impossible in the heat of Blantyre.

While in Blantyre they stayed at the Mount Soche Hotel in the centre that stood in a beautiful array of flowery trees and shrubs. In order for them to gain access to their room on the third floor they had to go up to the fourth floor and then down the stairs to the third floor. The lift had not been designed to stop on the third floor for some reason. Well, this was Africa!

Following a few days in Blantyre they took the long and winding road to the central region, where Terry had worked as Farm Manager for the University of Malawi at Bunda College, twelve miles from Lilongwe. He was delighted to find a few old friends at the farm who showed him around discussing their past experiences together and recalling events from Terry's days of running the farm. The new Principle invited them to have lunch with him at the college. They all sat in one of the college dining rooms chatting as they waited for the lunch to be brought to the table. A large bowl of rice and cabbage plus a bowl of beef casserole was put before them. It was surely enough to feed an army of people. They thanked the Principal for his kind invitation, took a plate and helped themselves to what was on offer. The heap of rice was enough to put them off eating and the cabbage, having had the life boiled out of it for several hours, was none too appetizing either. However, they tried their best to give the impression they were enjoying it. They slowly managed to eat a little while, at the same time, chatting to the Principal. Having made a small hole in the offering they took their leave and set off to visit again Mlale Mission, about five miles from Bunda College. Terry had first come to meet the Missionary Sisters of Africa there in 1978 after Ann had helped with a sewing class at the mission. It had become a favourite place for him to take rest and enjoy the company and warmth of the sisters. The Sisters he'd known had now moved elsewhere and the mission had been taken over by another Order, but he was still keen to show it to Andrea. The road was dusty and full of potholes, far worse than Terry remembered. The sun now high in the sky was burning down on them unmercifully.

Terry looked at Andrea who seemed a little pale and uneasy. 'Are you feeling alright?'

'Well no I'm not, I'm desperate to use the toilet. It's my stomach it's rolling and churning around.'

'Mine too, desperate is the word. I might have to stop at a tree but I'll try and make it to the mission as fast as I can.'

The rough dirt road did not help their plight as they both felt their stomachs churning noisily, feeling every bump in the road.

'Not sure I'm going to make it,' said Andrea as they pulled in to the house of the Sisters.
  'If they're not there I think I'm going to die.'

'Me too,' Terry replied as he rushed from the car to bang on the door.

Fortunately, a Sister answered the door quite quickly. She was Spanish and Terry soon established that she spoke no English.

'Toilet please, toilet please, emergency, emergency,' he screamed at her pointing in a circular motion to his and Andrea's stomachs. She seemed to understand and directed them to the place they desired more than anything else in the world - the toilets! What joyous relief. Pale and exhausted, after some time they both emerged feeling considerably more comfortable. They came to the conclusion that the lunch taken at Bunda College must have upset them and gone straight through.

The Spanish sister made them a cup of tea as they recovered sitting in the lounge trying to make themselves understood, which remarkably they seemed to achieve. After a look around the mission they thanked the sisters and drove off the twelve miles to Lilongwe, the new capital city of Malawi, one that had mushroomed out of the original old colonial town. They stopped overnight at the 'Lilongwe Hotel.' It was a pleasant but short stop-over, enough for them to recover and to prepare for the journey north to visit Jack Banda and his family. Jack had been an old colleague and friend who had worked at Bunda with Terry in 1978/79 as 'Tobacco Manager.' He was a very talented and able Malawian, for whom Terry had the greatest respect. Together they had worked long hours developing the tobacco unit and the acreage grown. They were producing over 400 acres of tobacco for sale in the auction rooms of Lilongwe and Limbi; with Jack's talent producing some of the best tobacco in the country. If that was not enough Jack, who started work at 6 o'clock every morning and finished at 7 pm, returned to his home to study. He went on to pass GCE exams in English, Religion, Maths, Economics and Biology. He studied by the light of an oil lamp. He also cared for his wife Emily and six children. How on earth he managed to achieve it all Terry had no idea, but his determination was an inspiration and his work on the farm was never rushed or suffered in any way.

Jack lived to the north of Lilongwe at Mkanda, near the town of Kasungu on the west side of Malawi. He had worked there successfully for a number of years since leaving Bunda College and was getting wonderful results. It was a long and dusty drive to the farm he managed on behalf of the government and they finally arrived as the sun was setting over the wide open stretches of this fertile farming area, to be greeted by his nine children, Jack and Emily and some of his workforce. Jack had been awarded many prizes for his work, by the government. They had even sent him to Zimbabwe to see how the tobacco was grown and harvested in that country. He had won so many financial bonuses that the company could not afford to pay them all in one payment, so he had to fight to get the amounts promised and hopefully eventually paid.

Jack and Emily were pleased and proud to have Terry and Andrea stay with them. It was a rare occurrence for a white man to visit and stay with a Malawian family. Jack's father now in his nineties said he would never believe it until he saw it. That evening a large gathering of Jack and Emily's family attended a welcoming party for them. They arrived one by one in their best suits to meet the strange white couple who had come from another world to visit them, deep in the bush of central Malawi and all in the name of friendship.

'Look at my father,' said Jack. 'I gave him some money to go to the village to buy a new suit for your visit, as he's always walking around in rags. But what did he do? He drank the lot so he's still in his rags and has come to meet you this evening with no shame. I've told him that he has paid you the greatest insult by turning up in that scruffy condition and he begs your pardon. He drinks far too much and never buys clothes, so we have to put up with him looking like that. Please forgive him.'

'Of course we do, we're so pleased to meet your father. We hope you will translate to him some of what we're saying as we don't share a common language, it's such a shame.'

As the family and the local people assembled in the house and garden it looked like becoming a long night. The Chief of Police and the Mayor were present and many members of Jack's church, his workforce and friends. They stood around with a drink in their hands, solemn faced with very little conversation going on between them. Terry and Andrea toured around like royalty shaking hands and greeting each one as was expected of them. Each one of them jabbered away and made motions of thanks. Towards the end of the evening there were speeches from all the main visitors thanking them for coming, carried out in such a humble and well-meaning manner. Jack asked Terry if he would say a few words to the gathered friends and family, which he did.

'You know they can't believe that a white man and his wife would come and stay in a Malawians house, it's beyond their comprehension, rarely if ever seen in these parts,' Jack explained.

Terry and Andrea felt very humble discovering what a wonderful caring and loving family they were, on the face of it at least. On the other hand, Terry knew from Jack they were often very jealous of him with all he had achieved and expected him to share it with no input from them.

After the excitement of their adventurous travels in Malawi, returning home to Yorkshire was not easy but necessary as the pressure of everyday life bore down on them. The end of 1990 saw Terry with flu and confined to bed for nearly two weeks. No sign of help from the sunshine of the holiday warding off the flu!

At the end of January 1991 Andrea's mother died after a short illness with pneumonia. They had always been very close so it hit her hard. Fortunately, she had Terry to help her, both physically and mentally during this period. She not only had to come to terms with the loss of her mother, but with it the loss of the long held family home that had been built by her father. Dark clouds hovered over the New Year as they struggled with it all and turned more to each other for comfort and strength.

Lynda celebrated her 19th birthday at the end of March followed by Paul's 21st in April. That and the advent of spring lifted their spirits somewhat as they worked hard bringing Osgodby House into shape with all that was involved.

On 26th August they again held a fund raising day for Africa in their garden for the sisters and their work. One of the projects the money was used for was to educate a young lady from Mozambique whose village had been subjected to attack by terrorists. She had hidden in a ditch and was not harmed by those ransacking her village, killing and raping as they passed through. Sister Laura met her one day while out in the villages on her motorbike helping people on the Mozambique border.

Hortencia the lady in question asked, 'could I become a missionary sister like you for I'd love to help others as you do.'

Laura explained. 'It's a very long process to train as a sister. First of all, you would need to return to school to get your standard eight exams and that costs a lot in fees. From there you would have to be accepted by the Order, followed by six years training as an apostolate.'

'I can do it,' Hortencia replied enthusiastically, 'but I don't have the money. Would you be able to help me Sister?'

'I might be able to,' Laura replied, 'but first I must speak to those that have given me some donations to ask if they are happy for me to spend it on your training.'

Terry and Andrea were delighted for Laura to use the monies in that way and thereby started a process that brought Hortencia to the missionary sisters and to commence her work in Africa. She promised to work hard and did so with all the difficulties that confronted her on the way. Part of the funds raised at Osgodby House each year went to support her. It was with tremendous determination and perseverance that she achieved her aim and when the time came to take her final vows in Rome, Terry and Andrea were invited to stay at the Mother House and to meet Hortencia for the first time and attend the service. It was a momentous occasion for them all and a real example of the proverb, 'Give a man a fish, and you feed him for a day; show him how to catch fish, and you feed him for a lifetime.' Her strength of character and hard work will have done more good than sending bags of food to Africa, as she will continue helping others for many many years to come.

CHAPTER ELEVEN

In February 1992 Lynda was engaged to Mark, a very nice young man she met at work. With such little experience and at her age, Terry and Andrea felt she was rather young and would have been happier to see her live a bit first. But it was what both she and Mark wanted and plans were made for their marriage to take place later in the year.

In March Jack and Emily Banda, Terry's Malawian friends, who they had visited in Malawi asked if they could come to stay for two weeks. It was quite an undertaking as they had never been to England and had a sort of fairy story view of what life was like in the UK. Jack had won a couple of trips to Zimbabwe in his work to see how they grew tobacco, but Emily had never been far from home and didn't speak a word of English. However, after careful consideration Terry and Andrea decided to let them come to stay. Terry arranged to pick them up from Heathrow airport as he didn't want them arriving in a strange country with no one to welcome them. It turned out to be quite an experience for all concerned but in the end they enjoyed their visit and of course learnt so much about life in England and were able to return home and tell their family all about it.

Jack was continually concerned for the family back in Malawi, ever conscious that the fifty or so members expected him to support them and if he didn't they would soon burn his crops or kill his animals. They were a complex people steeped deep in their traditions, with the young often lazy and expecting to be given everything from those who had jobs or a business and to share it with them. In the end, sadly, Jack's family were to overcome him with their jealousy and greed destroying the farm that he had worked hard for and purchased by his own efforts. They killed the animals and destroyed his crops, just because he would not share everything with them. Those not prepared to work, expected everything in return for nothing and, in the process, dragged them all down. It was a tragic demise of a good family, and painful to watch them implode as they did.

In the post, a voice from the past showed itself by way of an invitation from Jenefer, Harriet and Sarah to celebrate the Golden Wedding of their parents – Lord and Lady Burnham. Terry was touched to have been remembered and was delighted to accept the invitation to the party on 27th June 1992 at 'Hall Barn,' Beaconsfield. It was eighteen years since he'd left Lord Burnham's employment and he looked forward to returning again and to see the family and other friends and acquaintances. Andrea decided to paint a plate as a gift to mark their fifty years of marriage. It had a pen and ink type picture on it of 'Hall Barn' house with the famous inscription and family motto, 'Of Old I Hold.' Lady Burnham sent a lovely letter of thanks assuring them that it would become a family heirloom! Sadly, within a year Lord Burnham died on 18th June 1993.

Three months passed and Lynda and Mark were married at All Saints Catholic Church in Thirsk on 26th September 1992. She did not seem excited or committed to the day and its events and Terry wondered if she really knew what she was doing. She insisted that she did, so there was no more to be said or done only to wish her well as he escorted her to the church with a heavy heart and launched her forward into her new life.

At work things were fast changing. Ken and his fellow directors decided to go their separate ways, due mainly to having different interests, so the group was split up. Ken took most of the properties from the portfolio, together with the northern bus companies and moved his offices north to Darlington. He asked Terry if he would like to join him, or if he wanted to stay on in Wakefield with the remains of the bus group. They had built up a good rapport and worked well together, complimenting each other within the business. Terry was delighted to join him in Darlington, which would mean far less driving each day as it was nearer to home. It was to be only for a year as Ken planned to settle in Harrogate; a town he favoured.

A new phase in working life opened up for Terry. He was pleased to have less driving to do as the long one-and-a-half-hour drive to Wakefield was getting very tedious each morning with so much traffic to contend with, and then again at the end of the day. It always seemed such a waste of time too, time that could be spent doing other things.

Moving office from Wakefield to Darlington was quite a task. They had to merge into the northern office of the bus group sharing all their staff and secretarial services. One of Terry's main tasks was to lease the original bus company properties that were now surplus to requirements. There was limited demand but, there were some very good possibilities. Some of the properties were easier to let than others. Those in the towns being easiest to find good tenants. But on the whole they did manage to sign up some significant retailers into full repairing leases of twenty-five years. Those affluent days would not of course last forever. However, in the 90's, it seemed as if they would, with property owners and retailers enjoying some very profitable times.

Andrea's working life was also going through another change. One of the problems of taking on the finances of a company is that once you have sorted out the inherited mess you can find that the company is not as strong as may have been thought. Things were not healthy it seemed in her fabrics company. Not enough income to match the outgoings and it was time for her to move on.

Looking again in the much-used Yorkshire Post she found an administrative job with a local building company. It was a large construction company and looked suitable. After an interview for the position she started the job on a Monday morning. It soon transpired this was not a good move and by Friday gave in her notice! The chairman was a real autocrat expecting everyone to run around behind him bowing and scraping as in Dickens's day. I suppose Andrea's first day didn't get off to a very good start when the chairman arrived in the office and shouted 'Tea' to which Andrea replied, 'oh yes please, but no sugar.' She had thought he was just being thoughtful and kind on her first day but as the day wore on she realised he was a dictator of the worst type and none of the employees could wait to find another job and get out.

Andrea then took her experience and talents to another building and development company in Ripon. It was a little further to travel but they looked like a good team. She settled in well and quite enjoyed the work and the people that formed the company.

Terry was busy trying to get to grips with life in Darlington and his new office. Going through the mail early one morning, Terry heard a man's loud voice at reception.

'I want to see the Property Manager,' announced the man who had walked in off the street.

Jackie, the secretary, was well able to deal with such people, asking him if he had an appointment.

'Nope,' the man replied briskly. 'I need to see him now.'

Terry, hearing the commotion from his office, went out and said it was ok for him to come in, brusque as the man was. Terry had become used to dealing with people who apparently knew it all, made the loudest noise, had no manners and were rarely of any significance. The man was, it seemed, in a hurry and swept into his office.

'Is this property for sale?' he enquired in a matter of fact way.

'Yes' Terry replied to the man's surprise, 'all our properties are for sale. It's only the price that has to be agreed!'

'I'll give you two million pounds for it,' the man quickly replied.

'Ha! Ha!' Terry laughed, 'You'll have to double it and then add a nought, then we might be interested. Will you please now leave my office. I'm busy and we don't take kindly to people bursting in like this.'

He looked surprised and crest fallen with the response. 'I'll be back, I'll be back.'

Another time waster, Terry thought, thinking they can walk in and make an offer for a property when it suits them and for a knock down price. Always someone out there ready to make a quick buck, he thought.

Two weeks later the same man returned. 'Remember me?' he asked.

'Indeed I do. What can I do for you this time?'

'I can offer you £4.5 million for the whole site.'

'Well it's a good try, but this is the centre of our operations in the north east, right on the edge of town therefore a prime site. We wouldn't even consider such an offer, sorry.'

He looked rather crest fallen once again, muttering as he left Terry's office that it was a good offer for such run- down and out of date buildings.

Within days he was back once more. 'OK I'll make you an offer you can't refuse. It will be my final offer.'

'Why are you so keen to buy it, what do you have in mind to do with it?' Terry asked this bombastic chap.

'Can't tell you that, but my offer to you today, and my final one is £7.5 million, here's my card you can contact me there anytime.'

'Well sorry but you have a way to go yet.' Terry replied. 'Who are you acting for? Clearly this is not for yourself but on behalf of a company.'

'Sorry I can't tell you; but if you accept the offer we would of course reveal our hand, ring me if you change your mind.'

Terry took the card and was beginning to wonder what this was all about.
   He was beginning to realise that this man had not casually dropped in on passing by, but had a plan and really wanted to purchase the two-acre site that formed the office and bus

depot. It was time he felt to speak with Ken. This man was serious.

'Ken I've had this chap calling a few times. He wants to buy this site. His name is Ian Gilmore. He won't say who he represents but has made a substantial offer and I feel he's serious.'

'Oh does he?' Ken asked as he sat at his desk going through what looked like a batch of accounts. 'How much is he offering us then?'

'£7.5 million.'

'Is he for real?'

'Yes, I think he is. He started out offering £2 million. Each time he comes back to me he offers more, but won't say who he represents. I do think he is a serious buyer, so I thought I'd speak to you and get your opinion.'

'OK, well get him in to meet us, but only with whoever he represents. I want to meet them face to face. Speak with Jackie for suitable dates. I'm off tomorrow for a BUPA health check so it can't be then.'

'Right I'll see what I can arrange,' Terry replied.

'You should have one of these BUPA checks you know,' Ken suggested.

'Mmmm I'm not that keen, typical man I guess!'

'Well you should and Andrea. The company will pay for it and you should ideally have one every couple of years as I do.'

'Well, thanks I'll think about it.'

Wisely Ken said, 'You know going to the doctor won't give you anything, but if you do have something wouldn't you like to know?'
Those wise words always stuck in Terry's mind.

It was a Monday morning when Ian Gilmore arrived to meet Ken in the more formal setting of his office. 'I understand from my colleague that you'd like to buy the property and the land here and offered £7.5 million. I need to tell you that we don't do deals with faceless companies, so unless you reveal who this is you may leave now.'

Ken, always direct but very shrewd in all his dealings.

'I can't tell you that, but I'll pass your message to them and see if they are willing to come and see you.'

'If they want to buy the property and are serious,' Ken responded, 'then they will; otherwise you are wasting our time. We need to know with whom we're dealing. You will also need to raise your offer considerably if we are to take you seriously. This is a prime site in the town centre. Would you please make an appointment with our secretary for a convenient date and we'll look forward to meeting you all?'

There was nothing else to say and Ian Gilmore left the office.

By Thursday morning Ian was back with his two colleagues and they all sat in Ken's office to hear what they had to say. Ian started the meeting by introducing his colleagues, Charles and James who represented a large National Supermarket chain and were from a company by the name of Foinavon; buyers and negotiators on their behalf.

Ken looking serious and composed said, 'We did think that you must be representing a supermarket as the site would be about the right size for such an operation and Terry has discovered you've also made an offer for adjoining land.'

'I see you have done your homework on us.' Ian replied. 'Our offer is genuine and we'd like to buy this site from you as soon as possible. Is it feasible for you to move the bus operation within a reasonable time frame?'

'If the price is right we'll make sure it is,' said Ken with a smile.

'What is the right price?' James asked.

'Eleven million pounds,' replied Ken without any hesitation.

James looked across at his two colleagues with grim expression. 'We would never be able to agree that figure with our client, it's far too high.'

They all sat there in total silence.

'Mr Hodgson, do you mind if I confer with Charles and Ian. Is there another room somewhere we could use?'

'Certainly you can. Terry, show them into the board room.'

They left the room and went to confer in the boardroom as they had requested. Terry returned to Ken's office.

'So what do you think?' Ken asked.

'Shhhhhhhh!' Terry said to a puzzled Ken. 'Shhhhhhhh!' as he pointed to one of the men's brief cases by the desk. 'Shhhhhhhh!'

Terry said nothing but picked up the brief case and took it to the men who were down the corridor, sitting at the boardroom table. 'I thought you might need this.' Terry suggested politely, and left the briefcase on the table, and returned to Ken's office.

'What was all that about?' Ken asked.

'Well said Terry in a whisper, I read recently about a new device that is being used at meetings such as this. Those negotiating go to another room, but leave behind a briefcase with a live microphone on and are then able to listen in to any conversation that might help them.'

Ken smiled, 'really? You could be on to something there. Well done I'd never have thought of that.'

After some considerable time, the three men came back into Ken's office.

'We've discussed our offer and we're prepared to increase it for one last and final bid - but I'm afraid not to the level you've asked. We'll increase it to £9 million and we'll pay all your legal costs. That's a 'take it or leave it' figure and far beyond our original expectation for the proposed purchase of this site.'

Ken was silent, his face showing nothing of his likely answer as he stared ahead. The three of them looked anxious - awaiting his response.

'I'd like to go into another room and discuss this with my colleague.' Ken responded.

Ken and Terry left the room and went into Terry's office down the corridor. Ken was beaming. 'I can't believe the amount they are prepared to pay, can you? What do you think about it, shall we accept or should we push on?' Ken asked Terry excitedly.

'I think we should accept. We do have to purchase another site to rehouse the new bus depot, but with all the new buses you're planning to buy with the profits, we'll not need as many maintenance areas, so can purchase a smaller area to set up a new depot to run the operation. Let's go for it I say.'

'I agree, lets tell them we accept if you are happy with that Terry.'

'Yes Ken, I certainly am. You'll never receive a better offer for the site that's for sure, it's way beyond the book value and our wildest dreams.'

They both went back to Ken's office to where the three were waiting for a response.

'Well gentlemen, we have made our decision. If you would like to place your offer in writing to us, then we'll accept it and get the wheels in motion to move from here to new premises within nine months.' Ken declared with a deadpan expression.

He was a master at this sort of negotiation and a joy to watch his uncompromising talent.

As the workload for Terry and Ken increased they needed skilled secretarial services. The bus company had helped out by sharing their staff but this was no longer adequate. They were keen to acquire a secretary/PA whose services they could share, training her to carry some of the growing work load and to keep good computerised property records before things got out of control. It would become an important and developing job for a person with the right skills. First interviews were held on 21st January 1993 and they went on to employ a new member of staff being fortunate to find Elizabeth Foster, a young lady from Thirsk who quickly blended in to the new office routine proving to be a great asset.

CHAPTER TWELVE

Elizabeth, the newly appointed secretary, started to work for the company on Monday 1st March 1993. What a great relief it was. At last someone who could share the ever-growing workload. In mid-April she followed them to Harrogate where they finally set-up their permanent office on North Park Road.

In May Terry and Andrea decided to go to Canada to visit her cousins who had a hotel business at Niagara Falls and so flew into Toronto to stay with them for a few days. It was exciting to meet them and to see the falls - a truly dramatic volume of water that thundered past her cousin's front door. From there they went on to Montreal to meet Sister Genevieve who Terry knew from his time working in Malawi. After a few days there and visiting many interesting sights they moved on to Quebec where they were met by Sister Claire of the Missionary Sisters of Africa. She too was a special friend from those days in Malawi and Terry had not seen her for fourteen years when, due to illness, she left Malawi where she had served as the Provincial for East Africa, covering Tanzania, Malawi and Zambia. She had become very ill and was not expected to live long when she returned to Canada to retire. Claire was so excited to meet Andrea and to see Terry again and enjoyed the wonderful days spent together after so many years. Claire arranged with a friend to take them around so many places of interest giving them a real understanding and love for the country and its magnificence. It was an exhausting but enjoyable trip and they were sorry to leave. Indeed, they returned again in 1994 to spend more time with Sister Claire and to see more of Quebec - a beautiful old city on the edge of the St Lawrence River.

Once back home, work and life in general quickly took over. The annual fund raising for Africa seem to take over life in the summer months, when they opened their garden for morning coffee, lunches and afternoon teas. On 17th July, a warm sunny day, they raised £460 that was sent out to the sisters in Malawi for them to use as they felt best, with part of it being used to help Hortencia with her training to become a Sister of Africa. It was always a very busy day and involved Andrea in lots of preparation for an unknown number of people. It was hard work shared by many loyal helpers, and always dependant on fine weather, which was not always the case.

Life took on a continuously busy phase for them both. Andrea had been studying to become a Lay Reader in the Church of England and attended a training session with Reverend Jack Marsden every Wednesday evening for two years. It was an intensive 'one to one' course, which involved her going to his house for two-hour sessions, a lot of reading, essays and studies in order to do the three-year course in such a short time. But Andrea applied herself to it, as she always did when taking on a project of any kind and on 20th November 1993 was licensed as a Reader by the Bishop of Hull at a service in York Minster. It was a proud gathering of family and friends that witnessed the service. Friends from as far away as Devon and Dorset as well as Margaret and Cecil from Shropshire and a coach load of parishioners from her church plus individuals from Terry's Catholic Church in Thirsk, all attending on that joyous afternoon in the splendid surroundings of the majestic and historic Minster.

This created a new chapter in Andrea's life always being in demand in the three parishes of her own church, as well as being called upon to stand in for services when requested for other parishes in the area. There was so much preparation required for each service, which week after week demanded her time and attention. Christmas added an extra task on top of her usual duties as she wrote and produced the nativity play for the children who played to a packed church. Andrea blossomed and enjoyed it all, giving it her enthusiasm and energy to the delight and joy of many.

At work Ken had continued to pester Terry about having a regular health check, at the company's expense, as he himself did every year. When Terry told Andrea she thought it was a very good idea, that he should take up the company's offer. Terry was not so keen to be put under the microscope, but could see that perhaps he should be brave and do it.

As Ken always said, 'Going to the doctors won't give you anything you know!' He was right of course. So he agreed to go; but only if Andrea would, as she had never had a health check either.

'If you have one then I'll have one,' he bargained with her. Suddenly she was not so keen!

However, she did agree, and Terry arranged for his check to take place in mid-March 95 and then annually after that. All was well he was relieved to hear after the vigorous procedure he was put through and arrangements were made for Andrea to attend in early August so that she kept her side of the bargain.

Terry was ever keen for Andrea to see all the places he had known and worked. To know them, was to know him, and perhaps understand why his love for Africa drove him on. They had both enjoyed Sydney Pollack's academy award winning film 'Out of Africa,' the romantic drama made in 1985 with Robert Redford and Meryl Streep. It fuelled his desire to return and for them both to see some of the places in the film like Karen Blixen's home in Kenya, which is now a museum. They decided to take a trip in June 95.

'How about if we take a trip to Kenya and then on to Tanzania and go and spend a few days at Hombolo Leprosy Centre, near Dodoma?' Terry suggested.

'Is there anyone you know still living there?' Andrea asked.
  'It's thirty years ago since you lived there. I thought all the missionaries had now gone?'

'They have, but there is a guest house there and I'm sure if I write to the Bishop's office in Dodoma he'll allow us to go and stay, as it's all still run by the Diocese of Tanzania.'

Within weeks Terry received a reply from the Bishop's secretary, a white lady he had known from his last visit over fifteen years ago, when he called there on his way to work in Malawi. They were delighted to welcome them and said they would inform the doctor in charge at Hombolo so that things would be made ready for them to arrive on 20th June for five nights.

They departed for Kenya on 12th June and flew into Nairobi where they had arranged to stay at the Norfolk Hotel. This hotel, in the heart of Nairobi, was opened in 1904 and had been totally and inescapably an integral part of the country's history ever since, and always a good and important place to settle the dust as you pass that way on safari, as so many did. There you can both feel, smell and taste the history of Africa with its rich and colourful past.

It was magical being back in Africa again and Terry enjoyed showing Andrea around, visiting wild life parks, feeding Giraffes, visiting places like Karen Blixen's home. It was a very moving place and they sat in her garden remembering her life and times in the early part of the twentieth century. They had wanted to go up into the Ngong Hills behind her home where her lover Denys Finch Hatton was buried after his tragic air accident, as portrayed in the film, but they were advised not to because bandits were operating in the area.

In order to get to Dodoma, they booked seats on one of the 'Mission Aviation Fellowship's flights. This was a service that covered most of Africa with two and four seater planes serving missions in remote areas. It took most of one morning to book the seats at the Mission's office on the outskirts of Nairobi, but Africa is like that.

They set out from the Norfolk Hotel a few days later to the airstrip north of the city to board the small Cessna plane that would fly them to Dodoma. They squeezed into the small cabin late on a hot, dusty morning together with two missionaries and their three small children who were also going to Dodoma. Terry sat next to the pilot with headphones on so he could be in contact with the pilot who sat on his left. It was something of a terrifying experience as they sped down the badly maintained runway and up into the blue African sky in what felt like a very flimsy plane.

'What's this Dad?' shouted one of the missionary children holding up a handle from the door of the plane just after take-off. The pilot looked alarmed as he glanced over his shoulder at the child who was holding up the door handle.

'Don't anyone touch the door,' he shouted.

I don't think anyone had any intention of doing so, but the child's father held on to the door for the rest of the flight.

It was strange flying so close to the majestic Mount Kilimanjaro as the tip of the mountain showed itself through the cloud as they passed over the Tanzania/Kenya borders.

As they flew over Dodoma Terry recognised Lion Hill, a landmark on the outskirts of the town as they dropped rapidly down onto the airstrip below, arriving noisily and in a cloud of dust at a small group of buildings that formed the airport.

Thankfully the door seemed to remain closed despite the absence of the handle. The pilot got out and opened the door from the outside allowing them all to tumble out with some relief onto the rough surface of the airstrip and make their way to the buildings.

The heat was overwhelming. Dodoma is set on an arid plateau with sand filled gullies and granite outcrops, and dry airless heat that Terry remembered so well. Shelia Horseman the Bishop's secretary met them. She took them to their accommodation for the night - part of the MAF base alongside the airport. She also handed over a small Suzuki four-wheel drive vehicle which she had arranged for them to hire from the mission during their stay. This was mainly for their visit to Hombolo, which she confirmed she had organised with the doctor of the leprosy centre.

Everything at the MAF base was very primitive, but it had most of the essentials of life to keep them going for twenty-four hours. After a hot and uncomfortable night under mosquito nets they made their way into Dodoma where they were able to find food in the tired shops to take with them to Hombolo for their few days stay. It was over forty miles of dirt road to Hombolo and Terry hoped he would remember it after so long away. The first ten miles were fine, but at the point where they were supposed to turn off the main road there was a notice to say that the road ahead had been washed away and they should turn left at the next junction, which they did.

The road continued for a few miles and then quickly became a track used mainly by animals and people on cycles or on foot, until it defused into bush with no sign of a track or road. Terry continued on his way following only his instinct, driving through the thorn covered bush. He looked to the sun for guidance and worked out that if he kept the sun on his right he would eventually finish up somewhere near Hombolo and the road that he should have arrived on.

'How do you know where you're going?' asked Andrea with concern, 'and what do you do if we break down?'

'Its fine, don't worry,' he smiled 'if we break down we'll call the AA breakdown service!'

She suddenly realised he was joking and the seriousness of the situation hit her. They stopped a few times for Terry to ask in his pigeon Swahili if they were going in the right direction. Unbeknown to Andrea he had no idea where he was and was, relying totally on keeping the sun to his right, hoping in that way he would be travelling more or less north and would eventually cross over the road that took them to Hombolo. As luck would have it that's exactly what happened. No one was more relieved than Terry.

It was exciting to be at Hombolo again - the place of his youth. It brought back memories of the people he'd known and loved there; the familiar surroundings and the lay of the land that he'd known and cultivated. They pulled up outside the hospital, little changed over the years. A male nurse greeted them at the dusty entrance.

'You are Mr and Mrs Reeves?' he enquired. 'We were expecting you yesterday.'

'Oh really, don't know why as we did tell them today.'

'But welcome, welcome. It's many years since you worked here but there are still a few people who remember you and will come and see you during your visit.

'Follow me, I'll take you to the guest house.'

They drove a few hundred yards down the dirt road towards the water tank towering over the centre.

'Your old house has been expanded and is now a school. You must go and see it while you're here. Now we have a new 'Guest House' behind your old house, turn in here please.'

It was a large bungalow as usual in these places. They pulled up and went inside. In one of the bedrooms a mosquito net hung at an angle from the ceiling, and the bed had sheets trailed over it from the last guest who had occupied it. In the main bedroom there were two single beds which looked very tired, but nothing else! The kitchen was just the same. There was no sign that they had been expected.

'Did you say you were expecting us?' they asked.

'Oh yes the doctor told us you were coming to visit us and that you were to stay in the guesthouse.'

'So where is the doctor now?' they asked.

'He's gone to Dodoma and he has the key to the cupboard where everything is kept for this house.'

'And do you know when he'll return? Is it today?'

'I've no idea,' he replied, 'but I'll go to the hospital and see if I can find some things to help you until he returns.'

Andrea and Terry were amazed, but not surprised. This was Africa, this was how it worked! Shortly the old face of Leonard, who Terry had known in years gone by, appeared. He brought them a few items of limited help. A large soup ladle, a pillowslip, a thermos flask, a large fork and an equally large spoon and two plastic boxes.

'Is that it Leonard, is that all you have for us?'

'Yes master, everything is locked away, but I bring you these things to help you.'

Thank you Leonard for your thoughtfulness!

'So what are we going to do now?' asked Andrea.

'Well we did bring some provisions thank goodness. Let's see if we can prepare something to eat, we'll feel better then.'

'It'll soon be dark. The light is fading fast, where are we going to sleep? I'm not sleeping in those used sheets, who knows who's been there before us?'

She went to the sink and turned on the tap, 'I don't believe it, there's no water; what now? What are we going to do?'

Outside the house there was a large round galvanised water tank that Terry remembered was used to collect rain water from the roof. Thankfully it was full so they were able to run water into a bucket. Its handles were broken but they managed to carry it into the house.

After having found a large pan they prepared the vegetables and sausages they had brought from Dodoma. The pawpaw and bananas with the large drinks bottle that contained honey, where placed on the table. Terry quickly removed the cork and the dead fly from the top of the honey, before Andrea noticed it! They tried to light the gas cooker but there was no gas in the bottle. That was the last straw. Then suddenly a car arrived. It was the doctor and his wife who had just arrived back from their Dodoma trip. After introductions and apologies, they quickly produced a key for the cupboard that gave them access to all the items locked away like sauce pans, plates, knives and forks, and the doctor's wife was soon able to find some clean sheets for their bed and a bottle of gas. Suddenly everything felt better.

The fridge was not working and there was no electric power, but that would come on at dark they were assured, as soon as the generator was started. It was necessary for them to reduce the hours it was running to save on the expensive diesel costs.

As if by magic, the power did come on as darkness set in. The lighting was dim but at least it worked and the fridge came to life. They busied themselves preparing a meal and began to feel much better. While clearing away they were aware of a burning smell and were concerned enough to start looking around the house to identify the cause. Out on the veranda Terry found smoke coming from a bulkhead light. He quickly turned it off and, with the aid of a knife blade, was able to unscrew the glass dome covering the fitting. As he did so, out fell a heap of dried insects that had accumulated inside and were slowly burning, hence the smell. There was never a dull moment and to do the simplest things was a challenge, as always in Africa.

They enjoyed the days at the Leprosy Centre meeting a few old faces amongst the patients and those living nearby who had worked there in Terry's day. One very proud old Masai man, Petro, the ex-house boy of Dawn and Guy Timmis, stopped in total surprise with his mouth open when, walking tall around the corner of his house he saw Terry standing there before him, after thirty years away, recognising him immediately.

'My friend you wait long before you treat me to a visit. It fills my heart to see you again,' he cried.

'I have waited for you, the one that cultivated so much of our land to grow us food. Now you have come home.'

He and his family immediately welcomed them to sit and chat in their mud hut using what little Swahili Terry could recall. It was one of those moments in life that you remember forever. Life for him and his family was so very fragile, living on incredibly little, only what they were able to grow in the plot surrounding their small hut. However, even with them owning and having so little, they wanted to share what they did have and insisted they take some nuts and limes away. Overwhelming generosity that humbled them.

Africa is like that, always stopping you in your tracks in some way. The real people of the country are so very special, warm, and generous and worthy of so much better leadership than they often enjoy.

While at Hombolo there was another moving visit to make, when they went to greet the wife of Michael who had been trained to take over the running of the leprosy centre on the retirement of George Hart. Michael had been proud to welcome Mother Theresa for a visit on 11th October 1986, when she flew into this remote centre in the middle of Tanzania, after her visit to the Sudan. Michael was one of five people killed as her plane crashed on take-off from the dirt airstrip, ploughing into the waving crowd who were mutilated by the propellers of the twin-engine Cessna. She and her children still heartbroken, welcome them and thanked Terry and Andrea for their kind words about Michael who Terry had known and admired.

At the weekend they returned to Dodoma and attended a service at the Anglican cathedral in the middle of town. Dome shaped, rather like a mosque, it was a place that Terry was familiar with but had never visited when he lived in Tanzania. The Bishop's secretary was there and she explained that today was a special service with all the clergy being there from the Diocese. There was to be the unveiling of a plaque in memory of Bishop Alfred Stanway who had been the Australian Bishop in charge of the diocese in Terry's time. It seemed appropriate that he was there for the ceremony to mark the Bishop's service in Africa. The Bishop had died in retirement on 27th June 1989 aged 81 and had served the Diocese from 1951 – 1971. It was a moving service and Terry, with his video camera, was able to make a film which he later sent to Bishop Stanway's wife, who was living in Australia. She told him later that she had sent out the plaque, but had never heard if it had arrived or been placed in the Cathedral, so was delighted to receive news as well as the video film.

The following Monday saw them back on the MAF flight to Nairobi's Wilson airport and to the luxurious surroundings of the Norfolk Hotel. They had only one more day in Nairobi but still had the urge to go and see the grave of Denis Finch Hatton in the Ngong Hills. By chance they met an American lady at the hotel who told them, 'Go, its fine. I've just returned from there today and there was no problem with any bandits.'

'But we were advised not to go,' they explained.

'So was I, but if you go to the police station in the village of Ngong and ask for the police officer by the name of Patrick, he'll escort you through the forest to the top of the hill and to the grave site. He is armed so you should be fine, but don't carry any valuables – just in case!' she advised.

The next morning, having stored their wallets, passports, rings and watches in the safe at the hotel, they hired a taxi to take them to Ngong village a few miles north of Nairobi. They made their way to the police station and asked for police officer Patrick as suggested by the American lady. Out came Patrick, saluting them military style.

'Would it be possible for you to escort us to Denys Finch Hatton's grave?' they asked.

'Certainly sir,' he replied with a smile. So Patrick with his rifle in hand took his seat next to the taxi driver, with Andrea and Terry in the rear.

'It's do or die,' Terry said to Andrea, as they started out up the mountain path through the bush. At every turn they expected to see bandits jump out of the bush, and were not very confident that Patrick would know how to use the rifle he was carrying, should he need to! It was about a fifteen-minute drive to the top of the Ngong hill driving around the edge of the woodland along a dusty dirt track. The driver pulled in by a roughly paint daubed sign pointing to the grave. There was a small mud house surrounded by a wooden fence where a lady emerged smiling.

'Jambo,' (hello) she greeted them.

'I ask you for 1000 Kenyan shillings (£6) each, to enter the garden and to visit the grave to help me and my family and to maintain the garden.' They were more than happy to pay and Terry gave her 4000 shillings and in return she gave him a printed note about Finch Hatton's grave. Clearly it was a little business that helped her and her family. The fenced area had been planted with flowers. They went through the gate into the garden and there standing on a raised plinth was a twelve-foot-high obelisk enjoying wonderful breath taking views of the land below. The trees around had, no doubt, grown up over the years partly obstructing the views that were magnificent stretching across the hills and looking down to Karen's house in the distance.

The brass plate on the obelisk read,

DENYS GEORGE FINCH HATTON
1887 - 1931
"HE PRAYETH WELL WHO LOVETH WELL

BOTH MAN AND BIRD AND BEAST"

They were so involved with their surroundings and not aware of anything else happening as they filmed the grave and the view from it. However, something spooky had taken place, because when they returned home and replayed the video recording there was the noise of a light aircraft flying overhead. The type of aircraft in which Finch Hatton had died on his way to Tsavo in 1931. Yet they had not heard or seen any aircraft while making the film on that remote hillside in June 1995?

CHAPTER THIRTEEN

The flight from Nairobi arrived back into a grey London at five in the morning. After the exhilarating sun drenched days in Kenya and Tanzania it was such an anti-climax returning from holiday, but they made their way back to Yorkshire to pick up life where they had left off.

While they had been away Margaret and Cecil had decided after many happy years at Vernolds Common in Shropshire that it was time to move to something smaller. They loved it there, living in the bungalow looking out to the Long Mynd hills with its wonderful views but, as they got older the garden was getting too much for them and it was, reluctantly, time to seek something smaller. Cecil, using his life time ability for seeking out the right place to live found 'Frongelyn' - another bungalow, at Ciliau Aeron, near Aberaeron in West Wales. They completed the purchase on 3rd July 1995.

It was a difficult day for them, as they left Vernolds Common where they had been so happy; happier than in any place they had lived; but as their energy levels fell away with age, they could not stay on unless they employed someone to do the garden and Cecil did not want that. They had found another lovely bungalow and soon settled into their new life in Wales, which was a brave move at their ages. Cecil made serious attempts at learning the Welsh language and at seventy-eight years was content not to have so much garden to care for, as he had most of his life. He enjoyed reading and did spend quite a lot of time writing down his thoughts about life, to leave behind for others to benefit from, should they choose to read it. Margaret, now aged eighty-two years, enjoyed the small garden at Frongelyn which was set on the hillside about four miles from Aberaeron and took the bus from time to time to do shopping at Aberystwyth, which she loved to do. They enjoyed Terry and Andrea's visits and always made them most welcome, using that time as an excuse to indulge in Fish-n-Chips or a Chinese take-away, both of which they loved.

15th July was again their fundraising day, held each summer in their garden for Africa. There were so many things to do and organise in preparation for that day, so it was a very busy period.

Andrea, who felt forced to keep her side of the bargain regarding their health checks, received her call up papers from BUPA and reluctantly went along to Leeds, as she promised Terry she would, to have the full onceover.

Terry had agreed to video the wedding of Pam and Frank Beevers, friends from Kexby near York, on 16th September, so was beginning to think and plan for that event. It promised to be a lavish affair with a huge marque erected in the field at their farm for the celebration. He was looking forward to producing a record of their special day.

Unbeknown to Terry, Andrea was planning a surprise 50th birthday party for him on 15th September. She was involved in all sorts of undercover operations, inviting family and friends from the south as a surprise on this special day, so there was plenty going on.

At work Ken and Terry were busy getting ahead with various developments in Durham, Wakefield and a new shopping centre in Ripon, to name but a few. Ken was not one to let the grass grow and pushed on with steady pressure as one scheme followed another. They were a good team and able to make instant decisions allowing them to take opportunities quickly. These were busy and exciting times.

Andrea was very surprised when she received the results of her tests from BUPA. Following the mammogram x-ray undertaken at the check-up they suggested she should make an early appointment to see her own doctor who would arrange for her to see a specialist at Northallerton for breast x-rays, to check out their findings. There was no lump or anything like that, so she was not worried and followed their advice. She felt and looked well and was confident there was nothing wrong, so was very surprised to be told by the consultant that he wanted to do a biopsy and had arranged for her to have an overnight stay on 30th August. He explained they had found what was called calcification in one breast and would need to check it out with a biopsy and more x-rays, which they did immediately.

Andrea dreaded having to tell Terry. She would have done anything to avoid that. She explained that it was just a precaution that she was, and felt, fine but must have it checked out once and for all. Terry collected her from the hospital the day after the biopsy, trying not to have any black thoughts. Surely not, he thought, not again surely, no it couldn't be. Could it?

Suddenly and cruelly on 8th September, the world stopped when Andrea went back to see the hospital consultant for her results. She insisted in going alone, expecting only the all clear. She was shocked and horrified when her consultant informed her that the cells that were removed did have the ability to change into cancerous cells and should be removed. The calcification was scattered throughout the breast tissue therefore he recommended a mastectomy as being the only sure way of preventing any possible future problems. They were not dealing with a single lump which could have been more easily removed.

Things moved fast. The consultant made arrangements for her to have the operation on 13th September at the 'John of God' hospital in Richmond, North Yorkshire. Andrea's first reaction was, 'No, I can't; its Terry's birthday party on 15th.' However, on further discussion, she agreed with the consultant's advice that it really was the only and the safest route for her to take and should happen as soon as possible. As he said if she was his wife he would make the same recommendations.

Andrea was in a state of shock as she left the consultants room and went to her car; she couldn't believe what was happening. More than anything else, how on earth was she going to break it to Terry? He had said to her soon after they met that it was his worst nightmare that anything like this should happen again, if he were to re-marry. He had great difficulty with that thought which came close to stopping any new relationship. Somehow he had overcome it, but now she was having to give him this news. How would he take it? She would also have to cancel all the arrangements she had made for his birthday party surprise and contact all those who were planning to come. Then there was Pam and Frank's wedding they were to attend where Terry had promised to do their wedding video. They couldn't let them down. What a mess she thought.

She rang Terry's office but Elizabeth explained he was out and most probably in Dewsbury but to try his car phone.

'Hello can we speak. Are you driving?'

'Go ahead, its ok, I'm not driving at the moment. I'm at the bus depot in Dewsbury trying to sort the rent review.'

'Ah O.K. - I've seen the consultant and …..' she stopped unable to continue for a second or two.

He froze, motionless in his car seat – waiting for her to gather herself.

Slowly she continued, 'The consultant advised that the calcification could cause problems in the future and the only way forward is to have a mastectomy……. There is no cancer as such at the moment, but it's a necessary precaution to prevent its possible development. There is no way with radiation or chemical treatment they'd be able to target it as it's scattered throughout the breast tissue.'

'Terry, will you still love me if they have to do that?'

He was stunned. Like Andrea he had been sure all would be well as she was so fit and busy and not suffering in any way. If he had not forced her to have a health check they would never have been aware of the problem.

'Are you sure that is the only way? Is it really necessary to take such a drastic step?' Terry asked.

'Yes, the consultant said that it's the only certain way of avoiding future problems. It would be too much of a risk just to leave it. We don't want to be looking back thinking 'if only we had done this' do we?'

Terry was shocked, it was like a bad dream, a nightmare in fact, and a dreaded moment in time he had hoped never again to visit. He knew how distraught she must be to have to give him this news and to have to go through such an invasive operation. His heart went out to her.

'I'll be alright you know.' She said trying to reassure him. 'I will. I'll get over this, we'll be fine. I have to go through with it, to avoid us having to face something worse in the future. If I don't take this drastic step now, we could regret it.'

'Do you have full confidence in your consultant? Is he good; the best?' Terry asked almost in tears.

'They say he's a very clever man with a good and successful history of treating people with cancer. I believe what he says and wouldn't be happy not to take his advice.'

'I only want what you want,' Terry replied. 'I don't want you to suffer any unnecessary pain or stress.'

'You haven't answered my question have you?' Andrea replied.

'What question was that?'

'Will you still love me if I have the mastectomy?'

'I'd hope you wouldn't have the need to ask me that,' he quickly and assertively replied.
  'Of course I will. You'll still be you. I love the whole of you, not just parts. You'll still be you, just a bit less of you.' Terry made a weak attempt at a joke.

'That's all that matters then. Together we'll fight this thing. I'm otherwise healthy I'm told, but this is something too risky to ignore.'

'OK, it seems we have to do it. Would you like me to come and collect you now? Are you alright to drive home?' Terry asked, as she was very upset.

'Yes don't worry I'll be fine. I'm just a bit shocked.'

'I'll finish here straight away and come home. I should be there in an hour or so' Terry explained.

He drove home with a heavy heart. Poor Andrea, he thought to himself, she must have been to hell and back with all this. It's a real nightmare and, a sadly, a familiar one he thought. At home they talked it all through. It really did seem to be the only sensible option. Andrea was so very brave about the prospect, facing it head on. Terry on the other hand was torn apart inside. His mind was wondering if this was yet again the beginning of a long, empty, heart breaking and familiar road. Andrea did not deserve this he thought and, yet, there she was confident and strong, going forward in faith. Her strength only served to help Terry who was trying hard not to compare the past with the present. He tried to live off her confidence and incredible courage and not to allow himself to indulge in his dark thoughts.

They had the weekend to digest it all before returning to work. Terry knew he had to tell Ken as soon as possible and his secretary Elizabeth. He was probably going to need to take a lot of time off, depending on how things worked out so he had to prepare them. He shared his news with Elizabeth on the Monday morning as soon as he arrived in the office. Tears filled her eyes. She knew what he must be feeling, how he would be thinking about his first wife Ann, connecting the two events. But, as he explained, this was a precaution, whereas before it was a case of trying to remove an active and vile cancer. He explained he would need to take time off as and when necessary and would depend on her to keep everything going for him in the meantime. He had every confidence in her.

At ten o'clock Terry heard Ken arrive in his downstairs office. Terry's office was on the first floor. He heard Elizabeth briefing Ken about Andrea and he immediately rushed up to see Terry.

As always with Ken it was straight to the point.

'Elizabeth told me your shocking news, I'm so sorry. What can I do, tell me please? We'll send her anywhere, anywhere in the world, just say and it'll be done; you mustn't waste time. What about another opinion? Who is this Consultant? Where is he based? How much experience has he? Can I have him checked out for you? We'll send her anywhere, straight away, just say and I'll find the best place in the world for her to be treated. We must not delay a second.'

'Slow down Ken, slow down,' Terry responded. 'We've every confidence that the consultant knows what he's talking about - that his advice is sound. It's very thoughtful and generous of you Ken to offer all that help and to be so concerned. I really do appreciate it, but we feel we've had good advice in the circumstances. There is no cancer you see, only material that could possibly become cancerous. It's a precaution, albeit a drastic one.'

'How is Andrea? How is she coping? Is there anything she needs?' Ken enquired gently and thoughtfully.

'She's being incredibly brave. I only wish I was half as brave.'

'You have to be,' Ken replied. 'You'll need to give her every support as I'm sure you will. It's physically and psychologically a huge operation for any woman to undertake.'

'Yes I realise that Ken, it most certainly is. So how is she able to be so incredibly brave when I'm falling apart?'

'Look, you take all the time you need to be with Andrea. Don't leave her side for a minute, and if there's anything I can do just say the word. As I said we'll send her anywhere at any time if there's better treatment to be had. I'd arrange it all for you. Don't worry about anything here. It will all be waiting for you when you get back, when all this is over. Elizabeth and I will manage.'

He paused and looked so concerned for Terry. 'Try not to worry,' he said gently with eyes full of tears, then he quickly left for his office.

Terry took Andrea to the 'John of God' hospital on Wednesday 13th September for 1pm where they prepared her for the operation on the following day. She had a private room and once settled in insisted that Terry went home, but he sat with her for a while. It seemed a long journey home on his own, and he was feeling numbed by events.

His birthday party for the 15th had, of course, been cancelled, which was of little concern to him. Andrea insisted that he carry on and film Pam and Frank's wedding as arranged, giving her apologies for being unable to attend. She was so disappointed but persuaded Terry he must attend as promised.

After the operation the following day, Terry went to see her. All had gone well and she was being amazingly heroic, already up and walking around the ward dragging a mass of tubes. Her brave and cheerful attitude, he suspected was partly for his benefit, being aware of how he must be feeling and his deep disquiet. Of course she was anxious to return home, but had to wait at least a couple of days to be discharged. Then a discussion with the surgeon would take place to see what happened next, once test results taken during the operation were in.

It's strange how things happen; there is no such thing as coincidence. Some things are meant to be. That night after seeing Andrea and despite the spirited manner in which she handled her situation, Terry felt very depressed. He reluctantly left her bedside to return home and made his way to the hospital car park. They had both been to the gates of hell over the past few days. Their world could now crumple and swallow them both, the future unknown. His faith was at a low ebb. As the shock of it all hit him, he felt very low, confused, hurt and aggrieved. Sitting in the darkness of his car in the hospital car park he physically crumbled and emotionally collapsed. He selfishly felt sorry for himself, as well as for Andrea. His eyes were half closed, wearily staring ahead and going over all the unresolved questions in his head. He felt desperately sad for Andrea and he hated to see her suffer. How quickly it had all happened. How could all this come to his door yet again he wondered glumly; he couldn't face it. Why? What now will I have to face he questioned? With that thought the car phone rang out. It was Margaret Cox from Devon. She and Philip were long-time friends and were so anxious for them both. She chatted away and must have sensed he was very subdued and unhappy and kept talking away to him, encouragingly and going over normal things to try and cheer him - lift his spirits. For nearly an hour her voice rang out over the speakers as he drove on through the night along the half lit streets and the country lanes, listening to her voice willing him on, giving him hope, lifting his spirits. Somehow that call, more than anything, gave him strength and the boost necessary to stop feeling sorry for himself, accept things and give Andrea the support she sorely needed. That, plus Andrea's own amazing determination to accept and overcome all she had to go through, catapulted him in to the future with a new vengeance.

Without a single painkiller Andrea made steady progress, her continued strength and optimism shining through. Terry went to Pam and Frank's wedding producing a video of their wonderful happy day. They made the completely unselfish gesture of mentioning Andrea during the reception and wishing her well by giving Terry a wonderful display of flowers to take to her with their love and good wishes.

Four days later Andrea was out of hospital and returned home with a new spring in her step. At a meeting with the consultant a few days later, he brought them tremendous relief, when he explained that no cancer cells had been found anywhere in her body. The operation, he reassured them, had been a necessary precaution, as the calcification might well have caused problems in the future. It was a risk too many to leave it and do nothing. He convinced them that it was the only sensible thing to do. Apart from six monthly checks, there was nothing else to be done. It was not necessary for her to take a single pill, have radiation or chemo therapy. Their relief was immense as they made their way home to go on with life with renewed vigour. But, Andrea did need time to come to terms with it all and to recover from the operation. She felt like taking a few days' retreat somewhere, in order to aid her physical, spiritual and mental recovery. The retreat centre of Parcevall Hall (c1584) in the Diocese of West Yorkshire and the Dales seemed the very place. It offered guests a unique experience of hospitality in the tranquil and unrivalled setting of Upper Wharfedale. Its peace was healing, soothing and gave her time for thought and contemplation. After a few restful days Terry went to bring her home, finding her refreshed, renewed and longing to return to home and a normal life. Together they thanked God for her deliverance.

A week later they took a holiday in Holland staying in Amsterdam at the Tulip Hotel, overlooking the canals. It was a relaxing and enjoyable time with chance to visit a dear friend, Sister Anny, from Terry's days working in Malawi, and now living in a convent at Sterksal near Heeze.

The year came to a welcome end with Ken giving a wonderful Christmas Party at the historic Ripley Castle, a few miles from Harrogate. He was as happy as they both were with the outcome of Andrea's operation and everyone was looking forward to new beginnings and a New Year.

CCC

CHAPTER FOURTEEN

1996 by comparison was a quiet year and welcomed for that alone. The fund raising for Africa in July was as usual firmly fixed in the annual calendar beating all records by raising £1,045. This sum was welcomed by the missionary sisters in Malawi who scrutinize every penny of the expenditure of this yearly donation, maximizing its benefits and making the work of fund raising so worthwhile for all the team involved.

In September Ken celebrated his twenty-five years of marriage with a lavish party at Rudding Park, near Harrogate. A grand affair attended by his family, friends and close business associates. He was a man of great skill and caliber in business, acclaimed by all who knew him, both in his business life and for his work in the Catholic Diocese of Leeds. There he was a tremendous support to Bishop David Konstant both in the organization of the Diocese and in taking 'Trinity and All Saints College' to become 'Leeds Trinity University,' that took place in 2012. It was a pleasure and a joy to both know him and work with him. He made big demands of his staff, but was a man renowned for his fairness, honesty and dogged determination: there had not been many in Terry's working life he could say that about.

On 7th December news came through of the death of missionary George Hart in New Zealand, he was seventy-six.

Terry had worked with him at Hombolo in Tanzania in 1965/66 and later of course had a relationship with his daughter Anne. Terry had the greatest respect for George who had boundless vitality and tenacity, working hard in serving the people of Tanzania, showing them the face of Christ. He seemed rooted in the country and to belong to the people. He had a tremendous faith, which carried him through the latter years of his life when his health failed; never underestimating the support he received from his wife Joan throughout their life's work as missionaries in Tanzania.

The latter years of the nineties were hectic for all and at times it seemed as if the world had gone mad. Terry & Andrea continued working on Osgodby House making improvements and developments, which took most of their non- working time. The house was in such a beautiful spot and they enjoyed every minute of it, sharing it with many friends who would drop in to see how they and the developments were progressing.

The nineties were a heady time. Most people enjoyed a better income than they had ever had and the man in the street was encouraged at every level to invest his spare cash in the stock market. This resulted in the emergence of private equity firms, culminating in the massive dot-com-bubble.

One after the other companies floated their shares with private enterprise being rife. Profits were made and spent encouraging more and bigger investment in the stock market. Many had no experience of such trading, but stories of profit in the buying and selling of shares encouraged many more to take the plunge and try their luck. At the peak technology companies were being set up for a few pounds and then sold for millions, based only on promise and hope. It really was a crazy period and could only end one way.

On the 1st May 1997, Andrea's birthday, the general election took place resulting in a landslide victory for Tony Blair who won 419 seats and became the youngest prime minister of the century, while John Major had no option but to resign.

So many events took place in 1997. Hong Kong ended British Rule on 1st July and, if that was not enough excitement for one year, the nation and the world was rocked by the death of Diana Princess of Wales, who was involved in a road accident, when the car she was travelling in crashed in the Pont l'Alma road tunnel in Paris. She died as a result of her injuries on 31st August. The nation was in grief. Her funeral service took place in London on 6th September, only a day after the Princess's mentor, Mother Teresa, the nun who tended the poor and the sick of Calcutta for forty years and won the Nobel Peace Prize, had died on 5th September. So often things come together like that, strange as it may seem.

Friend and parish priest of All Saints Catholic church, Fr. O'Brian retired at the end of September 1998 with a farewell party. He had been a faithful leader of the church with good 'old school' values and a dry sense of humor. When Terry was invited to be a school governor Fr. O'Brian stopped him in church one Sunday asking,

'What are you doing next Thursday?'

Terry replied, 'Nothing special, why?'

'Well be at the school at 7.30. You are to be a School Governor,' he barked.

'But Father, I don't have any children at the school,' Terry replied.

'And do you think I have?'

'I have no idea,' Terry said with a smile. From that day Terry served four years as a governor, something of a new and mind bending experience for him and the administration at the school!

Paul moved his work on 21st October 1998 to the Dresdin Bank in Frankfurt using his expertise in the I.T business of the bank. He and girlfriend Carolyn rented a very nice flat in the town of Oberursel where they were to spend many happy and full years, before going to live and work in France.

Andrea was working flat out as a Lay Reader and called upon in so many of the churches of the Thirsk area to take services as well as to support her own parish of Kilburn. It was a busy time but much enjoyed using all her skills. By day she found fulfillment in her new work having moved to a new position with 'Youth Clubs North Yorkshire' near Thirsk as a fund raiser. There she gained much experience and was a big success.

1999 marked ten years at Osgodby House and the stress and strain of life with the Bowman property company was slowly becoming lost in the mists of time. Terry had settled into his new career as a commercial property manager, now based in Harrogate, and was presented with a silver shield in recognition of his service.

Andrea had cousins in Australia who had for many years wanted her to visit. It was somewhere neither of them had been. So they decided to fly out to visit the country for three weeks, calling at Singapore and then on to stay in Port Douglas in Queensland for four days, before dropping in on the cousins in Sydney. It was exciting for Andrea to see them after so many years and all enjoyed a happy time together exploring the area around and right up into the Blue Mountains.

On 13th August 1999 Paul announced his engagement to long term girlfriend Carolyn Young from Newcastle. They had been together for some considerable time so it was always when, rather than if, they would get married. So the family were looking forward to their wedding day in July 2001.

The other big celebration of the year was Cecil and Margaret's Diamond Wedding at the end of October. Terry and Andrea had organized a surprise party for all the family members, relatives from Kent and friends, to a luncheon at the Conrad Hotel, south of Aberystwyth. It had been very difficult to get them to agree to go out to eat until they were told it was to be a quiet lunch for the four of them. But what a wonderful surprise it was for them and how they enjoyed seeing everyone as they were introduced one by one to the guests. It was a fantastic achievement to get everyone there which brought them great pleasure in the renewal of friendships. It was sadly to be the last occasion they were all together.

It seemed as if the whole world had gone mad and lost all common sense when, towards the end of the year, people were asking if, at the turn of the century when the year 2000 arrived, everyday things would continue to work? Would computers all operate; would the toaster make toast; would the kettle boil; would the electric clocks, refrigerators and every imaginable household gadget continue to work? It was as if, at midnight, everything was going to stop! Terry and Andrea were fed up; it had gone too far, with serious discussions taking place on the media about it.

Coming in from work one evening Terry said, 'I've had an idea with regard to the millennium celebrations which everyone seems to be talking about and what we might do. What do you think to us getting right away from it all and going as far away as possible to a cottage on the north west corner of Wales? I've seen a cottage at Uwchmynydd that overlooks Bardsey Island not far from Aberdaron. It's about as far away as you can possible get from all this madness.'

'Now that sounds a brilliant idea,' Andrea said smiling. So that was what they did and at midnight 1999 at the gateway of the new millennium, they were standing on the cliff tops looking out towards Bardsey Island with two chocolate bottles of champagne and the radio balanced on a farm gate, listening to the chimes of Big Ben; it was wonderful.

The new millennium got off to an immediate regretful start when Lynda's marriage broke down. She announced that she was to separate from Mark. It created a lot of sadness and upset for everyone in the family.

A welcome distraction and a bundle of joy came into Terry and Andrea's life, quite by chance three months after their dog Bonnie had died, in the form of 'Tricks' a West Highland/Jack Russell that had been picked up in Northallerton and taken to a rescue center. She was a wonderful personality and a real joy to them bringing much, love, happiness and fun into their life. She went on to travel everywhere with them over the years, a real characterful dog and never a minute's trouble.

For some time, Terry and Andrea had considered submitting once again their case to the local authority for the removal of the agricultural clause that blighted their house; despite the setbacks from previous attempts. They had twice before made representations and these and the appeals had been turned down. As they did not give up easily in these matters it was time to try once more as it would make so much difference to the sale value of the property and encourage them to develop the property further and be able to build a double garage alongside the house. They went to speak to a solicitor and property expert in Newcastle who specialized in agricultural matters. He agreed to look through Terry's files showing the history and correspondence that had taken place. Expensive as it was to go through this exercise they felt they should have one last shot at having it removed.

Meanwhile, once again Africa called them! Having had such wonderful support at their yearly fund raising day for Africa, now over £1,400 each year from their garden party, they thought it a good idea to take a trip out to Malawi to make a film to show their faithful supporters how the monies were spent and what happened after the fund raising day. Some of the money raised went to educate and train Hortencia, the girl from Mozambique, who had shown an interest in becoming a Sister of Africa. Other money went to support the orphans trapped at Dedza on the border with Mozambique, who lived in poverty with no parents to care for them.

On 15th April 2000 they arrived at Lilongwe airport and were met by a welcoming group of Missionary Sisters of Africa based in the city, together with friend Luigi who was still working in Malawi. They had lunch together at the Capital Hotel and then drove south to Dedza where they met Mother Luiza, a dedicated sister who tried to care for over 2,000 orphans in the area. Through the fund raising 'Africa Day' held in their garden at home in Yorkshire, they had happily supported her for many years. Mother Luiza was delighted to meet them after so many years of only written contact and assisted them in making a film showing her work in and around Dedza. It was a momentous occasion as they toured around seeing the heart breaking conditions and the poverty. Many of the children had no parents or grandparents and were being cared for, six and seven together, in the house of other relatives and some with strangers. Those carers were given maize flour, a staple food of their diet, to help feed the children and themselves and, if very fortunate, a piece of soap if funds for the sisters allowed such luxury.

It was good to see the library that had been established as a result of previous donations being well used, as was the photocopier that had been provided by earlier contributions which enabled people to copy items of interest and take them home for study. They were able to film this and to interview all concerned, together with Bishop Remi Ste Marie who was from Canada and in charge of that area together with Malawian Bishop Moses Chisendera. They were working to acquire funds for the building of an orphanage so that the children no longer had to be scattered around the different villages amongst relatively unknown carers.

On 'Good Friday,' from early morning, hundreds of people from the surrounding area arrived at the mission. They sat under the trees waiting for the service to commence at 3pm. They had built their own 'Way of the Cross' having created a life size wooden cross up on the hillside several hundred feet up behind the mission. All the way down the hill there were various stations of the cross, where the assembled crowd would pause to pray and to remember one episode of the passion of Christ. This took over an hour and was followed by a Mass in the church that continued for three hours, carried out in the heat of the day. In Malawi the tradition is that the men and the women sit on different sides of the church, so Andrea and Terry sat at the back in the middle! After two and a half hours they withdrew to their room exhausted, admiring the stamina of those who remained.

The following day they continued making their film, visiting the surrounding villages with Mother Luiza to see how she cared for the orphans. It was a long hot dusty day and they returned to the mission in the afternoon exhausted from touring around on foot, and chatting to the people and absorbing all they saw. They were met by Sister Marie-Paul from the mission as they walked up the track to the house.

'You have two visitors to see you,' she told them.

'Really, how can that be? Nobody knows exactly where we are.'

'Well,' said Sister Marie-Paul, 'these two do and asked if you were here and if they could speak with you. They've been waiting for over an hour. I gave them some food and drink as they looked very tired. They're from Mozambique and crossed the border this morning, but have to return home later today. Apparently they urgently needed to see you.'

They wondered who, from Mozambique, knew them by name and also knew they were there.

They went into the house which was a simple, single story brick building with a tin roof, only slightly cooler than it was outside, but standing amongst trees in some shade.

'Go through into the sitting room,' Sister Marie-Paul instructed, 'Your visitors are there waiting.'

Coming in from the bright sunshine it was dark inside and their eyes needed time to adjust. They were just able to pick out the two figures sitting sideways to the door, surrounded by a considerable amount of bags and baggage. They immediately stood up. The lady, proud, elegant and dressed in a traditional design skirt and silky white top with a colourful headdress, held in her arms a young baby wearing a yellow bobble top hand knitted woollen hat, red jacket and booties. The man, with his white long sleeved shirt and brown jacket, looked as if he had made every attempt to be tidy, but looked uncomfortable with it all! He had a stern determined presence with a furrowed brow, looking tired, worn and perhaps a little uncomfortable in his surroundings after the wait and the hot and dusty journey.

They smiled at them as they entered the room, looking shy as they all greeted each other.

Sister Marie-Paul began to translate for them.

'We are the parents of Hortencia who you have helped so much over the past few years.'

Andrea and Terry stood speechless listening unbelievably to what they were saying.

'Hortencia's parents? How on earth did they know we were here from England and visiting Dedza? They live miles away from here, how did they get here?'

Sister continued her translation.

'We heard from Hortencia that you might be here today so we've come hoping to meet you and to thank you for all you've done for her. We would like you to please accept these gifts from us, as appreciation of your kindness.'

They began to open the various packages and baskets which they had carried the seventeen or more miles from their village, across the border in Mozambique and to present the contents to Andrea and Terry. There was a bag of wheat grain, a bag of dried beans, bananas, a bag of nuts, some dried fruit, various vegetables and potatoes and two LIVE chickens.

'These are for you to say thank you. We are so happy to have found you here.'

Terry and Andrea were dumbfounded as they began to understand the magnitude of what Hortencia's parents had done in coming such a distance to say thank you.

They felt so very humble and about one inch tall. There were no words. This couple, who had no wealth or worldly goods, had walked miles carrying all these items from their garden and home. They had crossed an international border, and carried a baby through the heat of the day on the 'off chance' of meeting them - a couple from England they'd never known. It was remarkable, unbelievable, and then to offer everything they had to say 'thank you.' Terry and Andrea were totally speechless.

'Then people ask me why I have this love for Africa and its people? This is why.' Terry explained.

They gripped their hands and thanked them for their kindness and generosity. There are few moments in life as sweet, to feel such unconditional love. It was a great leveler. They were, at that moment, made very aware of life's true values. Hortencia's parents had nothing, but were prepared to give all they did have in thanks for our simple gesture of support.

'Sister we can't accept these things – it's just too much. We can't take live chickens to England with us, British Airways would have a fit!'

'You have to accept the gifts. It would be the biggest insult you could pay them not to accept, but don't worry you can give them to the people around the mission here, but you cannot refuse their gifts.'

'Could we give them some money to help them get home, on a bus perhaps, if there is one?'

'Yes that would be fine, and I'm sure it would be acceptable to them.'

They said their goodbye's, allowing them to start their long journey back to Mozambique before darkness fell. It had been a privilege to meet such amazing people, something they would remember and treasure all their lives.

'You know, if nothing else, life in Africa has given me one very important value, 'Perspective' Terry said reflectively, as they stood watching Hortencia's parents with their baby walk back down the hot dusty road and out of sight.

The following day Terry and Andrea drove down the challenging dirt road to the Lakeshore forty miles away to visit another small mission station and to continue making the film. There they met Sister Rose - a young sister struggling to feed more orphan children that had gathered there from the surrounding countryside. She had the minimum of supplies and assistance and just did what she could each day with whatever she had to give them - food if she had any, to bury the dead if necessary - anything. She sat on the edge of life with them. They had brought them a small bag of oranges from Dedza so Sister Rose sat the children down in the dust, in the shade of a tree and handed one to each child. They accepted it with glee. A bar of gold would not have made them happier. It was heart breaking to witness such thought-provoking need, such poverty.

Further along the lake and just off the lakeshore was the ancient Mua Mission. It had started life as a Leprosy Centre founded by the White Fathers in 1902, where they worked with the White Sisters making it the oldest in Malawi. The buildings of the first big mission house were built about that time and still stand. The first church was finished in 1905 and opened the following Christmas, Terry and Andrea had the opportunity to join the local people for Mass in that church during their visit. It was a very special occasion. Terry had last visited Mua when he worked in Malawi and visited the mission with his good friend Luigi in 1979. He remembered how they had sat on the steps of the mission house and watched the eclipse of the moon.

Part of the mission is now given over to the Chamare Museum that provides visitors with an introduction to the richness of the Chewa, Ngoni and Yao cultures of central and southern Malawi, as well as a little on the Batwa people, the original, and now vanished, inhabitants of Malawi.

It is also the site of the KuNgoni Centre of Culture & Art, established in 1976 by a Canadian Missionary Fr. Claude Boucher Chisale who Terry had met in 1979. He was still there to welcome them and show them around on this visit, explaining all that had been achieved. Fr. Boucher had dedicated his life to researching, recording and preserving Malawian culture. The Centre had grown from an art co-operative to a vibrant cultural centre. It provided valuable insights into the history and culture of Malawi through the Chamare Museum, the Carving Centre, and the new Research Centre/Library. The museum describes the Chewa, Ngoni and Yao cultures; their rites of passage; their interaction with one another and their encounter with Islam and Christianity. It also holds a unique display of masks, collected over the years by Fr. Boucher which were absolutely amazing in their variation and style.

However, it was time to move on, so it was back up the mountain road winding its way up to Dedza where they stayed one more night before setting off again. This time it was for a week's holiday at the Wilderness Lodge, Mvuu Camp overlooking a broad stretch of the Shire River in Liwonde National Park in the south of the country.

It was hard saying goodbye to the Bishop and Sisters at Dedza Mission. They thanked them for their wonderful kindness and the generosity shown to them throughout their stay.

Sister Simone summed it up beautifully.

'Before you arrived we were a little concerned, as we did not know you or how you would fit in with us here. But as you leave us we are sad. You have been like a brother and sister to us.'

To leave Dedza with so many problems and in conditions so terrible and after such an experience - one that touched them deeply, was not easy. However, they had to continue with their tour and follow their set plan and time schedule, promising to carry the plight of these people back to Yorkshire with them and to do all they could to find means of supporting the work at Dedza. Apart from their own continuing yearly support, they did manage to acquire some help from the bankers Rothschild's and others who went on to see the film on their return home.

Their four-day stay at the Wilderness Lodge on the Shire River was a wonderful experience and time for a well-earned rest. Their accommodation was at No. five, the honeymoon suite. The Lodge nestles discreetly on the banks of a lagoon on the western boundary of the wildlife-rich Liwonde National Park. It is set high above the water for long views up-river that are full of every sort of wildlife. There were eight tents set inside thatched roofs for a maximum of sixteen guests, each with en-suite bathroom facilities and a private viewing platform looking out on the lagoon. There was a dining room, bar, lounge area, wildlife library and a swimming pool, so everything to help you relax and they certainly did. The day got underway at seven in the morning when the familiar cry of 'I bring tea' was heard as a tray was left outside the tent.

From the sultry heat of the Liwonde Valley they moved on to Zomba Mountain for a cooler overnight stay at the Ku Chawe Inn before returning to Lilongwe in the central region to be ready to take the return flight to Gatwick where they arrived at three in the morning after their flight had been delayed in Lusaka. The end of yet another African adventure.

CCC

CHAPTER FIFTEEN

Returning to work after such a contrasting holiday was as always, very difficult, with your head in one place and your body in another, but slowly normal everyday life took over.

September brought the reward for ten years' hard fight against the planning authorities for the removal of an Agricultural Clause on their house, when it was finally agreed that it could be removed. They were absolutely delighted. Their investment in the legal representation and the risk they had taken had, in the end paid off, but in great-part due to their own persistence and work over the years, slowly eroding away the case for its retention. As their hermit monk friend at Ampleforth Abbey always said to them, 'Be happy, take risks.' Well it had certainly been a risk to spend so much on fighting it, but it paid off this time increasing the ease at which they could sell the house when the day came, leaving it open for anyone to buy, not just those working in agriculture. Maybe it was this achievement that started to change the way they looked at their life, opening new thoughts, other scenarios.

In September 2000, Terry received a strange phone call at his office in Harrogate from Andrew Bowman's solicitor asking if he could make an appointment to see him. Why would he wish to come and speak to me he wondered? However, he cautiously agreed to meet him and invited him to his office the following day. Knowing how tricky Bowman could be and not having any idea why his solicitor would wish to meet him, Terry decided to set up a recording machine in the boardroom in which the meeting would take place. He arranged a heap of books on the table with the recorder hidden amongst them. That way the whole meeting could be secretly recorded. Terry was not going to take any risks with this man. Bowman was a slippery character.

When Mr. Desmond arrived, Terry switched on the recorder hidden in the books and went to great him at reception inviting him to the boardroom.

'Well Mr. Desmond, what can I do for you? It's over eleven years since I left Bowman Properties I have no idea why you should wish to speak with me after all this time.'

Mr. Desmond sat there in his dark pinned striped suite looking extremely pompous.

'Mr. Reeves, Andrew Bowman has to attend the Royal Courts of Justice in a very serious case brought to court by his sisters and needs you to help him to give witness in the case against him.'

'I see,' Terry responded. 'Is that in order to support his case?' He was wondering what on earth it was all about.

'Yes sir it is.' Mr. Desmond replied.

'Well, anything I have to say about Andrew Bowman in court or anywhere else for that matter will not help his case. He treated me and many others in his employment very badly indeed, I've nothing good to say about the man. You do know, I assume, the way we were treated and how I came to leave his employment? It was nothing short of constructive dismissal. Had I not myself found a new job when I did I would have taken him to court with, I am told, a cast iron case.'

'That maybe sir,' Mr. Desmond kept saying in a very annoying and arrogant manner, 'but you are requested to attend and give witness and if you refuse you will be subpoenaed and forced by law to attend.'

'I see, and are you going to tell me what the case is about?'

'Well Sir, I cannot go into all the details with you here, but it's to support something that Andrew Bowman did while you were in his employment. You are to give witness to the judge at the Royal Courts of Justice.'

'When is this likely to be?

'The court will be in touch with you. Sir, this meeting is just to inform you that you'll be called and must attend. All your expenses of course will be paid, so keep receipts and submit them to me, when repayment will be forthcoming.'

'I see, well I can only repeat to you Mr. Desmond that, as far as I'm concerned, nothing good will come out of what I have to say about Andrew Bowman. He damaged and destroyed too many people's lives.'

'That Sir, is up to you,' Mr. Desmond replied sheepishly.

Three weeks later while shopping in Northallerton one afternoon, Terry received a call from Mr. Desmond's office telling him that he had to attend the Royal Courts of Justice in London the following morning and to be there for 10 o'clock where he should wait to be called into court! This gave him little time so Terry quickly made arrangements to be off work, which was less than convenient. Recognizing that he was about to go into a lion's den, Andrea said she was not letting him go on his own and insisted on going with him to the courts.

They arrived at Kings Cross shortly after 9 am the following day and took a taxi across London to the Strand and the Royal Courts, arriving in good time. They reported their arrival and were directed to the corridor outside the court where the case was in progress. They sat there in the grand surroundings watching people dart in and out of various rooms looking earnest and important. Men and women in wigs huddled together in deep conversation, then went off to other rooms around the wide corridor looking worried and concerned creating a busy and earnest atmosphere. Terry and Andrea sat there watching all this for two hours until they began to get a little fed up. At around midday they were still waiting to be called but nothing had happened. They noticed that there was a great deal of hammering and banging going on outside. Terry, in jest, said to a gathering of men dressed in wigs, 'I see they are building the scaffolding already then.'

'Oh no sir,' they replied, quite seriously, 'they don't do that any longer!'

They were told that they could go for lunch at 1pm, so finding a pub across the road they indulged. By this time, they were tired of sitting around waiting for some action. At 3pm nothing had happened so they hailed one of the men in wigs as he came out of the court where Bowman's case was being heard.

'Can you tell me how much longer I have to wait here,' Terry asked.

'You may have to return tomorrow. They will not be rushed,' the wigged man replied.

'I can't do that. I have a business to run,' Terry informed him.

'I will see what I can do,' the bewigged man replied.

Finally, at 4pm Terry was called into court. At last he thought, as they both went into the court room. Andrea sat in the public area and Terry was guided to where the action was taking place. The Judge, with all his advisors and officials, was sitting on one side with rows of ushers, barristers and others on the opposite side, as well as Andrew Bowman. Terry had not seen him for over eleven years and was surprised to see how he had aged. He was instructed to go up onto a high rostrum at one end of the court where he assumed he was to be questioned. A man in a long black gown, and with what looked like a dead cat on his head, approached Terry.

Standing only feet away and looking straight at him he said, 'Say these words after me.'

O K thought Terry, waiting.

The man looked anxious.

Again he repeated, 'Say these words after me,' in a slightly more raised tone.

Terry was waiting for either a card to read or to be told what the words were; not unreasonably he thought.

Again the man with the dead cat on his head stared at Terry and almost shouted at him, 'Say these words after me.'

Well, Terry did not know what to do, or say, not having been given a card or told what words he was to say. So Terry repeated what the man had said, 'Say these words after me.'

With that the court burst into uproar and laughter at Terry's response.

Either the man with the dead cat on his head was drunk, or didn't have a clue what he was doing.

A card was then passed to Terry and he duly read the appropriate words required of him.

The judge then asked Terry to look at a letter that was in file 23 – section 3, subsection D. The files were not presented to Terry. He had to search through a row of twenty or more box files on a table to one side of him.

He pushed his chair back, which was on wheels, to inspect the files and to find the one required. As he did so he was aware that behind him there were no rails and a drop of about ten or more feet which he found alarming and nearly toppled over the side. He gathered himself together and eventually found the appropriate file. Glancing across the court he could see Andrea, now doubled up with laughter, had put a handkerchief in her mouth to stop herself from laughing out loud. She later told him it was like watching Norman Wisdom! The judge was getting somewhat frustrated by all this as Terry searched for the letter required, which he finally did locate after ploughing through the contents of numerous files.

'Did you write that letter?' the judge boomed out.

Terry looked at it and replied, 'Yes I did, my signature is on the bottom of the letter so clearly I wrote and signed it!'

Really he thought, have they dragged me down here all the way from Yorkshire, kept me waiting all day just to ask me if I had signed a letter that had my name on? It seemed as if they had.

'Is there anything else you would like to tell the court?' the judge asked Terry.

'Yes there is.'

This is the moment I've waited for he thought to himself. Terry then set off with all the things he wanted the court to know about this man they had on trial, glad to have the opportunity to express them in public. He was going to nail him once and for all. He then commenced his verbal attack on the man who had caused so much heartache and sorrow to himself and his family, colleagues, employees and their families over the years, some now sadly passed away. They were all good people that Terry had seen destroyed by this man and he told the court in no uncertain terms something of those events. When he had finished, Andrew's sisters, who were sitting in the court and who had brought the case against him, surprisingly applauded Terry's outburst, with the Judge and his team looking rather taken aback.

A silence fell over the court.

'I think, Mr. Reeves, you were going to tell us that, whatever question I'd have asked you?' the judge remarked.

'Yes, that was my plan. It needed to be said so that you know the sort of man you are dealing with. I hope it will help you come to the correct decision about him and his nephew and their appalling conduct at that time.'

'Thank you very much Mr. Reeves. Is there anything else you wish to add?'

'No thank you I've covered everything.'

'Then you may stand down,' the judge informed him.

With that they left the court and made their way in sombre mood to Kings Cross and the train back to Yorkshire, 'first class' of course. They later heard that Andrew's sisters had won the case at the Royal Courts which had lasted for two weeks. Bowman had been stripped of his control of the company and all assets as a result of his activities. His sisters fell short of taking away his company house, but they could have done so. He was very fortunate.

CCC

CHAPTER SIXTEEN

Paul and Carolyn were busy planning for their wedding day which was to take place on 21st July 2001 and thoughts were moving towards that exciting day. They were still living in Oberursel in Germany but had purchased a small house in France for holiday use at Bagnols-en-Foret, 50 miles west of Nice. They were thinking that one day they might move there to work and live but, in the meantime, Terry & Andrea were welcome to go and have a holiday there at any time, which they did and enjoyed their first taste of France.

On 1st November 2000, Andrea moved to a new job as a Co-ordinator for the Alzheimers Society, over-seeing six day-care centres throughout North Yorkshire. She grew to enjoy the contact with people, but it was a very demanding position, especially dealing with all the employment issues.

The twelfth Africa Day took place at Osgodby House on 14th July 2001 raising an all-time record amount of £1,700, despite afternoon rain. It was very good for a simple attempt to raise money for all those causes they had recently seen on their visit to Malawi. The wonderful group of loyal supporters who, year after year, came together to assist and take part always made the day such an occasion and such a success.

That behind them it was time to look to Paul and Carolyn's wedding day on 21st July. It was to be held at Holy Trinity

Church, High Usworth, Washington, Tyne and Wear followed by a reception in the splendour of the beautiful Langley Castle, Hexham, Northumberland. It was a magnificent setting surrounded by family and friends for an emotional but happy day. Paul and Carolyn had planned and organized the whole event. It was one of the many days in his life when he sorely missed his Mother's presence, as he movingly stated at the beginning of his speech to the assembled guests. Everyone agreed that his mother would have been so proud of him that day, how he had grown into such a fine and caring young man. Terry found the whole day a very moving experience, feeling for his loss, wishing it had been different. He took comfort that Andrea was always there for him and, although not Paul's mother, he would always be her son in every way possible and he knew Paul would always treat her with love and respect as he would have his own mother. For that Terry was grateful to him always.

Somewhat exhausted by the emotion of the event they spent a few days exploring the area and enjoyed a visit to Holy Island. It was there they spent their thirteenth wedding anniversary, walking around the island enjoying its relaxed atmosphere. They passed a small school where there was a sign outside inviting visitors to midday Mass. They enjoyed the children's service and, by coincidence, the hymn sung was the same as on their wedding day, 'Make me a Channel of Your Peace.'

They went onto Scotland visiting the David Livingstone museum situated in his old home and birthplace in Blantyre, near Glasgow. It was fascinating to see it, bringing back many memories of his own time in Africa when he followed in the footsteps of Livingstone. A few days were then spent in and around the beautiful Loch Lomond before returning home to Yorkshire when Andrea had yet another tremendous surprise for Terry and the family.

Terry at that time was still attending the Catholic church in Thirsk after Fr. O'Brian's retirement. He was not happy with the replacement priest, finding him a rather odd character, so he often attended Mass at Ampleforth Abbey finding great inspiration there, while keeping his allegiance to Thirsk and the parishioners and friends he had made. Andrea was continuing as a Lay Reader in and around the Kilburn Parishes, taking in Bagby and Thirkleby. She had become an important support to the vicar who appreciated her services. She was often called upon to help out at one of the other churches of the surrounding area, to stand in when someone was ill or on holiday. It was very challenging and Terry did sometimes worry that she was being taken advantage of, but she enjoyed it and clearly did it well.

Then, one Sunday when they had both returned from their respective churches and were chatting over coffee as usual, Andrea suddenly said,

'What would you say if I told you that I was thinking of becoming a Catholic?'

'Why on earth would you want to do that?' A surprised Terry enquired.

'I've been thinking about it now for some time and feel that I'd like to attend weekly worship with you and not for us to be going to different churches. Do you remember when we were last at Aylesford Priory in Kent for that break and retreat and the priest there at Mass welcomed anyone that was a Christian to come up to receive communion?'

'Oh yes I do,' Terry replied, 'but I don't think he was obeying the church's rule when he allowed that.'

'I was very surprised at the time that I could receive,' Andrea replied, 'but he opened doors in my mind. I suddenly felt I was welcome in the church, that had, until then, put up a barrier. It was where I wanted to be - alongside you. However, I still have obstacles in my mind and I have to sort them out. As I understand it I'd have to take some sort of instruction by a priest, which is fine. But I wouldn't want those to be from your priest at Thirsk. We are definitely not on the same wavelength. I always enjoy going to Ampleforth with you. Would Fr. Paul Brown, the monk we often chat to and who ran our last retreat, be allowed to take me through the motions and do what's required? I can sort out the remaining things in my mind with him I'm sure. He'd do it so well and is such a spiritual man, a bit crazy sometimes, but that makes him human and I'm sure he and I could sort out things, if he's allowed too.'

Let's go to Ampleforth next Sunday and ask him if he would be prepared to take you on?' Terry said smiling, 'if you're really sure it's what you want.'

Fr. Paul was both delighted and surprised to be asked and told them he would have to ask the Abbot first, as it was slightly unusual for a monk to be asked but, in principal, he was delighted. He told Andrea that he would really put her through the mill, to make sure that she really understood what she was taking on!

The following week Fr. Paul came rushing up to them after mass waving his arms around and shouting,

'The Abbot – he say yes!'

They were both delighted and Andrea looked forward to the beginning of her six week course that was to start the following week.

Terry and Ken continued to work closely developing the property company together and seemed to complement each other in the various activities, trusting each other and becoming good friends. They were working on projects in many areas from Shopping Centres, Health Centres and Commercial Units, as far apart as Wakefield, Sheffield, Ripon, Dewsbury, Sunderland, Whitby, Darlington and at Stockton-on-Tees. This was on top of the day to day activities involved in managing a multi-million-pound property portfolio. Ken also carried out a lot of private activities associated with the Catholic Diocese of Leeds. He had tremendous drive. As soon as one project was complete he was raring to get on with the next.

One of these developments was not moving at speed and he wanted it resolved. The bus depot at Hartlepool had received a compulsory purchase order served on it by local government for a new development corporation they were backing. This meant the bus company was forced to sell it to them for the development of a new marina they were looking to build. The depot was in the way and had to go. The price had first to be established between the two parties so estate agents were appointed to agree the figure within a set framework, but time was slowly running out with no agreement in sight.

'Have you any news from the agents yet as to what figure they might agree?' Ken asked Terry for the third week running.

'Only that they are stuck at £300,000 and neither side will budge.'

'I see,' Ken replied thoughtfully. 'Well that's nowhere near enough is it? We have to find a new site for our bus depot in the town and very quickly, so we need a resolution. Who is the Chief Executive of the development company?'

'Not sure,' Terry replied, 'but I'll find out.'

'OK, do that straight away and tell him we want a meeting tomorrow morning in his office at nine, this has to be settled but if we wait for these agents we'll wait forever,' Ken sharply declared.

Terry arranged the meeting and he and Ken met at eight thirty the following morning to discuss tactics before their meeting at nine at the development company's head office. It was an extremely expensive looking office building towering high above the development site at Teesdale.

'What do you think we should ask?' Ken enquired from Terry thoughtfully.

'How about we ask for a million?' Ken suggested.

'We'll never get that,' Terry laughed as they made their way up to the top floor of the building for their appointment. They quickly found the smart, plush offices of the chief executive and informed the secretary they had arrived. She ushered them in to his office.

He greeted them in a sharp, efficient and friendly manner. They all shook hands and were invited to sit down.

'Now gentlemen, what is the problem here?' he enquired forcefully.

'We are getting nowhere fast with our respective estate agents over the land that you are to compulsorily purchase from us and we need to get it settled so we can plan ahead,' Ken put forward in his usual business like way.

'I see,' the C.E. said, 'and how much are you expecting for the site?

'One million pounds,' said Ken boldly and without a flinch.

'That's fine,' the C.E. replied. Now would you like some coffee before you go!

Ken, never slow to wring out the last drop from a deal said, 'There will also be legal costs for the transfer and the agent's fees.'

'Of course,' the C.E. replied. How much will those be?'

'Around two hundred and fifty thousand pounds, including the stamp duty for the purchase of a new site,' Ken replied brazenly.

'O.K. that's fine. Now, do you gentlemen take milk in your coffee?'

That was it, the deal was done!

As they both took the lift down to the ground floor and to their cars Ken, smiling, said to Terry,

'I wonder if I should have asked for two million?'

'That would have been very greedy wouldn't it!' They laughed at the speed the deal had been made and were delighted with the settlement, proving again their expertise over the bickering estate agents.

CCC

CHAPTER SEVENTEEN

2002 was a memorable year for the whole country when they said farewell to Queen Elizabeth the Queen Mother who died peacefully at the Royal Lodge, Windsor on 30th March, aged 101 years. She was queen for fewer than 15 years, during a period which is now beginning to pass out of living memory. Yet her personal popularity continued through 50 years of widowhood, unimpaired by changing public reactions to her children and grandchildren, and their broken marriages.

When she married the Duke of York (later King George VI) on April 23 1923, her impact on the crowds was comparable to that of Diana's, 58 years later. She had been reluctant to marry royalty, afraid never again to be free to think, speak and act as she felt. But, having accepted the life, she threw herself into it, and carried her husband through the trauma of the 1936 abdication, which brought him to the throne.

During the war, her seemingly indomitable spirit provided moral support to the British public. In recognition of her role as an asset to British interests, Adolf Hitler described her as, "the most dangerous woman in Europe." After the war, her husband's health deteriorated and she was widowed at the age of 51. Her elder daughter, aged 25, became our new Queen.

Terry and Andrea often returned to Weymouth to visit friends and family during the year. With the usual difficulty in locating good accommodation, they decided to purchase a static caravan at 'Cove Holiday Park,' on the Isle of Portland. There was a particularly beautiful spot available on the park overlooking the sea, so they decided to purchase a new static caravan there overlooking 'Church Ope Cove.' It was an amazing spot which they went on to enjoy for twelve years.

Easter 2002 was a very special time when Andrea was received into the Catholic Church at a wonderfully spiritual service that took place during the Easter Vigil Mass at Ampleforth Abbey. In a memorable and moving service, the packed candlelit abbey welcomed Andrea. A monk came down into the congregation from the high altar to invite her up to join them, where Fr. Timothy Wright, the Abbot of Ampleforth, carried out the ceremony welcoming her into the Catholic Church. Terry was especially happy that they would be sharing their spiritual life together, with all its joys and challenges.

At the end of September one of the developments in Ripon that Terry and his team had been working on for a number of years, which included a new library for the city, was finally ready. Prince Charles came to do the honours, as always in his beige camel coat! The attached shopping centre opened weeks later, with the whole development conceived and constructed on what had been a large and poorly utilized bus station and car park. It was an enormous improvement for the city, as well as an improved value and income stream for the company.

At this time there had been a great deal of discussion within the media about people from UK going to France to buy property and stories about those who went there to live. Terry and Andrea had watched the television programs and had been to stay at Paul and Carolyn's house near Nice and were attracted by the laid back life style, the people, the countryside and the food. They were very tempted to give it a try themselves once they retired. Thousands had moved there to take advantage of the cheap property prices, compared to the U.K. and to enjoy the more laid back, less congested way of life. For years many French citizens had come to live in the UK and, at this time, there were said to be over 100,000 living here, with London becoming known as France's sixth biggest city! According to the media, 20,000 Britons a year were packing up and moving out of the overcrowded UK in search of more elbow room in France, just across the water. What is often overlooked though is that about half of those who decide to move "permanently" to France do not stay more than a year or two, or else give up the "permanent" notion, and become seasonal migrants. Moving to live in another country can be a traumatic experience, but the challenge and excitement tempted them both.

In June of 2003 they decided to visit mid France to look around at property and to explore and understand the market, but with no serious intent. It was with a view to 'perhaps' making an investment in the property market. The share market in the UK was not as good as it had been and Terry always felt more comfortable investing in things that he understood, so he wanted to see the possibilities and assess them. Thinking the middle of France would be cooler than the south of France, but warmer than the north which would really be little better then living in Cornwall, they chose to explore the area around Bergerac in the middle of the country. With only a handful of French words between them and little experience of driving on the other side of the road, they set off for a week's holiday with a purpose.

They had flown into Bergerac on the Monday morning. By Thursday lunch time they had signed contracts on a fantastic house on the edge of the village of St. Barthelemy-de-Bellegarde! They had looked at about four houses which were of no interest then, walking through the town of Riberac at lunch time, Terry spotted the picture of a rural house in an estate agent's window which attracted him. They went in and asked for more information. The agent, Mr. Bigley, an English man, asked if they would like to go and view it and phoned the owners, Mr. and Mrs. Coles. They said they were having lunch with friends at the house and so it was not as tidy as it might be, but they were welcome to come and view it. So accompanied by Mr. Paul Bigley they drove the thirty minutes to St Barthelemy-de-Bellegarde. He told them how he and his family had been in France for several years and they chatted to him about his experiences. He explained that the current owners of 'L'Etang Des Vias' the house they were to view, were English, so it would be easy to discuss matters with them. Terry had warned Andrea before setting out not to show too much emotion about the property, either to the owner or the estate agent, 'buying property is like a game of poker' he explained.

They arrived at the small village of St. Barthelemy de Bellegarde, a sleepy looking spot in the middle of nowhere, surrounded by agricultural land and forestry. It was though only a few miles from the town of Montpon where all the usual services could be found including, on Wednesdays, a colourful market which took place in the streets. They drove about a mile out of the village and on the left, set back off the road, was 'L'Etang Des Vias' (house by the lake), with its green gates and cream coloured walls. The electrically controlled gates slowly opened, at the same time and speed as their mouths! Remembering what Terry had said, Andrea did not say a word, but her face was a picture and relayed Terry's own thoughts (Woweee!). The opening gates revealed a well laid out and cared for garden with a large gravelled area surrounding a central garden full of colourful shrubs. Attached to the single storied house was a double garage with electric doors. All this was set within a large lawn area planted with shrubs and trees, illuminated at night by large globe lights all around the garden, making it look spectacular. At the rear was the most fantastic swimming pool and tiled terrace complete with built-in BBQ dotted with Victorian style tree lights, looking out to the agricultural and forestry land beyond the garden.

They could hardly look at each other. It was stunning. The owners, Mr. and Mrs. Cole, welcomed them and showed them around the spacious house, garden room and the large covered terraced area. The faint smell of the roast lamb lunch only added to the wonder of the place as they gazed around, trying hard not to look too excited or approving. They do say that you decide on buying a house within the first few minutes of arriving. They certainly found that to be true and, without even discussing it with each other, they both instinctively knew this was the one. There was no going back after seeing that and as they left the property to return to the estate agents office, they did once dare to look at each other with a knowing glance of satisfaction and desire! Once back at Riberac they told Mr. Bigley that they wanted to have a few minutes together to discuss what they had seen. They adjourned across the road to a café for coffee, promising to return to his office in a short while.

Spell bound they discussed the situation and both agreed it was a beautiful house and a fantastic property, with the opportunity to develop it further if they wanted, making it a good investment too. They both loved it. Out came the calculator and notebook and over coffee they did their homework and decided that they could and would make an offer for 'L'Etang,' as it had become known to them. Throwing caution to the wind they offered five thousand below the asking price which was refused. In the end they had to settle at pretty much the asking price, but were happy to do so for such a dream place and the price of a new adventure. Subject to the usual surveys and checks it was in the bag. They would, in the short term, let the house with the thought that when they retired they might move to France, but that would not be for many years. Or so they thought! The Cole's said they would like to rent it for a while as they had not yet found the house they were looking for. That certainly suited Terry & Andrea, so a tenancy agreement was drawn up as part of the legal transaction.

In less than a week they had gone to France, purchased a house and now were returning home hardly able to believe all they had done and achieved. Were they completely crazy they wondered - probably?

It took quite a lot of time to sort out the details of the purchase, with it being in another language and country, but with the aid of the FAX machine and an English speaking Notaire, on 30th October 2003 completion took place with the exchange rate then at euro 1.41 to the pound. The Cole's agreed to rent the property while they continued their search for another place in France with less garden and in an area that they favoured.

2004 came in with the news that the Coles had found a house and so would be moving out. This was not good news as Terry and Andrea were very happy to have them staying there and to receive the rental income knowing they would take good care of the property. Now they had to decide what to do next - find another tenant, or to furnish it and seek holiday lets during the summer months, as per the original plan. They decided to go out again to see the house at the end of February once the Cole's had left and hopefully come to a decision. They had started doing French lesson one evening a week in Ripon, so hopefully some of it would rub off before their next trip!

Going back again, sitting on the sun terrace in the February sun, eating fresh prawns, they decided they couldn't bear not to live in their beautiful new house, as they fell in love with it all over again. They were of course concerned about grand-parents Cecil and Margaret, now living in Wales, but it was not so far away, only across the channel, so they could easily return for a few weeks at a time, also allowing them to make good use of their static caravan on Portland at the same time. So two days after their return to England they went to see a couple of estate agents to obtain a valuation for Osgodby

House. They were amazed at the value that had built up in the house over the years, but it confirmed their ability to take early retirement if they wished.

The bureaucracy in Andrea's job was getting out of hand, not allowing her to care for the people in need which was why she had come into the job in the first place. It was driving her and many other good people away, to the extent that she felt it might be a very good idea to take early retirement at fifty-four. Terry, now fifty-nine, was happy in his work and enjoyed being part of a fair and honest company for a change, enjoying the daily challenges. He and Ken got on well and enjoyed the cut and thrust of the property world of the early twenty first century. Together they had made a fortune for the company over the years. But, as far as Terry was concerned, always on the horizon were Ken's two boys who were out of college and considering their futures. One was heavily into the music business and went on to make a big name for himself in a very successful and well known group. The other son was looking to be involved with property and this sounded alarm bells. Terry had seen, when working for other companies, that sons often move into a business and before long your job is on the line. He expressed this view to Ken who made it quite clear that there would always be a job for Terry in the company, no matter what his sons decided to do. Terry wanted to believe this but life's experience had shown the reality to be different, blood being thicker than water. So it was after much consideration that they both decided to take early retirement and enjoy the fruits of their labour. It was an exciting prospect to have the new French experience ahead, whatever it should bring.

Terry had to tell Ken which was one of the hardest tasks he had to do. He found him one morning sitting at his desk going through the endless lists that he always made and used as a prompt.

'Ken, I have a bit of a surprise for you.'

'Oh yes' he replied calmly, never one to get over excited. He took things very much in his stride.

'Remember how I told you we'd bought a house in France as an investment and were going to use it for holiday lets. Well, after a recent trip to France and finding the existing tenant had given notice, we've decided to take early retirement and go and live there. It's a huge step folding up life here to go and live in another country, but we'd like to give it a go and see how it works out. Sorry, but this means of course I'll have to give you three months' notice, as per my contract.'

It was rare to see him shocked or surprised but Terry's news seemed to stop him in his tracks. He wished there had been an easier way to tell him, but there really wasn't.

'Can I ask you why?' he asked.

'Well, life is short Ken, Andrea's health problem a few years ago underlined that fact. We feel we can do this now, even without our pensions, which aren't due to pay out for five years. It's an adventure, while we're both young enough to do it and enjoy it. I'm sorry Ken, I really am. I've loved working with you it's been a time of excitement and challenge. Be assured I'll do all I can to hand over everything as smoothly as possible.'

He sat there as if frozen to the spot, his face pale and motionless.

'I'll leave you to think it over Ken, I'm upstairs if you need me.'

Terry felt bad and was a little surprised that Ken had seemingly taken it so hard, but he was sure he would soon come to terms with it and think upon it as another opportunity, after all that's what Ken did. That was his way.

However, about an hour later Terry passed Ken's office and, to his amazement, Ken seemed to be sitting in exactly the same position, just as Terry had left him, starring ahead with an open vague expression.

'Are you OK?' Terry enquired.

He gave a half smile, but continued to sit there looking dazed. That moment was to stay with Terry in the years ahead. He always hoped he was wrong and that he had not been the root cause of what was to transpire several years later.

House sales, as always are never straight forward and the sale of Osgodby House was no exception. The first buyer gave back word after three days, but a second buyer came along at the same price and it proceeded to contract, subject to a long completion date. The first date slipped by but it was finally settled for 9th September 2004 completing a fifteen year, three-month stay! On Wednesday 29th September it was goodbye to North Yorkshire and to England as they stepped aboard the Brittany Ferry to embark on their new life in France.

CCC

CHAPTER EIGHTEEN

It had been a very emotional time leaving North Yorkshire. Not only was it Andrea's place of birth, but they had left behind many good friends built up throughout their sixteen years of marriage. It felt as if they had died and were reborn in France where they were nobody but Andrea and Terry, a retired couple, otherwise a blank canvas. However, after the vigours, stresses and strains of work, they had no problem with it and were happy to become Mr. and Mrs. Nobody.

Arriving in Cherbourg they drove into the town centre to look for somewhere to stop for the night before embarking on the journey south to their new home. As luck would have it they saw a magnificent looking building ahead of them which stated, 'Hotel de Ville.' Fantastic, they thought, we could do with a night of luxury in this wonderful hotel after all the work and emotion of leaving England. It would set them up for the next phase of their journey and the beginning of their new adventure. Terry, being unsure where to park and unable to read all the French signs, pulled up outside the hotel building while Andrea went in to check whether they had a room available. A few minutes later she returned to the car looking a little flushed!

'Whatever's the matter?' Terry asked.

'You might well ask. In my very best French I asked them if they had a room for the night. They all looked at me puzzled, so I asked again, feeling my French had been quite correct. They were still looking suitably vague and I was wondering what was wrong with these French people who didn't seem to understand their own language. Then one of them spoke to me in English. She said. This, madam, is not a hotel.'

'Really? But it says Hotel on the front of the building.'

'No Madam, it says 'Hotel de Ville.' It's the town hall!'

They went on to find a suitable hotel and, after their overnight stay in northern France, they drove the five hundred miles south to the Dordogne and the village of St Barthelemy de Bellegarde. Driving on the right was always going to be a challenge. It made the journey a little more stressful having to remember to keep on the correct side of the road, especially in the country where there were no other cars to follow. But, slowly, they adjusted and at 15.30 they pulled up outside the familiar green gates of their new French home, relieved to have completed the trip with no real problems, and feeling very excited. Pressing the button on the key fob the gates slowly opened – immediately confirming that they had done the right thing - made this decision to retire early and enjoy this stunning and peaceful spot for as long as they chose, with no real work or employers to satisfy or other such daily pressures.

The car was full to its roof, with things jammed under the seats to use every possible space. Tricks, their West Highland x Jack Russell bitch, had travelled lying in the back in her bed with everything stacked around her. She too was pleased the journey was over. They all almost fell out of the car and made haste to explore in case it had all been a dream. They were proud of their achievement and were looking forward to their exciting new adventure in France.

Apart from a new bed that had been delivered to the house, and the plastic sunbeds from around the pool, there was no other furniture. Their house contents from the UK would take three weeks to arrive so, for the time being, they were sort of camping with only the contents of the car to get them started and keep them going. The first thing they noticed was how quiet it was. Osgodby had never been noisy, but somehow L'Etang was even quieter with only the occasional car passing by. They started to place their few things around the house and excitedly found out how everything worked, or in some cases didn't, and where things were to be found.

The built-in hob had four rings but only three worked! The house had a septic tank system which they had been used to in Yorkshire, but they would have to learn its little idiosyncrasies. All the electric plugs in the house were two pin, which meant every electric appliance would need new plugs to suit the system. Every morning, in his yellow post van, the postman delivered all their correspondence to a box built into the outside garden wall. It had a door on both sides of the wall for delivery and collection, but where was the key? The pool was a nasty shade of green – what had happened to the man they had employed to look after it? and why had he not cut the extensive lawns around the house as he had been paid to do? How did they get their telephone to work and what would they say when they received a call and picked up the handset with their very limited French? The water was turned off, so they had to go in search of the stop-cock in order to bring life giving water to the place? Some of the lights around the house worked others did not. Where were the light switches to the garden and the pool? How did they get into the little brick garden shed near the gate? So many questions. But first, the most important thing was to put the new bed together and make it ready for the first night in their new home.

Slowly, answers were found to all the new challenges and having brought the plastic poolside sunbeds into the house to use as arm chairs, they began to find their feet, still amazed at the quietness and lack of any people or manmade noise. The next day they decided to venture out to the near-by town of Mussidan to find a supermarket and stock their empty cupboards. They drove the three miles through the Foret de la Double (Double Forest). They did not see another car or person and were beginning to wonder if they were the only people left in France! They found a Lidl supermarket, which was a surprise name to find in France. There were only two cars in the large car park and they wondered if it was open. Fortunately, it was. The content of this Lidl was similar to the UK but with a number of very different lines relating to French taste. It was good to find some things that were familiar and to their taste. After the supermarket shopping they fell into a common French trap. When they went to the Bank they found that it was closed until after lunch! Everywhere seemed to close for two hours from midday. This was very frustrating meaning they had to wait around for the bank and shops to reopen before going home, making the whole quick shopping process an entire day's trip! Slowly they became used to this, but it was never natural to them and they were often caught in the same trap. The French attitude, they soon learned, was to make enough money to survive for today - no more than that. Perhaps, in a way, they have it right and don't spend their lives rushing around trying to make more money as was the case in the UK. It soon became very apparent that the French had a very much more laid back way of life - the wine, the sun, all contributing to their philosophy!

One of the reasons for moving to France and living a new life and challenge included their continued interest in property development. They could see that the new house, beautiful as it was, would benefit from beautification. There was a large number of fir trees in the acre garden, some of which should be removed as they were making the house dark. The double garages provided a wonderful space, but were part of the house. They planned to make them into a fourth en-suite bedroom and then build a freestanding garage at the side of the house which would improve the property considerably. They started on this work almost immediately employing the services of a local architect who would guide them through the complicated planning procedure. So, together with a young

French lady who would translate, they put that plan into action within a month of their arrival, as well as removing some of the fir trees ready for the development.

The excitement of the year culminated with their first Christmas living in France. It was the first time in sixteen years of marriage that they were able to spend Christmas alone together - just the two of them. It was wonderful. They attended midnight Mass at the Echourgnac, 'Abbaye de la Trappe' just a few miles up the road. It was a beautiful spot where the Sisters of that order, playing a Celtic harp, sang like angels.

2005 swept in with plenty of frost and snow which was a bit of a surprise to them. The large log fire burned throughout the day at these times, but it was a huge area to keep warm, so they did not stray far from its blaze during the cold winter months.

With a large area of grass to cut they decided to purchase a sit on tractor mower ready for the new season, much to Terry's delight. For fifteen hundred euros it was delivered to the door proving to be a useful tool in keeping the grass under control with the minimum of effort.

The village Mayor, Maurice Ruelle, and all the members of the Council invited them to the traditional exchange of views at the Sale des Fete (village Hall) at St Barthelemy de Bellegarde one evening early in the new year, as was the tradition. It was a new experience but a useful one where the intention was to explain how the local taxation had been spent. It sounded like a very good idea, something they would do well to adopt in the UK. It was a pleasant evening with the opportunity to meet all the locals and to fly the flag for the few British people living in the area.

When they arrived they were greeted by the Mayor and his members with much kissy kissy all round. They stood with a gathering of around one hundred local people in the hall, who had come to hear how their taxes had been spent and the plans for the coming year's expenditure. They were all keen to learn what was happening to the newly converted building in the village. They had understood it was to be a restaurant and a butchery. They were also waiting for news of a new Post Office. The opening hours of the old one were ridiculously random and never when you needed it.

The hall was set out with tables and chairs to accommodate the crowd that had attended the meeting. Strangely enough, everyone stood to hear the speech given by the Mayor, Monsieur M Ruelle, who was standing on the stage at one end of the hall. The microphone was very base and flattened his voice completely, making it even more difficult to hear what he was saying - especially for the English couples, of which three had attended.

Following a speech of about twenty minutes everyone sat at the long tables stretched across the hall, and food was served. First the bottles of wine and water were placed on the table, then small plastic beakers and cardboard plates! It was clearly going to be a stylish affair!

After a long wait bread appeared, sliced and in small bowls carefully distributed along each of the tables. Then steel knives and forks were given to each person. They were then served two slices of meat (not sure what it was?) which they ate with the bread that had been passed around the table.

This was followed by a serving of more meat - a sort of Ham and Parma Ham together. As they started to enjoy this a man from two tables away jumped out of his seat and started choking while at the same time rushing to the door, hotly pursued by his wife and others. Within minutes the wife returned shouting for help. Others jumped up and rushed outside to the man's aid. After a few minutes someone dashed in for a mobile phone in order to call the ambulance indicating the seriousness of the situation. It, reassuringly arrived quickly with its blue flashing lights.

While this was going on they sat at the table feeling some-what alarmed, worrying about the poor man's fate. However, all around them the show was going on as if nothing was happening. Bread was being passed around and second help-ings of meat, bottles of wine and water were dished out!

Through the window they could just see the man's feet. He was now lying on the concrete floor, receiving attention, but completely motionless. They were very concerned for him and distressed that it was all happening just a few feet from where they were sitting. Meanwhile inside, people were feasting and passing food and wine to each other seemingly unmoved by what was happening! The blue lights of the Ambulance were turned off. They could only see the man's feet - his body was now covered by a white sheet – it did not look good. Long faces went in and out of the hall, but still the food and drink was being distributed to the gathered people. Through the window they saw another vehicle arrive which they were told, was, in fact, the undertaker! The body of this seventy-two-year-old man was then taken away.

'Would anyone like another piece of cake or a glass of sweet wine?' they were asked.

Terry and Andrea and the other Brits were shocked and wanted to leave, not wishing under the circumstances to continue with the dinner. They left in a state of astonishment that the meeting had not been brought to an end immediately. They heard the following day that the man had died choking on Parma ham.

Their choice of the Dordogne for a place to live in France was largely based on the fact that the north would be cool and the south of France very hot, so they worked out that the middle would be best suited to their needs. As it happened their first winter experienced some of the lowest temperatures for years. Snow fell all around for the first time in twelve years and daily they were fighting against the cold, both inside and outside the house. They used vast quantities of oak timber to fuel the open fire in the sitting room from dawn until midnight and with the aid of the odd electric radiator dotted around the house, they managed to keep reasonably warm.

Mother's day on 6th March was a special day in more ways than one. Paul rang to inform them that Carolyn was expecting a baby in mid-October. That was exciting news - the best Mother's day present possible. They were very happy for them and excited at being made grandparents for the first time.

Living away from England seemed to attract more visitors than ever, probably due to curiosity with a chance to visit France. They were delighted to have friends and family come to stay which made the distance from home seem less and it was always good to know they had not been forgotten.

As they grew to know more of their ex-countrymen living in the area they began to realise that not many had come to France just for an adventure. A large number of them seemed to be running away from life; broken relationships, failed businesses and the like. It was interesting, when meeting other Brits, to study them to see which category they fell into. This often became very clear!

The long arduous task of getting planning permission together and a bill of quantities agreed with a builder, for the alterations they planned to the house and the conversion of the garage to a fourth bedroom were finally agreed and work got underway. They found a local English man and his son to do the work. They were known to them as they were supposed to have cared for the house and the pool when the house had been unoccupied. They had worked for another English couple nearby, so they gave them the benefit of the doubt, knowing that at least they would be able to discuss the project without the complications of translating everything. With Terry's assistance, ten large fir trees were removed from the garden. This made the house much lighter, opening up the garden wonderfully. Slowly the builder and his son started the work as per the planning permission. They seemed to work in complete chaos and mess leaving Terry and Andrea to clean up behind them each evening at the end of their day.

In the Spring and Autumn of each year they returned to England for a break of about three or four weeks staying in

Portland in Dorset using their static caravan at Cove Park. It was a seven-hundred-mile journey door to door but it enabled them to visit the family and the grandparents in Wales, as well as family in Yorkshire. They enjoyed the trip, but it probably did not help them to settle to life in France.

They continued to take French lessons on a one to one basis, having a teacher come to the house. It helped a little, but they were never going to be fluent. It enabled them to get by, but speaking on the telephone would always be difficult. They kept at it in the hope they would slowly progress as it was so necessary for everyday living! They chose to avoid too much contact with other British people and tried to have both French and English friends, hoping it would improve their language skills. The house next to them, a few meters up the road, was owned by a French couple who used it as a holiday home. He was a trouble-shooter manager for Carrefour, one of the main supermarkets in France. Marie his wife, spoke some English but her husband Fredric spoke none so conversation was limited, but they did become very good friends. Terry first met Marie as he was taking Tricks for her walk one morning. He greeted her in his poor French and invited her to join them for coffee which she seemed to understand and accepted. Together they made reasonable conversation, although it was mainly in a 'form' of English. Marie was a lovely lady and she seemed happy to have them as neighbours. She had been to England some thirty years ago, but her English was reasonable and certainly better than their French and they struck up a very good relationship.

A few days later Terry again met Marie while walking the dog. In jest, Terry said, 'Ah hello Marie, my mistress.' She looked shocked.

'Oh no,' she replied, 'I cannot be, I'm very happily married, I cannot be your mistress.'

Terry tried to reassure her that he was only joking! She looked very puzzled and concerned for a while, but then seemed to understand and replied, 'It is a Yoke?'

'Yes Marie it is a Yoke.'

They both laughed and were forever very good friends after that and she could not do enough for them. Whenever they had any problems she told them to ring her and she would deal with it. Marie was a master at sorting things out and took no prisoners, as they say. She told it how it was, and wanted everything done 'now' when she was dealing with the inevitable slow French bureaucracy. They in turn dare not ignore her requests.

In May, Paul and Carolyn, eager to see where they were living, drove the nine hours from their home in Nice to St Barthelemy de Bellegarde. It was a long journey, making them realise how big France was. It was good to see them and be able to show them around their corner of the country.

In June, shortly after returning from a visit to North Yorkshire where they had stayed with friends in Kilburn, a team of French workmen arrived at L'Etang to replace the Septic tank. It was deemed necessary because the old one did not fulfil the regulations, discharging its contents into a ditch. So at the heady cost of 9000 euros a French builder and his team arrived with their JCB and were excellent. They did what they said they would, were very clean and tidy and left the whole area as they had found it. Terry and Andrea were most impressed with their work and the speed in which the task had been completed successfully.

Two of the very memorable visitors to L'Etang were Jeremy and Gabrielle. It was a joy to welcome them. Jeremy had been such a wonderful friend and support in the years since Terry first met him in 1980 when starting his new job as Property Manager in Yorkshire. They had shared so much together.

Jeremy had shown Terry around the confusing mix of land and property all over North Yorkshire, helping him to make some sense of it all. He was there throughout the period when Ann was fighting cancer and Terry needed so much practical and emotional support. When Ann died it was Jeremy who dropped everything to be at his side the very next morning, helping with the many distressing arrangements that needed immediate attention. It was Jeremy who was there. He was a trusted friend and colleague, helping to fight the battles with their employer who was trying to constructively dismiss them from their respective jobs. Later, when his Boroughbridge house was flooded in 1981, the lone figure of Jeremy was there at seven the next morning to help pick him up and to restore some normality. On so many other occasions too, when a good friend was desperately needed, he was there at his side, so was a very special man.

Jeremy loved France. He and Gabrielle often had holidays there, and now Terry felt he could repay some of the love and friendship he had so freely received over the years by giving him and Gabrielle a holiday to remember. On 23rd July 2005 they arrived in their Morris Minor 1000 Traveller Estate, as only they could do, having driven across France to be at L'Etang with them. They enjoyed a wonderful feast on the terrace prepared by Andrea to welcome them and then showed them around their new home. It was such a relaxed and happy time with Jeremy delighting in the use of the pool that warm and sultry afternoon of their arrival.

Together, with a large bottle of Saint-Emilion red wine, they sat by the pool in the warmth of the evening, Terry and Jeremy chatting long after the ladies had gone to bed. They remembered and revisited all the events they had shared; the happy, the sad and the mad ones – there were so many! Midnight passed but they continued to chat and walk around the garden which was lit-up by countless electric lamps scattered around. They were entertained by the croaking of frogs hiding in the hedge rows, seemingly willing them to stay up and be entertained by their quirky sound. In a way it seemed that they didn't want the evening to end. It was as if they knew it would never be repeated and were hanging on to their deeply held friendship and experiences. They both savoured that friendship and their escape from the trials which they had both endured whilst in the employment of Bowman Properties.

Little did Terry realise how much this was going to be remembered by them all. Twelve months later, Jeremy rang to tell them he had terminal cancer. Within three months of that call at the age of 58, he died leaving behind a heart broken family - Gabrielle, his wife and daughters Marianne and Laura and all his dear friends.

CCC

CHAPTER NINETEEN

As well as the mess the builders seemed to work in while converting the existing garage to a fourth en-suite bedroom, progress too was painfully slow. Fortunately, it did not upset the rest of the house as it was taking place at one end. Part of the garden was looking like a bomb site because the rubble and rubbish was never taken away. They had laid the concrete slab for the double garage and were now in the process of building the oak wood frame. That was a huge and time consuming task but would be worth it once complete. It later transpired that one of the building team, a married man, was also busy having an affair with his neighbour's wife at the time, which may well have contributed to the speed of progress that took place!

The pool at five x ten meters required a circulation pump to maintain the water in good condition and in August when the temperature was at its highest the pump suddenly decided to give up and needed Terry's immediate attention. The pump, along with many control valves, lived in an underground chamber deep in the ground at the side of the pool. It was into that hole, in the heat of the day, that Terry had to descend to extract the pump. Adjectives were heard flying out of the chamber but after a few hours he had managed to remove it from its underground cavern. To find a replacement was never easy at the best of times and much worse when you do not speak the language with all the complexities of the different pumps. It was time yet again to call on the services of Marie, their stalwart neighbour, who was at that time back in Marseille where Frederic was working. As always Marie came forward to help and to accept the challenge. She soon found a new pump, all arranged on the phone from Marseille. Terry was able to collect it from Bergerac and in two days had it fitted and working before the pool turned green. Once again Marie had come to their rescue as she did on numerous occasions.

Another example was when the landline for the phone had stopped working and French telecom did not have a very good reputation for speedy repair work. They had been informed that it would be two weeks before anyone would come to look at it. However, they had not reckoned with Marie. She rang French telecom to report the line fault and they had to sit up and take notice. She explained that the lady in this house had a serious heart condition and that if anything were to happen to her due to the faulty phone line preventing her from making an emergency phone call, they would be held responsible! Next morning at 8 o'clock the repair men were up the pole in the garden carrying out the necessary work to reinstate the line. Marie had warned Andrea not to rush out to greet the repairmen as she had told them Andrea was ill with a bad heart and for that reason it was so important for her to have a reliable phone line!

Terry and Andrea attended the catholic church in the market town of Montpon just a few miles from where they lived. They had attended the 'Echourgnac Abbaye' that was also nearby but felt they should mix with the local people as much as they could so they decided to attend Mass in Montpon. The priest, six foot four, Fr. Michel, did speak a little English and they grew to like him very much and enjoyed his wonderful sense of humour. He had introduced them to Elaine, an English lady in the church who had lived in France for some twenty years and they became good friends. She, too, was always very concerned about them, helpful and keen to do anything she could to assist them in settling into France. Her family from Bath in England were due to come to see her. Fr. Michel asked Andrea and Terry if they would welcome them to the church by going to the choir and saying a few words. No other instructions were given to them other than he would give them a signal when they were to speak and for them to prepare a few words of greeting ready for the following Sunday Mass. Despite a threatened baggage strike in Bristol Elaine's family were still expected to come.

'So where is the choir exactly?' Terry asked Andrea. 'The French have different names for things. For us the choir is up in the organ loft, surely it's not up there we're expected to go?'

'I have no idea, but I'm guessing it's at the lectern on the altar,' Andrea replied.

The following Sunday they arrived in church where there must have been around the usual one hundred and fifty parishioners present. They sat there wondering what sign Fr Michel would give them and when. Would it be at the beginning, middle or the end of the service?

They kept a close eye on him during the service waiting for the signal. Every time he scratched his nose they wondered if that was it and were on tenterhooks.

The time came for them to receive communion and they both went to the altar to receive. When Fr. Michel reached Andrea he whispered something to her. Having returned to their seats Terry asked,

'What did he say?'

'He said, it's OK.'

'What's OK?' Terry asked her.

'I don't know, he just said, it's OK'

They knelt waiting and watching. Then at the end of the Mass, sitting in a chair at the side of the altar, Fr. Michel started to wave his hands around so they took that to be their call to the altar. Slowly they walked up the aisle like a bride and groom and almost as nervous.

When they arrived at the altar rail they stopped, waiting for further instructions. Everyone was looking and wondering, but there was silence as they both just stood there not knowing what to do next!

Suddenly the eccentric Fr. Michel waved his hand wildly for them to go onto the altar to the lectern, which they did. Andrea spoke better French than Terry, but he was able to understand French better than Andrea, so they had agreed that she would speak and standing at the lectern started to address the congregation in her best French to explain about the visitors from England and to welcome them. Fr. Michel immediately leapt from his seat and did a sort of dance while shouting and waving his arms at them both.

'No! No! No! not in French. In English!' he yelled at them exasperatedly.

Language and understanding were always going to be problematic but somehow they did, on the whole, get by and manage to make themselves understood, but they began to wonder if that would ever be enough.

The summer was long and hot with temperatures in the 40's. With not a breath of air, it was overpowering. They tried to purchase an air conditioning unit but they were sold out and no more expected until the following year; something that would never happen in the UK. Each day was hotter than the last and the lack of air movement made it feel even worse. They did have a couple of free-standing floor fans to try and move the air around which were on day and night. So desperate were they that they tied a frozen ice block on the front of the fan to try and cool the air as it was propelled out. At night they had hot water bottles that had been filled and frozen solid to try and help cool the bed. After weeks of this and having, late at night, tried to cool down in the pool which was as warm as a bath, they became so frantic that they took to the car with Tricks their dog and sat there with the air conditioning on full in order to get some relief from the heat. It was at a time, when their friend Fr. Philip Dyson from UK was staying with them for a couple of weeks, as he tried to do each year. He, a non-swimmer, was forced to submerge himself in the pool every night, but found little relief. When one evening the heat wave did eventually break they were all sitting on the open terrace enjoying a meal. The storm with its dark black clouds moved threateningly towards them. Every tree in the garden was bent almost horizontal by the strength of the wind. Clearing everything from the table they rushed inside to take shelter from the fierce wind, wondering whether the whole roof was going to be lifted by the power of the storm. Fortunately, little damage was done but it was a terrifying experience.

As summer moved towards autumn it was time once again to pay a visit to the UK to visit friends and family and of course, the grandparents Margaret and Cecil in Wales. They spoke weekly on the phone with them which helped to keep in touch with their everyday events and needs. The round trip worked out at around two thousand miles and was not taken lightly. So they broke the journey at the northern port of Boulogne and took the speed ferry the next day to Dover. This took only an hour, which suited them, as they tried to reduce the time on the water not being very good sailors. The fares were very good too at £50 for the return crossing, compared with £350 from Poole.

Whilst in northern France they took the opportunity to view some of the beaches used during the war and to visit especially the war cemetery at Bayeux, where Terry's uncle Jonathan Reeves was buried. He enjoyed his life in the army and had been in the 1st Battalion of the Dorset Regiment serving in Palestine before the second world war. At the time of the Dunkirk evacuation he was in France and had, after receiving an injury, to be invalided home for hospital treatment. His train at that time had been bombed and he was missing for quite a few days before getting back to his unit.

He later returned to France with his regiment on D-Day 6th June. But on the 19th June, together with the 2nd Battalion of the Dorset's in a fight for the village of Hottot-les-Bagues, south of Bayeux and west of Caen, he was again wounded. There was an almighty battle between the Dorset's and the German Panther tanks who were defending a Chateau on the edge of the town when he was taken prisoner and died of his wounds near the village of Tesse-la-Madeline on 21st June 1944. He was first buried there, in the community grave yard, but as the cemetery was very wet and flooded they later moved him to Bayeux.

It was a very moving experience to go and visit his grave. Terry had never known his uncle but had read all the letters he had sent to his mother and warmed to him. He was a very intelligent and well educated man, as well as a real idealist. Like so many others he gave of his life that we may be free of dictators and enjoy freedom. The words accredited to John Bunyan were written at the foot of his headstone;

> 'so he passed over and all the trumpets sounded for him on the other side.'

The day after their return from England they received a call from Paul to inform them Carolyn had given birth to a son, Adam, who had arrived at 5pm on Thursday 13th October, weighing in at 7.6 lbs. They were delighted to reach such a milestone as having grandchildren and to hear of Adam's safe arrival. Life would begin to change for Carolyn and Paul, but they too were very happy.

Christmas was soon upon them with the temperatures being much the same as they were in England at that time. The French seem to carry Christmas better with less emphasis on the commercial side and more on the family which was good to experience. The holiday too was shorter with no Boxing Day which meant they only had one day as a holiday.

On 7th January 2006 Cecil was 89 and still enjoying good health. He was of course less active than he was, but enjoying their life in Wales. He often enjoyed a chat with them on the phone always interested in what they were doing in France and delighted to see them on their visits to England.

The building works at L'Etang were finally completed on 1st May so they were able to move into the fourth bedroom and enjoy the extra space it had created. It would be very useful for all the visitors planning a visit that year, from Australia, England and from France. Temperatures had not been quite as high as the previous summer, but it was early yet. Between visitors they were able to enjoy the garden, the pool and visiting some of the lovely villages around them, enjoying the French experience. So many people asked if they had yet visited the shrine at Lourdes, so they decided the time had come to take a trip to the shrine.

They set off from L'etang des Vias with a friend who took them to the Railway Station in Montpon, just 8 km away. They boarded the 11.59 Train to Bordeaux, where it was necessary to change for Lourdes. The small, three carriage train from Montpon was full and after walking through the train they found a seat for Andrea at one end, where she sat squashed amongst many others who all seemed to be using their Ipods, Pea Pods, Blackberries and mobiles! Terry made his way back to the suitcase that he'd left at the entrance of the train, not wanting to be separated from it for long.

He stood by the door as more and more people came aboard, people with cases, pushchairs etc. Then, just as he was sure that nobody else could possibly fit in the carriage, a young man crushed in with his cycle, followed by two young ladies. The door squeezed closed and Terry spent the journey sandwiched between two pairs of bosoms, a suit case and a bicycle – not the best start to the journey, but that, of course, depends on your point of view!

In fifty minutes they arrived at Bordeaux where the train poured its contents onto the platform and Terry and Andrea were reunited. They crossed to another platform and joined the TVG that was to take them to Lourdes. They were very careful to get on the correct numbered carriage as the train, later, split and went in different directions at Drax and they did not want to be in the wrong half.

Their tickets bore the number of their seats, so they made their way to the appropriate carriage only to find that the whole Argentinean Football/Rugby team were there too, with all their gear piled to the ceiling.

As if that were not enough, the contents of a Filipino Convent had joined the carriage also on their way to Lourdes. All their cases had to be stored in the central aisle due to a lack of space! One of the Sisters, who could speak no French, asked us if we could speak English, to which Terry was able to answer, 'Yes a little.'

She asked if the train was going to Lourdes, so he was able to put her mind at rest.

'Ah' she replied 'God has sent you to us.'

He was at that moment wishing that he hadn't.

Life in the carriage was somewhat crammed, to say the least, and was not helped by the lady who clearly had bladder problems and insisted in passing up and down the carriage every few minutes to go to the toilets. This required everyone in turn to lift their case out of the aisle on to the seat to let her pass! This improbable collection of bodies hurled its way along the track towards Drax, Pau and Lourdes. At Pau the Football/Rugby Team had to leave the train. If you have ever had to prise sardines from their tin, you will understand something of the task. The Team – of course all shouting away in Spanish – made a human chain along the centre of the carriage and started throwing cases to each other along the length of the carriage out onto the platform, accompanied by much jabber shouting and jeering. Cases that anyone would find very difficult to lift off the ground were flying above their heads on the way to the exit. One false move and someone might have finished up in hospital for a month.

There was a wonderful silence as the last case and member of the team left the carriage, leaving them with just the convent full of Sisters, all looking rather stunned.

They sped on arriving in Lourdes at 16.00 hours and picked up a taxi which drove them the short distance to the 'Hotel Solitude.' Driving down the hill into the town of Lourdes was just as they had imagined it would be. It was more like entering Blackpool, with shops on each side of the road selling - not rock, funny hats and the like - but row after row of icons, rosary beads, candles, medals, holy pictures etc. One shop after another and then the shop to end all shops of this nature, a supermarket given over to selling nothing else but these items! You collected your basket or trolley and went along the shelves picking up the items you wanted and then to the checkout to pay – can you imagine anything more repulsive and off putting? Needless to say, they did not enter into any of those.

The hotel was all that was required, a good clean on-suite room overlooking the river all very tranquil, with bar and restaurant if they needed it. There were two hundred and ninety-three such rooms. After unpacking they thought they would go down to the bar and find some refreshment before going off to see the Shrine a few hundred yards away. It was there that they experienced their first Lourdes Miracles! On walking into the bar they found 'Emmerdale' an English television program playing on the television. The second miracle was that, unlike any other place in Europe, they were able to produce a first class cup of tea, which they enjoyed on the riverside terrace while recovering from the day's events.

They went on to visit the shrine a short distance down the road and walked straight to the area of the Grotto. They joined a short queue walking along the side of a rock and into the shallow cutting of the cave. There a small glass window in the ground showed the place where Bernadette was said to have dug down with her hands and found the spring that has continued to run since 1858. It was somewhat disappointing. They felt it should have been more of a feature being the central part of the shrine, to add to the joy and beauty of the rock cave setting. As it was the insignificant little window in the rock floor could easily have been missed.

The rock around the shrine was shiny from the passage of thousands of people jostling past over the years. Above, in a little cutting in the rock face about twelve feet above the ground was the place where Our Lady was said to have appeared to Bernadette on eighteen different occasions between 11th February and 16th July 1858. After walking through that small area they stood and looked back on the scene as if expecting something to happen.

At the side of the Grotto was, what exactly? It was a few minutes before they were able to work out what was going on. There was row after row of what at first looked like tin market stalls with a roof over each of them, at least thirty of them all blackened and covered with smoke stains. In each one they noticed, as they walked down between the rows, there were hundreds of candles burning. They realised that pilgrims purchased the candles at a huge candle dispensing machine, took them to this area and placed them in a large container to await a free space for them to be individually placed in position and lit. 700 tonnes of candles are burnt there each year. By the size of the heap waiting, it would be months before they were used. Again they felt the use of these candles could have been put to better and more prayerful effect, to highlight and decorate the shrine, perhaps having moving trays of smaller candles.

On the top of this huge rock three churches had been built, The Crypt, The Basilica of the Immaculate Conception and The Basilica of Our Lady of the Rosary. They attended their first Mass in the Basilica of Our Lady of the Rosary.

There was also an underground basilica at the shrine which, because of its concrete structure, felt a lot like an underground car park. An International Mass is said there every Sunday and Wednesday. There were twenty-five thousand seats but when they went to attend the Mass an hour before the start there was standing room only. As they had stood the day before at the Grotto Mass and at the torch light procession, they gave it a miss in favour of a Mass in a smaller chapel with an Irish group.

The torch light procession each evening was quite something to witness, with the square in which it was held able to accommodate 40,000 people. For them, whatever you might believe, they found the event a wonderful witness to Christianity that goes on every day of the year. While they were there, the square was full every night.

The shrine will certainly have to expand in the years to come, the only way it can is in front of the Grotto, perhaps with a wide bridge over the adjoining river that surrounds and confines it, allowing development up into the hill beyond. Time will tell.

Meanwhile back at the Hotel starting at midnight every night and going on until 2am there was a noise you would only expect from the football stadium at Wembley. They could not make out where it was coming from but it was terrible. They closed the bedroom windows and turned on the air conditioning to drown out the noise. They later told the management, 'If that is not somehow stopped, it will clear Lourdes faster than St Bernadette was able to fill it.'

So what did they think of Lourdes? Well, either Our lady did appear there, or there was a very enterprising Mayor who came up with a great idea to secure the financial future of the village. Each has to decide for themselves!

They had an uneventful and pleasant journey back to Montpon contemplating all they had seen and so pleased they had spent those few days at Lourdes to experience the shrine for themselves.

CCC

CHAPTER TWENTY

France, they both agreed, had a lot going for it but, if you were not fluent in the language, it was never going to be easy and could create difficulties in every aspect of life. Sitting on the decking of their caravan at Portland at the beginning of 2007 they reviewed their situation.

'The French lessons have not exactly been that encouraging, but have helped,' Andrea declared.

'Books and cd's are fine, but we're never going to learn the language that way are we? I think we've learnt more by being with the people in their everyday life. I'm sorry to say I feel we're never going to be fluent. We've come to the language too late in life and don't have a natural talent for it.'

'I think we've come to a cross roads and must decide whether or not we'll stay in France or return home. We're making a lot of new friends, French and English, but I don't want to go through all the emotions of having to say farewell to everyone if we stay on now, and then in a few years decide to go home. I really feel we should make that decision now don't you?' she asked.

'You're right of course,' Terry agreed. 'Leaving Yorkshire and all our friends was an experience I'd not like to go through again. It was unbearably hard and not to be repeated. We couldn't endure all that again, it hurt too much.'

Once they began to think on those lines they knew it was not going to be the place where they would live out their days and, slowly, other considerations came into mind which encouraged them towards a move back to England.

'We've also to consider Cecil and Margaret, now in their early nineties. They are pretty strong and do look after themselves quite well living independently in Wales, but they may not always be so able.' Andrea said with concern.

'Quite right. It seems we're forced to move back to England. As you say, I don't see either of us becoming fluent so we have to be big and brave and make the move. It's been a fantastic experience though. I'd do it all again.'

It was with much sadness that they decided to put their house in France on the market and see what buyers were out there and what interest there might be. It was such a beautiful house, set alone on the edge of the 'Double Forest' just a mile from the nearest village. They had loved it from the start. A great deal of beautification work along with the extension had now been completed. It should prove to have been a good investment they thought, even if the heat had gone out of the property market recently.

So, on arrival back in France they instructed estate agents and put in progress advertising on the internet for the sale of L'Etang. They also informed their friends who were all very surprised at their decision, but understood the reasons. The first viewers arrived by mid-April and the process got underway. There was steady interest and on 18th August 2007 a sale was agreed and contracts exchanged with an English Eye Specialist and his wife who were looking for a holiday home in that region. They also purchased the contents of the house which cut down on furniture haulage costs.

Terry and Andrea subsequently left L'Etang des Vias almost as quickly as they had found it three years previously. They moved out on 12th November following the usual hiccups during the final contract stage. How did anyone sell a property without complications of some type? What a wonderful experience it had all been, providing many happy memories and a lifelong love for France and its people, who had welcomed them and showed them nothing but love and affection throughout their stay.

In a way the next decision was a more difficult one. Where would they seek to live now? They were like children in a sweet shop, being free to live anywhere.

Andrea quite liked the thought of retirement in the south west of England.

'As a child we had some lovely holidays in Dorset. My father loved it there and we did have relatives in Wareham of course – I'd really enjoy Dorset or Devon if we could find something suitable.'

Terry agreed, 'Mmm yes it's a beautiful coast line. Although I was born in Weymouth I have no ambition to go back and live there, it's so 'dead-end' I always feel. The only good thing about it is the sea front. There is of course Portland, where we have our caravan. Not that I'd really want to live there either, as nice as it is. Dorchester or Bridport would be my first choice if we really have one, but it'll depend on what we can find.'

However, they did feel a responsibility towards the grandparents Cecil and Margret and felt they should start their search in Wales to see what was on offer. They knew the country quite well and loved the countryside and the beauty of the place, even if it seemed to have much more rain than anywhere else on earth. This was probably why it always looked so lush and green. They searched the area around Aberaeron in west Wales, renting a cottage for a couple of weeks to enable them to explore and view some of the available houses. They were shown some very tired and dull looking places but there seemed to be nothing on the market to attract them. They cast their net wider but it seemed as if Wales was not going to be the place for them. They looked at Shropshire attached to Wales, with its beautiful countryside and where they had friends, but still they couldn't find what they were looking for.

The quest went on for months when they finally had to return to their caravan in Portland to reconsider their position. On searching the internet, they found little of interest to them except one they kept coming back to. It was a house in the village of Petrockstow, not far from the town of Okehampton.

'OK, let's go and see what we think. If you want to.' Terry agreed, but wasn't keen.

'The house looks perfect only two years old with four bedrooms. There'd be no repairs or refitting to do and it's set amongst seventeen other new houses,' Andrea declared.

Terry was not so sure, 'I don't think I could live on such an estate, not when I've become used to living in the country over the years, not to mention Africa with its wide open spaces. I'd feel so claustrophobic.' It did not sit well with him.

They were shown around by a suited gentleman, the owner, a sharpish man who had bought the house off plan to sell it on again when the time was right. As they were unable to find anything more suitable they decided to buy the house and if it did not work out they would move on in a few years when there might be something more suitable available. Completion of the contract to purchase 17 Townland Rise took place on 21st May 2008, when they moved in. They remained there for three years, knowing it was not really the sort of surroundings they were looking for. Terry was not happy there, as nice as the house may have been. It was too overlooked on a newly built village development and really not his scene.

It did give him time to do something that friends had been telling him he should do for years and that was to write a book about his life experiences. Andrea had continually told him and tried to convince him he should. Then, when in touch with author Billy Hopkins, (Wilfred Hopkins) having read a number of his wonderful books, he was swayed by him. Wilfred, from Manchester had worked at the University of Malawi, like Terry, but a few years before him so they had much in common and exchanged many emails. He encouraged Terry to write and asked him to send a few pages of text about his life and what he had done. He came back so positively that Terry decided to take up the challenge and write his autobiography. It was something outside his normal experience, but he was prepared to have a go in order that generations of his family, yet unborn, would understand something of his life and times, and their roots. After all, he thought, how fascinating it would be today if he had a book written by his great grandfather all those years ago and to be able to read about his life. And so 'African Harvest' by Terence Reeves was born. An autobiography of his life and all he had harvested from his time in Africa.

He was helped by being able to use all the letters he had retained from the past as well as personal diaries. Some, like Ann's diaries, he had never read and he would now have to go through everything before starting the long and involved process of writing. It was an immensely emotional but necessary experience trailing through the past and reliving those moments. He found it amazing how much the memory was triggered by reading the events of that time. So much was still stored away in his mind. For the first time in his life he was able to read both sides of events - his own and that of Ann's through her in-depth letters and diaries, which he had been aware of, but had never read. Ann had written them in a way very different from most diaries, recording what she was feeling, as well as what she was doing, which opened up a whole new understanding for him and their relationship. The process took over a year of very concentrated work and was completed by the middle of 2011 which was the time they decided to seek a buyer for 17 Townland Rise as they had seen a more suitable house in Devon for which they had made an offer.

On the 28th August 2008 he was reminded of why he was writing the book when into the world arrived their second grandson, 'Ewan George Reeves' born in France and weighing in at nearly eight pounds. Maybe, one day Ewan's son or daughter would read the book with some fascination.

It was January 2009 when Cecil had his ninety-second birthday that they had a good chat on the phone. He told Terry that he thought he'd done well, to live so long, and was probably one of the last surviving members of the 'Desert Rats' from the war in North Africa. It was always something of a rarity to hear him speak of his days spent in the army. Cecil didn't enjoy using the phone more than he had to either, so conversation was short and to the point. In April he had to go into hospital after he collapsed at home. Fortunately, the nurse was present at the time treating Margaret's leg ulcers. He hated hospital more than most and rarely attended the doctors for anything. However, he had been having some breathing problems and had a very deep husky cough. Sadly, he never came out of hospital and on the evening of 22nd June 2009 he passed away. They later found he had lung cancer. Margaret, who was now confined to a wheel chair due to her leg ulcers, had been totally dependent on him so was immediately taken to the local nursing home in Aberaeron, not far from their home in Ciliau Aeron. Terry and Andrea were visiting a friend in Penzance, Cornwall at the time and as soon as they heard what had happened to Cecil they rushed to Wales to her aid. It was a very sad time for all. Margaret had lost her husband of seventy years. Terry had lost a friend and mentor, who he would miss desperately, Paul and Lynda their grandfather and Adam and Ewan their great grandfather - one they never met. As Terry told the congregation, when giving the eulogy at Cecil's funeral service, Cecil had told him in conversation more than once, that he had no fear of death - maybe the process, but not what followed, saying,

'It's the beginning of a new and exciting adventure which I look forward to.'

They hoped he was now enjoying that new life but they missed him so very much and the wisdom and support he had brought into the family.

They received an offer for their house in Petrockstow and in June 2011, they moved into their investment house in Yeovil, which they'd bought before going to France and rented out. Now was a good time to use it for a few months while waiting for the owners of the bungalow which they had agreed to buy in Newton Poppleford, Devon, to move out.

Almost two months had passed when they received devastating news from Yorkshire. Terry's ex-boss and colleague Ken Hodgson had been diagnosed as having Alzheimers Disease. He was only fifty-nine. For some time he had not been well and, when Terry had taken him out to lunch the previous June, he remembered how he had disturbing memory problems. Terry could only think back to the day he had given Ken his notice and how he had just sat there in a daze. Was that the beginning of the problem he wondered?

Terry wanted to see Ken and went to Yorkshire where he and his ex-secretary Elizabeth visited him at his nursing home. It was a very distressing visit, an unbelievable and very sad experience, for he was not the Ken who had cut so many deals with Terry in the past. The change was incredible and very upsetting.

On 9th September 2011 Terry and Andrea were able to move in to their new home in Devon. It was the same day that Terry received copies of his book 'African Harvest' that were waiting for him at their new home, so a momentous day in every way.

The house looked out over the rolling Devon countryside with not too big a garden. They were through with large gardens, lovely as they were, and didn't want to be slaves to another as they grew older. This one had lots of beautiful shrubs, very colourful with not too much maintenance and a wonderful rural view. The house needed refurbishment with a new kitchen and bathrooms. They also decided to build a new garden room to take advantage of the wonderful views from the front of the house. There was a great deal of work to do to make it how they wanted it, but they expected to be there for a long time. They managed to find a builder to carry out the work. He was, as is often the case, a bit of a nightmare! It took nearly a year to complete the works before they were able to settle and enjoy their new surroundings, not being too tied down and able to travel as they wished.

It was distressing to receive the news that Terry's friend and colleague Ken Hodgson, who he had worked with for fifteen years, had died on 23rd September 2011 aged only fifty-nine.

'It seems wrong that such a decent and brilliant man should die so young,' Terry declared.

'He offered and achieved so much, always sharp, fair, considerate, thoughtful, determined and keen in business, as his success showed. I've learnt so much from him over the years. He will be missed by many.'

Terry was overwhelmed at the loss of such a good man.

Ever since Terry had met Andrea he had wanted to show her all the places he had lived and worked. The places that had formed part of who he was.

'It's not so much that I live *in* the past, but *with* the past,' he explained to her one day.

'They really are two very different situations. The past makes us what we are and we do well to remember that fact. So far I've dragged you around Tanzania, Kenya, Malawi, Buckinghamshire, Wiltshire, Hampshire and Dorset. It's all been great fun and we've enjoyed it haven't we? It must mean that you're getting to know me quite well,' he laughed. 'There is one place we haven't yet visited. A place of great beauty far away in time, distance and way of life. A place I've never had the courage to return to since leaving forty years ago. It is of course the Seychelles, where I spent two years working from 1974–76. It was there Ann developed skin cancer and all our troubles started. For a long time, I couldn't return, but I now feel I could and would love to show you something of the beauty of the islands. Let's think about it and see how we feel.'

The following week they were speaking via skype to Andrea's cousins Neville and Sylvia in Sydney, Australia, as they often did. They had become very close over the years. They suggested it would be lovely to have a holiday together and what did they think about the idea. Immediately Terry & Andrea remembered their discussions about going to the Seychelles and suggested to Neville and Sylvia that it might be a good place to meet up, being half way between Oz and UK. They loved the idea suggesting that Andrea's other cousins, Cheryl and Bob from Australia might wish to join them. Terry said he could make all the arrangements with 'Seychelles Travel' based in Dorset. He knew they were very competitive. Derek, a director of the company, was known to him and had forty years' experience of the Islands, so could guide them through. It was agreed that Terry would obtain a quote for the trip. In the end Bob and Cheryl decided not go to the Seychelles, but they did meet up with them in Dubai on the return leg of the journey and went on to have a holiday in the UK with Neville and Sylvia.

To arrive again in the Seychelles after forty years was quite something – a really emotional experience. The beauty of the place was as striking as ever. From the moment you arrive you are under its bewitching spell. They spent the first five days on the second largest island of Praslin staying at the Hotel L'Archipel set in a marvelous position on the beach and perfect to unwind for five days after the long journey. They enjoyed a day-trip to the smaller island of La Digue, cloaked in thousands of coconut palms and home to some of the rarest birds like the paradise flycatcher, sparrow-sized and metallic blue. At one time they had been reported as extinct, but were later found inhabiting the forests on the island.

After five days recovering on this unique little island they returned to the main island of Mahe, where the plane had brought them on arrival. They had booked to stay at the 'Hanneman Residence' at Beau Vallon in a two-bedroom spacious air-conditioned apartment that suited them all very well. When they were not in the pool they were in the sea and enjoyed exploring the island in their hired car seeking out many of the places Terry had known from the past.

Neville and Sylvia were as enthusiastic to see 'Sawa Sawa Farm,' where Terry had worked all those years ago, as he was. Terry, fearing he might not recognize many of the places had brought some old photographs to help them find their way around. They drove past the entrance the first time but with the aid of the old pictures found where the small track was hidden which lead them off the main road to the farm. It had changed almost beyond recognition. Many of the farm buildings had gone, probably fallen down over the years and the old farm house where Carly and Anna Brooks lived had been replaced by a new one, but built on the same site. They followed a single track up the steep hill and through the coconut plantation. Suddenly for Terry it was all becoming familiar. It's astonishing how the brain can store such information to be recalled even after forty years away - amazing! At the top of the hill there was a sharp bend that he remembered well. It turned towards Terry's small house hidden behind a building and an enormous granite rock. They had to walk the last twenty meters as the road became a path. It was so emotional to be once again walking that path towards his old house. As they turned the corner Terry could see that his house was no more. It had been replaced by a new single story one that looked out to the sea just as his had done.

As they all stood there staring, a man came from the house asking if he could help. Terry explained that he used to live on this spot and asked him to confirm that it was Sawa Sawa Farm, as Terry knew it to be. The man confirmed that most of the farm had been sold off by the government, who now owned it, for house building plots. He had no knowledge of the Brooks family who had lived there and had employed

Terry in the 70's, or what had happened to them. Terry was keen to find out, but it was a very long time ago and he was unlikely to find anyone who knew, but he felt he wanted closure on that episode of his life, of the Brooks family and what happened to them. However, the man said if they were to walk around the corner they would see the remains of the old steel framed chicken houses that Terry had worked in and helped to build in 1974 and were still standing. They were amazed to see these relics, standing there like dead skeletons of by-gone times. Terry walked around inside the shell of the building remembering so many things about those days forty years earlier.

But it was time to leave the past where it was and they all returned to the car, driving back down the steep hill to the main road and continued their exploration of Mahe, new places and the old.

Terry still remembered the name of the doctor and his wife who worked for the local health service back in the 70's and who had lived opposite 'Sawa Sawa Farm.' He decided to check the name in the phone book back at their hotel, just in case they were still there or, if not, another member of their family. To his surprise the doctor's wife's name was listed - at least he thought it was her. If she had been around forty then she would be in her eighties now, so it was possible. He rang the number and spoke to a lady who confirmed she was Jan. Her husband had died ten years earlier, but his wife Jan continued to live in their beautiful house by the sea. Terry was elated and asked if he could go along and see her, explaining who he was. She said she did remember him and Ann and would be delighted to see them the following afternoon, inviting them to tea.

Fortunately, Terry had taken some of his old photographs which would help in prompting memories. She was delighted to meet them, holding on hard to Terry's hand as they met again after forty years apart. It was a truly tear-jerking and astonishing moment as they sat together unravelling the years. Her house was set in the rocks on the edge of the sea with the rocks themselves forming part of the structure, truly a unique place. She explained that her husband had died about ten years earlier and now her niece took good care of her. Terry could recognize the old face hidden away under the years and could remember her and the kindness she had shown to them back in those difficult days. She spoke of the compassion that Ann had shown to her friend, Denise, who lived near-by, and was suffering from multiple sclerosis. Ann used to go to her house every week to help her with exercises which were of great benefit to her. It was something she never forgot and was ever grateful to Ann.

Terry was keen to hear what had happened to the Brooks family who had run the farm opposite her and where Terry had worked for two years. She was able to give them the full and fascinating story.

After Terry and Ann left the Seychelles in 1976 life went on pretty much the same, she told them. Carly and his wife Anna Brooks continued running the farm with son Philip and his wife Pauline. After two years Anna became ill and had to go to hospital in Victoria on Mahe. She was diagnosed with cancer and was kept in the hospital. Carly in the meantime had a lady friend move in to the house and was having an affair with her! After sometime it was clear that Anna was dying and against the doctor's advice Carly wanted her to die at home, and not in the hospital, so insisted she was brought home. Carly continued his relationship with his new lady friend who was living with him, while Anna was dying in another room. After a few weeks Anna died and was buried at the cemetery in Victoria.

Anna was the main workhorse at the farm so after her demise it began to fall apart. Carly sold the farm as it slowly slipped into decline and he went to live in South Africa with his new lady. Philip and Pauline had not been getting along well and were divorced. They moved to Darwin, Australia where they both went on to re-marry. After a few years, when Carly died, Philip who was responsible for settling his father's estate, went to South Africa to bring Carly's ashes back to the Seychelles, due to him having been a Seychellois. Carly had requested he be buried next to his wife at the cemetery in Victoria. Philip carried the ashes to the grave that had been prepared alongside his mother's. But, he being very upset by his father having another woman in the house when his mother was dying, could never really forgive him. He just stood there, unable to place the ashes in the grave.

'My mother would turn in her grave if she knew what he had done and wouldn't want him buried anywhere near her.' He told Jan.

So, instead of carrying out his father's wishes, Philip, who was so disgusted with his father's behavior, walked away from the grave and threw the ashes in a swamp!

That was the end of the Brooks family story, as far as it is known. Terry was immensely grateful to Jan for telling him all that she knew as he had so often wondered what became of them. She knew the story to be true, as Philip always visited her when he came to the islands, as he did when winding up his father's affairs in the Seychelles, when he told Jan the whole story.

Jan had enjoyed their chat and was sad to see them leave as they said farewell at the entrance to her beautiful house in the rocks by the sea. They had enjoyed a very special couple of hours together, but it was time to go. They thanked her for seeing them and for revealing the final chapter of the Brooks family in the Seychelles.

CHAPTER TWENTY-ONE

Here this autobiographical story has come full circle and perhaps it is time to reflect and bring it to a close. The story has travelled from the early days of childhood, as set out in the first book 'African Harvest.' It has covered the insecurity of childhood, to the drive and idealistic ways of youth, with its enthusiasm to right the world and abolish hunger, single handedly - the arrogance of youth! It then continued with the adventurous journey to a mysterious and exciting new country, where the sun shone from dawn through to dusk. Falling in love with the country and its people allowing them to take over such a great part of his life. To go on and find such a wonderfully gentle person as Ann hidden in the beauty and wilds of Africa to share his life. There are few things in life as sweet, but to appreciate the value of sweetness you have to know bitterness too, which is never as pleasant; how could it be?

Like wisdom, which is found in the most unlikely of people and places, often from those you might consider had nothing to give. Their clutter free lives can provide a clarity of vision that most never see or benefit from. Like the ninety-year-old, two-meter-high man, sitting in the sun of the Tanzanian bush, ravished by leprosy, his toes destroyed, his fingers buckled and bent, grinding a living from making rope from the bark of the majestic baobab tree, who sought only a few grains of maize to fill his empty and distorted frame. Who said to Terry, 'contentment is not comprised of possessing much, but in wanting little.'

There was occasionally in Terry's life adventure and excitement, as well as intense drama and darkness, the feeling that a cosmic battle was taking place. But faith and hope despite all remained and brought him through the darkest hours. Acceptance was necessary and the only way to become yourself and a better stronger person.

Whilst in one of those loneliest and darkest of places God sent him the delightful gift of Andrea. He sent her to fill the empty space in his life with her love, attractiveness, talent and beauty. A gift for him and his children for which they could never express the full extent of their intense gratitude, always receiving far more than they could give. In life you sometimes have to get to the bottom of the barrel or the last coin retrieved from the bottom of a chair, as Terry did, to make you appreciate your life fully.

Terry's 70th birthday was approaching. The question from Andrea was,

'What are we going to do for your birthday? What would you like?' she asked.

'Have you any ideas? Would you like a party? Or to travel somewhere?'

'I really have no idea. We had that wonderful Viking River Danube cruise for our 25th Wedding Anniversary a couple of years ago. That was nice but I'm not sure I want to do it again.'

'My wedding ring has become very thin and sometimes cuts into my finger, perhaps a new ring would be appropriate. The same wife, but a new ring,' he said laughing.

A few days later Andrea asked, 'Where are the wedding rings that you and Ann exchanged at your marriage? You showed them to me years ago and must have stored them away.'

'Why do you ask?'

'Well I've had an idea. What if we had those and the worn wedding ring that I gave you all melted down to make one new wedding ring? Sort of three in one!'

'That's an amazing idea, I love the symbolism of it.' 'Three in one.'

'Would you mind me wearing the rings of both wives?' he asked.

'Why ever should I? I already feel I know Ann so well, I see her in Paul and Lynda and often feel her presence with us. We share many of the same interests – as well as you of course,' She laughed.

'That is so very generous of you, I'm touched,' and so the three became one.

------::------

POSTSCRIPT

Sometimes in life unexplainable occurrences take place that have impossible odds. If they were anything but true, you would say, 'that could never happen!'

The day after Terry had completed the writing of this book and sent it to the publisher to be typeset, feeling somewhat relieved that it was now finished and behind him, he decided to spend the morning working in the garden and enjoy his freedom from the keyboard. After only ten minutes, Andrea called to him. 'There is a phone call for you, its Anne Baxter' (ne Hart).

Having just written his story that included much about Anne and their time together in the 1980's she was fresh in his mind. However, thirty-three years had elapsed without any contact with her, as this story described so graphically so why now?

Terry took the call and spoke to Anne. She told him she was still living in New Zealand, but had returned here for the first time on a four-week holiday. She explained that she was in Exeter for a few days and would very much like to come and see him.

Terry was stunned, shocked and surprised. First, to hear from her at all after all this time, and secondly that it should be at this moment, one day after sending off the story to the publisher having so recently trailed through their days together for the writing of this book.

Thirty-three years is such a long time, and uncanny that it should happen just at this point, unbelievable. How on earth can you possibly bridge that period of time as well as the intense and heart breaking period experienced in the 1980's?

After a short chat Terry said he would be delighted to see her and Anne agreed she would come the following day. Her friend was to drive her over in the morning when they could spend a few hours together.

If that were not enough Terry discovered, on tracking back through to those days, when Anne had written to say she could not marry him and had decided to go and live in New Zealand, that letter, as this book explains, had arrived on Thursday 16th June 1983 – Anne was now coming to see him on the same day and date – Thursday 16th June 2016! It was beginning to feel somewhat eerie.

Anne duly arrived the following morning, 16th June 2016, Terry and Andrea went out to greet her. Anne looked a little nervous, but soon that was to change, as Terry embraced her warmly, melting away all that had gone between them with a flowing of love and forgiveness. It was a very emotional day as they skimmed the years.

Andrea watched the scene unfold with loving generosity of spirit.

Lightning Source UK Ltd.
Milton Keynes UK
UKHW010657220820
368653UK00002B/52